Trigger Warning

Trigger Warning

*Is the Fear of Being Offensive
Killing Free Speech?*

Mick Hume

WILLIAM
COLLINS

William Collins
An imprint of HarperCollins*Publishers*
1 London Bridge Street
London SE1 9GF
WilliamCollinsBooks.com

First published in Great Britain by William Collins in 2015

1

Mick Hume asserts the moral right to
be identified as the author of this work

A catalogue record for this book
is available from the British Library

ISBN 978-0-00-812545-5

Printed and bound in the United States of America
by RR Donnelley

Find out more about HarperCollins and the environment at
www.harpercollins.co.uk/green

For Stella and Isabel, may they always think
what they like and say what they think

Contents

Trigger Warning (noun): a statement at the start of any piece of writing, video, etc, alerting the reader or viewer to the fact that it contains material they might find upsetting or offensive.

Author's note

This is not a book about the *Charlie Hebdo* massacre. When I began to write *Trigger Warning* in late 2014, *Charlie* was a small French satirical magazine known by relatively few and read by far fewer, particularly in the Anglo-American world. The murderous attack at the magazine's Paris offices in January 2015 did not really alter the argument about the urgent need to defend free speech, but that massacre and the reactions to it certainly brought the issues into focus.

Two concerns had already motivated me to write this book, both of which were highlighted in the aftermath of *Charlie Hebdo*. The first was an awareness of the widening gap between the rhetorical, ritualistic support that Western societies pay to freedom of speech in principle, and the increasing preparedness to compromise and restrict it in practice. The sight of world political leaders declaring 'Je Suis Charlie', whilst simultaneously trying to outlaw opinions they found offensive, illustrated that chasm.

My second concern was that the political and cultural attacks on free speech were often being led, not by Islamist extremists, but by those in the West who would consider themselves liberal or left-minded. The flipside of this was freedom being dismissed as of interest only to right-wing cranks, accused of 'hiding behind free speech'. As a veteran of radical struggles who still considers himself on the left, even if not of its modern incarnation, I have always understood that fighting for free speech is indispensable to those who want to argue for radical ideas and social change. When I first wrote in defence of 'the Right to be Offensive', twenty-five years ago, it was as the editor of *Living Marxism* magazine. Those opinions were in a distinct minority on the British left even then. Today, with campaigners demanding post-*Charlie* purges of both 'Islamophobia' and 'Islamo-fascism', the need to resist the tide and make the radical case for the right to offend is more urgent still.

This polemical book is intended as a contribution to that resistance. The case it makes for free speech has developed through years of argument as a campaigning political journalist in both the alternative and mainstream UK media. In 1988 I was the launch editor of *Living Marxism*, which we relaunched as the taboo-busting *LM* magazine in the Nineties until it was forced to close in 2000 after being sued under England's atrocious libel laws. Then I became the launch editor of *Spiked* (spiked-online.com), the UK's first and best web-based current affairs and comment magazine, of which I am now editor-at-large. I was also the only libertarian Marxist columnist at *The Times* (London) for ten years, and now write as a guest columnist for the *Sun*, among others.

The development of the arguments in the pages that follow would not, however, have been possible without the input of others. I want to recognise and thank my overworked and underpaid colleagues at *Spiked*, where many of these ideas first germinated and where the crisis of free speech in Anglo-American society has been brilliantly brought to light by editor Brendan O'Neill, ably backed by deputy editor Tim Black and managing editor Viv Regan. *Spiked*'s transatlantic 'Free Speech Now' campaign, especially its work to combat censorship on campus led by Tom Slater, is a model, online and off, of how to breathe new life into a dormant political principle.

I also want sincerely to thank my old friends and collaborators Frank Furedi, whose inspiration and advice was as indispensable for this book as it has been for longer than either of us might care to remember, and Michael Fitzpatrick, who first tried to teach me how to write properly more than thirty years ago, and is still trying now. Thanks are due to Martin Redfern, my editor at William Collins, for bringing the idea to fruition. And most of all to my wife, Ginny, the managing editor of all that I do, for making me start and finish writing it. The responsibility for the text, warts and all, is of course mine.

Mick Hume, London, April 2015

Prologue

'Je Suis Charlie' and the free-speech fraud

Free speech is threatened on two fronts: occasionally by bullets, and every day by buts.

Copenhagen, Denmark, 15 February 2015. A meeting in a café to discuss the issues of free speech and blasphemy, just over a month after the massacre at the Paris offices of the satirical magazine *Charlie Hebdo*. Inna Shevchenko of the Ukrainian feminist protest group FEMEN opens the panel discussion, talking about her relationship with the cartoonist Charb – *Charlie Hebdo*'s editor – and their shared insistence on their right to freedom of expression (FEMEN are famous for protesting topless).

Shevchenko gets to the nub of the argument: 'I realise that, every time we talk about the activity of those people, there will always be, "Yes, it is freedom of speech, but ..." And the turning point is "but". Why do we still say "but" when we ...' At that precise moment her speech is ended by the sound of sustained gunfire from outside the meeting.[1]

The timing of the Islamist gunman's attack on the Copenhagen free-speech meeting was so precise it might almost have been scripted. Just as the speaker raised the problem of people within the West saying 'Yes it is free speech, but' to signal the limits of their support, the murderer added his own full stop to the debate from outside by opening up with an M95 assault rifle, leaving Finn Noergaard, a Danish film-maker, dead. (The gunman later killed another man in an attack on a synagogue in the city.)

There is no equivalence, of course, between bullets and buts, between violent assaults on free speech and equivocal endorsements of it. Might it be, however, that the weakening of support for free speech in the West, signalled by the rising chorus of 'buts' attached to it, has encouraged those few willing to take more forceful action to put a stop to what they deem offensive?

Two crimes were committed against the satirical magazine *Charlie Hebdo* in January 2015.

Islamist gunmen committed mass murder at the paper's Paris offices. They shot dead eight cartoonists and journalists, two police officers and two others, in a graphic demonstration of their hatred for freedom of speech and of the press.

Then the great and the good of Western society committed a mass free-speech fraud. They sold us the line that they all supported free speech, making rhetorical and ritualistic gestures of support for the *Charlie Hebdo* victims. Yet at the same time many were acting out their contempt for the real freedom of expression that allows such provocative publications to exist in the first place.

The massive 'Je Suis Charlie' demonstrations in Paris and many other cities, which followed the massacre and the connected murders at a Jewish supermarket, were uplifting displays of human solidarity that made an impression on us all. They also, however, gave a misleading impression of the state of play with free speech in Europe and America.

Here, it might have appeared, was a clear cultural divide: on one side, a free world united in support of *Charlie Hebdo* and freedom of expression; on the other, a handful of extremists opposed to liberty and 'all that we hold dear'. Behind those solidarity banners, however, Western opinion was far less solidly for free speech. Many public figures could hardly wait to stop paying lip service to liberty and start adding the inevitable qualifications, obfuscations and, above all, 'Buts ...'

Those who took a dim view of genuinely free speech in the aftermath of *Charlie Hebdo* were not confined to Islamist terror cells. It quickly emerged that the threat to freedom came not just from a few barbarians at the gate. Free speech faces more powerful enemies within the supposed citadel of civilisation itself.

The moving displays of solidarity were primarily showing sympathy with the murder victims. Support for freedom of speech as embodied by the consistently offensive *Charlie Hebdo* was a lot less solid. It might have been more appropriate if many of those placards had named individual victims – 'Je Suis Charb/Wolinski/Elsa' – rather than *Charlie* the magazine. From the *Guardian* to Sky News, media outlets in the UK which expressed outrage at the murders still felt obliged to apologise for any offence caused by allowing a glimpse of the post-massacre cover of *Charlie Hebdo*, with its cartoon image of Muhammad.

Even before the dead had been buried, it turned out that the 'worldwide' support for *Charlie Hebdo*'s right to free speech was far from universal – and that those of a different persuasion were not confined to the hostile parts of the Islamic world.

An international consensus of a different hue quickly emerged, to agree that the *Charlie Hebdo* massacre showed the need to apply limits to free speech and restrict the right to be offensive. This consensus included some unusual bedfellows, notably His Holiness Pope Francis and the Communist Party of China.

Soon after condemning the murders, the Pope almost appeared to suggest that those cartoonists he called 'provocateurs' had been asking for it. His Holiness declared that 'There is a limit' to free speech, that 'You cannot insult the faith of others. You cannot make fun of the faith of others', and that it was 'normal' for those who do so to 'expect a punch'.[2]

The state-run Xinhua News Agency, official voice of the Chinese Communist regime, was a couple of days ahead of the Pope in stating that 'the world is diverse and there should be limits on press freedom'. Its editorial made clear that, for China's authoritarian rulers, 'unfettered and unprincipled satire, humiliation and free speech are not acceptable'.[3]

To which the natural response might be: 'Is the Pope a Catholic?' and 'Do Red bears dump on the press?' Nobody should have been too shocked to hear such views on punishing heretics from the head of the Church whose Inquisition condemned Galileo, or from the Chinese state hierarchy that has kept its press on the shortest leash and freedom in a noose.

More surprising was that the joint Vatican–Beijing statement setting 'limits' to what the likes of *Charlie* ought to say seemed to become the accepted party line for many in the supposedly liberal-minded West, who also want to rein in 'unfettered satire and free speech'. No sooner had they got the niceties of paying respects to the dead out of the way than they embarked on wholesale free-speech fraud.

There were loud accusations of hypocrisy after the appearance of autocratic governments from the Middle East and Africa at the Paris 'Je Suis Charlie' demo. As one US professor at George Washington University tweeted, 'Glad so many world leaders could take time off jailing and torturing journalists and dissidents to march for free expression in France.'[4]

Yet double standards flourished much closer to home.

The French authorities led the way, responding to the murderous assault on free speech in their capital by ordering a crackdown – on those whose speech they found offensive. The Justice Ministry sent a letter to all French prosecutors and judges 'urging more aggressive tactics' against suspected hate speech and those accused of defending terrorism. A week after the *Charlie Hebdo* attack, more than fifty people had been arrested for speech crimes.

Among those scooped up was the notorious anti-Semitic comedian Dieudonné M'bala M'bala, arrested as an alleged 'apologist for terrorism' after he posted on Facebook that: 'Tonight, as far as I'm concerned, I feel like Charlie Coulibaly' – a fusion of 'Je Suis Charlie' with the name of the assassin in the kosher supermarket, Amedy Coulibaly. Whether you consider that an ironic joke or an attempted justification for violence, it was only words – and only one word, 'Coulibaly', made it controversial. Yet that word could have cost Dieudonné up to seven years in prison. In fact he was convicted of 'condoning terrorism' and given a two-month suspended jail sentence. The French authorities thus spelled out their version of standing up for free speech: they would fight to the last for the people's right to say things that government and judges approved of.

Across the Channel, the free-speech fraudsters turned out in force in the UK. Some overcooked their disdain for *Charlie Hebdo*: the European editor of the *Financial Times* sparked a backlash by writing a column which accused the 'stupid' satirical rag of 'editorial foolishness'.[5] In an apparently irony-free move, the *Financial Times* then felt obliged to 'update' (meaning censor) his column for paying too little heed to *Charlie Hebdo*'s right to freedom of expression.

At least he was trying to be honest about it. If anything, it was more objectionable to witness the display of double standards from UK politicians and liberals who have led the campaigns to criminalise 'offensive' speech and sanitise the scurrilous, dirt-digging British tabloid press in recent years, yet now expected us to believe that they are freedom fighters for the satirical and scandal-mongering French press's right to offend.

Straight after *Charlie Hebdo*, Conservative prime minister David Cameron told parliament that 'we stand squarely for free speech and democracy'. In later interviews Cameron even said that 'in a free society there is a right to cause offence'. This was the same UK prime minister whose government was presiding over a state where people were being arrested and jailed for posting unpleasant jokes and messages online or singing naughty songs at football grounds, and whose justice secretary had just pledged to quadruple prison sentences for offensive internet 'trolls' found guilty of speech crimes.

Cameron also insisted after *Charlie Hebdo* that as a politician 'my job is not to tell newspapers and magazines what to publish or what not to publish'. That would be the same prime minister who in July 2011 set up, with the support of all party leaders, the Leveson Inquiry not merely to probe the phone-hacking scandal but to cleanse the entire 'culture, ethics and practices' of the offensive UK tabloid press and propose a new system to tame it. On that occasion Cameron had a very different message for parliament about what he could tell the press to do, asserting that: 'It is vital that a free press can tell truth to power ... it is equally important that those in power can tell truth to the press.'[6] One can imagine what the increasingly offence-sensitive British authorities would have said to any *Charlie*-type magazine whose front covers had dared to mock Muhammad in the UK.

On the day of the *Charlie Hebdo* massacre, Labour Party leader Ed Miliband stood with prime minister Cameron in the House of Commons and vowed to resist all attacks on 'our democratic way of life and freedom of speech'. Away from the cameras, Miliband's Labour team was busy finalising plans to create an official 'blacklist' of those convicted of speech offences online that would warn prospective employers not to hire them – the sort of thought-policing measure some might think has more in common with McCarthyism and witch-hunts than democracy and freedom.[7]

A month after parliament had united in support of *Charlie*, an all-party committee of UK MPs went further still down that slippery slope and called for persistent online 'hate speech' offenders to be issued with 'internet ASBOs [Anti-Social Behaviour Orders]' that would ban them from Facebook and Twitter, a punishment currently reserved for convicted sex offenders. It is not too hard to imagine the name of the allegedly racist, Islamophobic, anti-Semitic, sexist and homophobic *Charlie Hebdo* being among those nominated for any such state hit-list of 'haters' to be denied free speech.[8]

And let us not leave out Harriet Harman, deputy Labour leader and the party's self-styled champion of press freedom. In a statement after the Paris murders Harman expressed her concern that 'this crime will cause a chilling effect and undermine free speech'. She declared that 'free speech is a basic human right for every individual and no democracy can function without freedom of the press', that the 'right to satirise, to lampoon and to criticise is a freedom which we must celebrate and defend', and pledged 'to take all the steps necessary to assure our journalists and media that we will do everything we can to defend that right of free speech'.[9] Strong and admirable words. A few weeks later, however, Harman was back to using slightly less freedom-loving words when she appeared at a Hacked Off rally in Westminster to warn those same journalists and the media that Labour was 'absolutely committed' to implementing Lord Justice Leveson's proposals for state-back regulation of the UK press and that, if elected, a Labour government would 'follow through on Leveson' with laws to bring a free press to heel. As well as Harman's promise/threat, that rally featured former funnyman John Cleese of *Monty Python* fame comparing journalists opposed to state-backed regulation to murderers, who would also 'like to regulate themselves'. 'The murderers would make a very good case,' said Cleese. 'They'd say we murdered a lot of people, we know people who have murdered people. We really are best qualified to regulate ...' No doubt the surviving satirical journalists at *Charlie Hebdo* would have found the comparison hilarious.[10]

Alongside the political campaign to tame the UK press, the police and prosecutors have been conducting their own war on the tabloids. British police chiefs stood outside Scotland Yard in solidarity with the officers and journalists killed in Paris. Meanwhile, back in the real world, the Metropolitan Police had arrested more than sixty tabloid journalists in what amounts to a three-year witch-hunt.

Much of the cultural elite in the UK wrestled with its liberal conscience in response to *Charlie Hebdo*, and lost. The novelist Will Self wrote that the murderers were 'evil' (while insisting that we all share their 'murderous, animal instincts'). Yet Self could not stop himself also complaining about how 'our society makes a fetish of "the right to free speech" without ever questioning what sort of responsibilities are implied by this right', as if there was something perverse about extending 'free speech' to irresponsible cartoonists.[11] Higher still in the literary stratosphere, the *London Review of Books*, a self-proclaimed champion of artistic expression, could barely disguise its lack of empathy with the *Charlie Hebdo* cartoonists. A 'deeply disappointed' reader wrote to ask why the journal had issued 'No message of solidarity, no support for freedom of expression' in the aftermath of 'the execution of the editorial staff of a magazine a few hours' journey from your own office'. *LRB* editor Mary-Kay Wilmers published a curt response stating that 'I believe in the right not to be killed for something I say, but I don't believe I have a right to insult whomever I please.' Perhaps the *LRB* thinks those whose insults go too far should be punished, but that the sentence was excessive. Wilmers dismissed those 'who insist that the only acceptable response to the events in Paris is to stand up for "freedom of expression"'. As with Self, those tell-tale inverted commas appeared to offer the same comforting support to 'freedom of expression' as a noose might to a hanging man.[12]

Even in the USA, land of the free and home of the First Amendment that gives constitutional protection to freedom of speech and of the press, the free-speech fraudsters were quick to distance themselves from *Charlie Hebdo*. President Barack Obama and secretary of state John Kerry both made bold statements in defence of free speech, Kerry winning plaudits for insisting that 'no matter what your feelings were about [*Charlie Hebdo*], the freedom of expression that it represented is not able to be killed by this kind of act of terror.'[13] The Obama administration was then criticised for failing to send any senior representative to the Paris march. However Laurent Léger, an investigative reporter at *Charlie Hebdo* and survivor of the attack, thought that was a more honest expression of the White House's true attitude to free speech. 'You have to be very happy he [Obama] didn't come to the march in Paris,' said Léger. '[His administration's actions are] an absolute scandal.'[14]

Elsewhere in the US at one end of a *Charlie*-kicking consensus stood Bill Donohue, president of the Catholic League, a group that claims it is 'motivated by the letter and spirit of the First Amendment' in standing up for the right of Roman Catholics to speak their minds, regardless of what anybody else might think. Yet Donohue quickly dismissed the free-speech rights of the French cartoonists, asserting that 'Muslims are right to be angry' at the 'insulting' depictions of their prophet. He conceded that killing should not be tolerated before adding the punchline 'but neither should we tolerate the kind of intolerance that provoked this violent reaction', and concluded by criticising the editor of *Charlie Hebdo* for failing to understand 'the role he played in his tragic death'. Clearly the spirit of the First Amendment would not be visiting atheist cartoonists.[15]

At the other end of the US consensus stood a clique of influential liberal and radical bloggers and tweeters, all seemingly keen to assure us that 'these killings have nothing to do with freedom of speech or expression, regardless of how much our rulers and France's try to cast them that way'.[16] Kitty Stryker, self-styled 'Geeky Porn Starlet/Lecturer/Presenter/Sex Critical Feminist', summed it up for many. Although she is 'generally pretty anti-censorship' and 'a big fan of art, and using humour to hopefully make people think and change their minds', Kitty the feminist fighter draws the line at the likes of *Charlie Hebdo*, since 'I do not believe that racist, homophobic language is satire' (like other critics, she felt no need to explain how *Charlie Hebdo* had managed to be racist). Then she gets to the point: 'I don't think that shooting up the *Charlie Hebdo* offices was ethically Right with a capital R, OK? BUT I do think it's understandable.'[17] So to satirise Islam is unacceptable, but mass murder of satirists is understandable. And it has nothing to do with any attack on freedom of expression. Got that? Or are you a racist too?

One illustration of how far the tide might be turning against free speech in the US came when the departing ombudsman of National Public Radio declared 'I am not Charlie'. In his 'farewell blog posting' Edward Schumacher-Matos wrote: 'I do not know if American courts would find much of what *Charlie Hebdo* does to be hate speech unprotected by the Constitution but I know – hope? – that most Americans would.'[18] What Schumacher-Matos seemingly 'does not know' is that there is no such thing as 'hate speech unprotected by the Constitution'; offensive 'hate speech' *is* protected in the US by the First Amendment, as *Charlie Hebdo*'s cartoons certainly would be. Yet a leading media figure, who has not only worked as a journalist on top American newspapers for more than thirty years but even lectures on the First Amendment as a visiting professor at the prestigious Columbia University School of Journalism, apparently thinks otherwise, believing that *Charlie Hebdo* could – and should – be legally thrown to the wolves.

Surveying the different strands of this discussion in America, the headline on Anthony L. Fisher's blog for *Reason* magazine captured the essential message of the free-speech frauds: 'I'm all for free speech and murder is wrong. But ...'[19] Of course, everybody with a shred of humanity condemned the cold-blooded mass murder by Islamist gunmen. Well done. They had far less to say about the right of *Charlie Hebdo* or any other section of the Western press to publish whatever it believes to be true or just funny, regardless of whether it upsets Muslims or Catholics, Tories, socialists or transgender activists.

Asked what he thought of the rhetorical sympathy from the normally hostile European and international establishment, one surviving *Charlie Hebdo* cartoonist, 73-year old Bernard Holtrop, responded: 'We puke on all these people who suddenly say they're our friends.' In the context that might seem harsh, but fair.[20]

The free-speech fraud around the Paris killings did not come out of the blue. It would be pleasant to imagine that the vocal 'Je Suis Charlie' reaction reflected the strength of support for freedom of speech and of the press in Europe and America. It would also be wrong. If there really was such solid support for free speech, it would not have taken the cold-blooded murder of cartoonists and journalists to prompt our politicians and public figures to mention it. The loud expressions of support for free speech have been so striking because they contrast with the everyday silence on the subject.

In normal circumstances we in the West now spend far more time discussing how to restrict and outlaw types of speech than how to defend and extend that precious liberty. Almost everybody in public life pays lip service to the principle of free speech. Scratch the surface, however, and in practice most will add the inevitable 'But …' to button that lip and put a limit on liberty. The 'buts' were out in force on both sides of the Atlantic and across the internet after *Charlie Hebdo*; to quote the American writer Andrew Klavan, it looked like 'The Attack of the But-Heads'.[21]

This was the culmination of a steady loss of faith in freedom of speech and the ability of people to handle uncomfortable words or images. In recent years it has become fashionable not only to declare yourself offended by what somebody else says, but to use the 'offence card' to trump free speech and demand that they be prevented from saying it.

Charlie Hebdo itself was in the firing line of the war on offensive speech long before the gunmen burst into its editorial meeting. In 2007 the magazine was dragged into court under France's proscriptive laws against 'hate speech' for publishing cartoons of Muhammad, in a case brought by the Paris Grand Mosque and the Union of French Islamic Organisations, with the undeclared support of some in high places. 'This is not a trial against freedom of expression or against secularism' was the free-speech fraudster's protest from the Mosque's lawyer, Francis Szpiner – who also happened to be a close ally of France's President Jacques Chirac.[22]

Charlie Hebdo won that particular case, but others embraced the underlying principle of Europe's hate-speech laws – that words and images which offend can be a suitable case for punishment – and expressed it in more forceful terms. In 2011 the satirical magazine's offices were firebombed. There were no mass 'Je Suis Charlie' protests on that occasion. Indeed back then some observers were keen to spell out their contempt for *Charlie*'s right to offend. *Time* magazine asked whether the firebombed weekly was 'a victim of Islamists or its own obnoxious Islamophobia?' For *Time*'s France correspondent, *Charlie Hebdo*'s 'Islamophobic antics … openly beg for the very violent responses from extremists' that they had received. This voice of liberal America in Europe apparently believed that offensive cartoons were not merely asking for it, but 'openly begging' for it. Presumably they got what they'd been begging for in January 2015.[23]

This culture of offence-taking censoriousness emanates powerfully from Anglo-American universities, traditional bastions of open-minded inquiry and debate. It came as no surprise, after the Paris massacre, to hear a leading student official at Bristol University in England suggest that *Charlie Hebdo* would have been banned from their campus anyway, since its potentially offensive images would certainly have contradicted the university's cocooning 'safe-space' policies, which treat adult students like delicate flowers and words and images as if they were automatic weapons. What price such a caustic magazine surviving at all in the UK today, where it is apparently considered suspicious even to read *Charlie Hebdo*, never mind write for it? Several police forces in England reportedly quizzed local newsagents about the names of those who ordered copies of the post-massacre edition.[24]

Perhaps we need to face the hard fact that the Islamic gunmen who attacked the offices of *Charlie Hebdo* acted not just as the soldiers of an oldish Eastern religion but also as the armed extremist wing of a thoroughly modern Western creed. The West today is dogged by a creeping culture of conformism. From the official censors of the police and political elite to the army of unofficial censors online, the *cri de coeur* of these crusaders against offensive speech is You-Can't-Say-That. The Islamist gunmen took that attitude to a murderous extreme.

A month later came the Copenhagen shootings, when a gunman attacked a café meeting called to discuss issues of free speech and blasphemy, and then a synagogue, leaving two dead. This too sounded like a repercussion of a familiar attitude. The idea of assailing meetings to prevent speakers even being heard has grown more and more popular in radical Western circles in recent years, especially on campus. The reactionary No Platform policy has evolved from one aimed at fascists and political extremists into a broader demand to ban anybody who might cause offence to somebody, from comedians to philosophical societies. Where No Platform protesters seek pre-emptively to shout down or shut down speakers they find offensive, the Copenhagen gunman sought to shoot them down. That is an important tactical difference. But the underlying attitude of intolerance of offensive speech seems familiar. Where do these gunmen get their ideas from? They might be inspired by Western-hating clerics. But they can only be encouraged by a Western culture that seems to have fallen out of love with its own core value of free speech.

The prevailing mood of intellectual intolerance in the upper echelons of Western culture is exemplified by the onward march of Trigger Warnings, from which this book takes its title. The habit of putting a Trigger Warning (or 'TW') at the start of any piece of writing or video, to warn readers or viewers of potentially upsetting or offensive content, has spread from US campuses across the

Atlantic and the internet. The implied message of a Trigger Warning is that it would probably be better if you did not read or see this. Those delivering a different kind of Trigger Warning in Paris and Copenhagen aimed to cut out the middleman and stop anybody reading the blasphemous *Charlie Hebdo* or listening to a debate about free speech and blasphemy.

That Copenhagen meeting on free speech and blasphemy was called on the anniversary of Ayatollah Khomeini issuing a fatwa condemning the author Salman Rushdie to death for his novel *The Satanic Verses*, first published in 1988. Rushdie's was one of few prominent voices raised against the attack of the but-heads after *Charlie Hebdo*. The author told an audience at the University of Vermont in Burlington that: 'The moment somebody says "Yes I believe in free speech, but" – I stop listening.' Rushdie ridiculed the free-speech frauds' familiar cop-outs that: 'I believe in free speech, but people should behave themselves … I believe in free speech, but we shouldn't upset anybody … I believe in free speech, but let's not go too far.' The 'buts' that began to be heard in the UK and US when Rushdie was accused of going too far and upsetting people twenty-five years ago have since become a deafening chorus. If he stops listening the moment somebody uses any of those weasel formulations these days, Rushdie must spend a considerable amount of time with his smartphone earbuds plugged in.[25]

That bitter controversy surrounding Muslim protests against *The Satanic Verses* a quarter of a century ago marked a turning point in attitudes towards offensive speech, when many in the West condemned the fatwa yet chided Rushdie for being too offensive to Islam. It was during that row in 1989 that I first wrote about the importance of the Right to Be Offensive. Then in 1994, as the editor of *Living Marxism* magazine, I published a declaration in defence of that right. It upheld two principles – 'No censorship – bans are for bigots and Big Brother', and 'No taboos – taboos are for the superstitious and the stupid' – and an imperative that has informed my attitude ever since: 'Question everything – Ban nothing'.[26]

In the two decades since, as the You-Can't-Say-That culture has advanced, the fear of offending Islam has grown in the West. There has been a sustained effort to bury the issue post-Rushdie, to avoid discussing sensitive or difficult questions about what our society stands for and what unites or divides us. The result has been to suppress free speech and censor what is deemed potentially offensive. As the author Kenan Malik puts it in *From Fatwa to Jihad*, in recent years the liberal elite 'internalised the fatwa'. There is now a quite lengthy list of plays, books and exhibitions that have been cancelled or cut in Europe and the US in order to avoid controversy or offence (and not just to Muslims) – often in acts of pre-emptive self-censorship without the need for protests beforehand.[27]

Having done their best to bury these issues and stymie debate for decades, our elites seem shocked when the tensions suddenly break through the surface of society and explode into view, as in the violent protests against the Danish Muhammad cartoons in 2011, and the murderous assault on the offices of *Charlie Hebdo* and the Copenhagen debate in 2015.

They then try to force the genie back into the bottle, cracking down on anything deemed to be 'extremist' speech. This has led to bizarre cases such as that of Samina Malik, the UK's 'lyrical terrorist', who was given a nine-month suspended prison sentence in 2007 (subsequently quashed on appeal) for writing doggerel in praise of Osama bin Laden. Sample: 'Kafirs your time will come soon/And no-one will be able to save you from your doom'. You get the idea. For penning this McGonagall-lite on the back of till receipts from the WH Smith store where she worked at Heathrow Airport, Malik was convicted of possessing material that might 'prove useful to terrorists' (it is hard to see how). As the lyrical terrorist herself had to point out to the learned court: 'To partake in something and to write about something are two different things.' No longer, it seems. She was convicted of a modern British thought crime.[28]

Not all exponents of radical Islamist doctrine and alleged apologists for terrorism are such harmless scribblers, of course. There are some far more dangerous Islamist demagogues around in the West, accused of effectively acting as recruiting sergeants for al-Qaeda or the Islamic State. In the aftermath of *Charlie Hebdo* it might be tempting to imagine going along with government attempts to crack down on 'radicalisation' and censor extremists in our universities. Wouldn't it be good if we could simply gag them with the UK's 2015 Counter-Terrorism and Security Act, and kick them off campus, if not out of the country, altogether?

But such simple authoritarian solutions won't work. Trying to defend freedom by banning its enemies, to uphold our belief in free speech by censoring those who disagree, would be both wrong in principle and useless in practice. What we need to do is to fight them on the intellectual and political beaches, not try to bury the issues in the sand. The big problem Western society faces is not how to stop radical Islamists expounding their beliefs; it is how best to make a compelling case for what 'we' are supposed to believe in. As ever in times of trouble, the only thing that is likely to work is encouraging more speech rather than ordering there be less of it. Free speech is the potential solution, not the problem.

Despite the initial upsurge of 'Je Suis Charlie' sentiments, the Paris massacre has not led to any major new campaign for free speech. Quite the opposite – it has reinforced the fear, reticence and confusion surrounding freedom of expression in the West today. This book aims to put the case for unfettered free speech and the right to be offensive. These are both non-negotiable principles and practical necessities to address the problems we face.

That must involve defending the right of a magazine like *Charlie Hebdo* to offend who it chooses, without any buts, and whether we like it or not. The truth is you don't have to be *Charlie*, read *Charlie* or chortle at *Charlie* in order to defend it. Free speech is always primarily about defending what a US Supreme Court justice once famously described as 'freedom for the thought that we hate'.

In passing we might note that wholeheartedly defending *Charlie Hebdo*'s right to offend need not necessarily mean reprinting its cartoons, as some insisted it must. Freedom of speech and of the press mean that media outlets must be free to make their own editorial judgements about what they publish – just as others must be free to pass judgement on those decisions.

In the free-speech fraud that followed the *Charlie Hebdo* massacre, many suddenly started talking about the 'right to offend' and the fact that there is 'no right not to be offended'. Quite so. What most of them appeared to mean, however, is that we must defend the right to offend Islamist extremists. Yet the right to be offensive has to be about much more than Islam. It means the right to question, criticise or ridicule any belief or religion – and the freedom of the religious or anybody else to offend secular sensibilities, too.

In the aftermath of *Charlie Hebdo* Clare Short, a 34-year-old Catholic mother of three and blogger, wrote of her concerns that a fearful backlash against 'offensive' speech might now make it hard for her 'to express my views without fear of prosecution'. She observed that she had 'never thought I would be appreciating the "right to offend", but today it seems I am'. Short concluded that 'Je Suis Charlie, and I would like to proclaim that Jesus Christ is lord, marriage can only occur between one man and one woman, and that abortion is murder. Or am I not allowed to say that?' If 'Je Suis Charlie' is to mean something more than a slogan on a discarded placard, she surely should be allowed to proclaim her beliefs, however out of step with the times they might seem.[29]

Any such tolerance of traditional opinion seemed seriously out of vogue just two months after the Paris attacks, however, when Sir Elton John led an international celebrity boycott of Dolce & Gabbana, after the two gay Catholic Italian fashion designers told an interviewer they believed gay adoption of 'synthetic' babies to be unnatural. The #BoycottDolceGabbana tag swept across social media as many thousands backed the celebs' demand to close the designers down, not for exploiting workers, overcharging customers or anything else they might have done, but merely for expressing an unfashionable opinion. 'Elton John is a Taliban,' said Italian senator Roberto Formigoni in response to the boycott, 'and is using with Dolce & Gabbana the same method used by the Taliban against *Charlie Hebdo*.' Not quite 'the same method' – no gun attacks by gay parents on D&G stores were reported – but perhaps a similar-sounding message.[30]

Defending the right to be offensive also means recognising that the work of such bold cartoonists, whether one considers it insightful or infantile, is not enough. The right to be offensive means something more than the right to ridicule Islam or any religionists. We should be free to question everything that we are not supposed to question in the suffocating cloud of conformism that hangs over our societies today.

France of course is the land of Voltaire, the eighteenth-century revolutionary writer whose views on tolerance and free speech are famously summarised as: 'I disapprove of what you say, but I will fight to the death your right to say it.' By contrast, as this book examines, we are now living in the age of the reverse-Voltaires, whose slogan is 'I know I will detest what you say, and I will defend to the end of free speech for my right to stop you saying it.'

It would be a fitting tribute to those killed in Paris and Copenhagen if we were to rekindle the spirit of the free-speech fighters of yesteryear for the twenty-first century. 'Je Suis Charlie' is not enough – we need to send out the message loud and clear that 'Nous Sommes Voltaire'.

The silent war on free speech

Compared to many countries elsewhere in the world, the UK and the US look like bastions of freedom of speech, holding the line against censorship and intolerance. The 800th anniversary of England's Magna Carta in 2015 is understandably being marked with much self-congratulatory talk about our long history of unbroken liberty.

Yet there is little cause for complacency when we come to consider the state of free speech in the Anglo-American world. There is a danger that we underestimate the importance of freedom of expression in creating and advancing our civilisation. There is a danger, too, that we overestimate how secure that liberty really is in Western culture today.

This first section of the book sets out to establish why we need to defend free speech more forthrightly. Against the background of the historic fight for free speech it aims to identify the new threats and challenges from inside the supposed free-speech citadels of Western society.

1

A few things we forgot about free speech

No subject (with the possible exception of football) has been talked about as much yet seriously discussed as little as free speech. Everybody pays lip service to the right to freedom of speech. Few of us appear to give much thought to what that means or why it matters. Sometimes it's necessary to remind ourselves of the obvious and look again at what we take for granted.

After all, it's funny how the simple little things can slip your mind. The first thing that seems to have been forgotten about free speech is that it's supposed to be Free. The second thing that is often forgotten is that it's simply Speech.

This chapter offers a quick reminder of why these things matter, alongside the third thing we often forget: that, when you put those two words together, you have the most important expression in the English language. Free speech is the single most powerful factor in creating and sustaining a civilised society. Without the advance of free speech, the development of life as we know it in the West is unlikely to have been possible over the past 500 years. There could have been little progress towards democracy in Europe or America without the ability to demand political change and to put forward competing principles about how society should be run. Many of the great scientific breakthroughs would have been unimaginable without winning the freedom to speak out and question the old accepted 'truths' about the world.

Few new artistic or cultural advances would have happened unless there was sufficient freedom of expression for writers and artists to go where none had gone before. None of the mass communications on which the interconnected modern world relies could have thrived without the fight for free speech – or if they existed, they would not be worth having. And the other freedoms we take for granted today, from the high principles of sexual and racial equality in law to the low liberty to gossip about the rich and famous online, would have been hard to secure without first demanding the freedom of all to speak out in public.

In short, without the willingness of some to insist on their right to speak what they believed to be true, we might still be living on a flat Earth at the centre of the known Universe, where women were denied the vote but granted the right to be burnt as witches. That is one good reason why it is time to stop kicking and 'but-ing' free speech around so casually today and get serious about discussing how to defend and extend our most precious liberty.

To begin with the dreaded f-word. It often appears to have slipped our Anglo-American society's mind that free speech is supposed to be Free. That's free as in 'free as a bird', to soar as high as it can and swoop as low as it chooses. Not as in 'free-range chicken', at liberty only to scratch in the dirt within a fenced-in pen and en route to the chopping block.

Free means speech should not be shackled by official censorship imposed by governments, police, courts or any other state-licensed pecknose or prodstaff. Nor should it be stymied by unofficial censorship exercised through university speech codes and 'safe zones', twitterstorming mobs of online crusaders against offensiveness, or Islamist zealots gunning for blasphemy. And nor should it be sacrificed by the spineless self-censorship of intellectual invertebrates.

If it is to mean anything, free speech has to live up to its name. This is the hardest thing for many who claim to endorse the principle to remember in practice. It means that what others say or write need not conform to what you, I, or anybody else might prefer. Bad taste or good, offensive or attractive, cutting or boring. Just so long as it is free.

Here is the terrible truth about free speech. Anybody can choose to write, blog, tweet, chant, preach, phone a radio programme or shout at a television set. Not all of them will have the purity of soul of Jesus Christ or Joan Rivers, the wisdom of Socrates or Simon Cowell, or the good manners of Prince Harry or Piers Morgan. That's tough. They still get the same access to free speech as the rest of us, whether we like it or not.

Defending the unfettered Free in free speech is not a question of endorsing whatever objectionable or idiotic things might be written or said. Nobody had to find *Charlie Hebdo's* cartoons insightful or hilarious in order to stand by its right to publish them. Nor is it a question of being soft and suffering somebody else's nonsense in silence. Free speech means you are also free to talk back as you see fit.

The Free in free speech does mean recognising that free speech is for fools, fanatics and the other fellow too – even if they want to use that freedom to argue against it. Like all true liberties, free speech is an indivisible and universal right. We defend it for all or not at all.

Remembering to put the Free in free speech makes clear why we should oppose attempts to outlaw or curtail certain categories of speech. Freedom is, unfortunately, indivisible. You cannot have half-freedom, part-time freedom or fat-free freedom. You cannot abolish slavery but only for white people or celebrities. Similarly you cannot declare your support for free speech, but only defend those parts of it that you like or that meet your preferred set of standards, however high-minded those preferences might appear. If one leg or even one gangrenous toe remains chained to the post, the entire body is still shackled.

In all the talk about free speech today, how often do you hear free speech spoken of as a universal and non-negotiable right? Instead the focus seems always to be on the buts, the exceptions, the limits to freedom. Everybody in public life might insist that they support free speech, but scratch the surface and it becomes clear that what many support is not so much free speech as speech on parole.

They want speech that is released from custody only on licence with a promise of good behaviour, preferably wearing a security ankle bracelet to stop it straying from the straight and narrow, having signed the rhetorical offenders' register. Speech that is free to toe the line, stick to the script and do what it is told. The reinterpretation of freedom to mean liberty-on-licence is a con that the free-speech fraudsters should not be allowed to get away with.

Once you forget the meaning of 'freedom' and start cherry-picking which people or what type of speech might deserve it, free speech ceases to be a right. Instead it becomes a privilege, to be extended or withheld to the well- or the not so well-behaved as those in authority see fit. This is the message of all those fashionable sermons about how 'rights come with responsibilities'. That is just another way of saying that it is not a right at all, but a selective reward for good behaviour. Rights don't come with buts or provisos.

Today's free-speech fraudsters will claim to support it firmly in principle, yet equivocate in practice. This often translates as supporting it for those who share your attitudes and opinions – less free speech than 'me speech'.

To defend free speech 'in principle' must mean to defend it for all. Otherwise, once a principle becomes negotiable it ceases to be principled at all (as in the old political joke, 'We have principles, and if you don't like them, we have others').

The indivisibility of the right to free speech is also a very practical matter. Once you make free speech a privilege and not a right, who are you going to trust to make the decision about where to draw that line through free speech? Government ministers? High court judges? Mary Berry and Sharon Osbourne?

This is an old lesson which many, especially on the left, still stubbornly refuse to learn. As far back as the 1930s, the British left campaigned for a ban on marches by Oswald Mosley's black-shirted British Union of Fascists. They got their wish in the Public Order Act of 1936 – and were quickly astonished to discover that the state used its new powers to ban their right to protest, too. Almost eighty years later, and British anti-fascist crusaders are still apparently outraged to find that, when they 'win' a legal ban on a little demonstration by some far-right grouplet, the police will use the same blanket ban to prevent them staging a 'victory' march.

This problem is even more acute now, when everything is judged by the subjective standards of 'offence' and things can be censored or banned not for threatening public order but for hurting some-body's feelings and making them feel 'uncomfortable'. There is no telling where the runaway train of censorship in the name of 'me speech' will end – witness the fate of the UK feminist comedians and speakers who have been surprised to find themselves protested against and even banned from campuses for being deemed offen-sive to some, shortly after they had demanded the same treatment for sexist blokes. Once you say that free speech is only for those who comply and conform and toe a fashionable line, you are asking for trouble.

The other practical problem with 'me speech' is that, by restrict-ing the free-speech rights of those you detest, you weaken your own and everybody else's rights. You deny others the right to listen and to argue, to test the truth and judge for ourselves. You effec-tively condemn yourself to being locked in your bubble cell, with only your own and similar opinions to listen to, like a solitary pris-oner with only one book to read (and even that is his own boring diary).

As Thomas Paine, the English radical who became a key figure in both the American and the French revolutions of the eighteenth century, wrote in the introduction to his classic *The Age of Reason* (a critique of religion considered so offensive that it was subject to serial prosecutions by the British government): 'He who denies to another this right, makes a slave of himself to his present opinion, because he precludes himself the right of changing it.'[1] It is not only those directly denied their freedom who are 'enslaved' by selectively chaining some forms of speech.

It is important to remember that free speech in the West, as chapter 3, about the history of the issue, argues, was never a gift from the gods or an act of largesse doled out by governments. From the Magna Carta 800 years ago to today, any liberties that are worth the parchment they are written on have been hard-won in a struggle to wrest them from our rulers. Once won, those liberties do not come with any moral commandments. Nobody has to pass through the eye of an ethical needle to qualify for the right to free speech. There should be no official test to pass or licence to obtain before you can express an opinion.

Free speech is not to be rationed out like charity, to only the most deserving cases. A right is a right, and is not limited by any incumbent responsibilities. Liberties do not come with strings attached, any more than freedom can be exercised in leg-irons.

This is not a plea for irresponsible speech. It is to be dearly wished that people exercise their rights responsibly and take responsibility for what they say. We might like to think that taking responsibility would always involve saying what you mean and meaning what you say; expressing the truth as you understand it as clearly as you are able, and then standing by it for all that you are worth. But wishing that could be true is no excuse for trampling on the speech rights of others in the name of what you imagine their responsibilities should be.

We should remember that the Free in free speech is not only about the freedom to speak and write as you see fit. It is also about the freedom of the rest of us to hear and read everything that we choose, and to judge for ourselves what is right. The flipside of freedom of speech is the freedom to listen (or not) and to choose.

We are under no obligation to take any notice of anybody's words; the right to free speech never entails a 'right' to be taken seriously. But nor does the speaker have any obligation to restrict what they say to what we want to hear. To mean something worthwhile, freedom must be first and foremost for the other person's point of view. George Orwell put in perfectly in his 1945 essay 'The Freedom of the Press' (originally written as a preface to his novel *Animal Farm*, though ironically the publisher refused to include it): 'If liberty means anything at all, it means the right to tell people what they do not want to hear.'[2]

As part of forgetting to put the Free in free speech, we also appear to have forgotten the meaning of tolerance. Today tolerance is talked about in two related ways: either it means allowing the expression of views without judging or criticising them, or it is used as the excuse for closing down views which are too offensive, as in 'we will not tolerate intolerance'. Neither has much to do with true tolerance.

Intolerance is always the enemy of free-thinking. But tolerance and the right to free speech does not mean a free ride. Tolerance is not about allowing anybody to rant away, offend and insult without challenge because 'everybody's entitled to their opinion'. True tolerance means allowing others to express their opinions, however disagreeable – and then being free yourself to tell them what you think of it, just as they are free to repay the compliment to you. In this, I am always with the great Englishman of letters Dr Samuel Johnson, who declared that 'Every man has the right to utter what he thinks truth – and every other man has the right to knock him down for it.'[3] Figuratively speaking, at the very least.

The second thing we have forgotten about free speech is that it is Speech. It is simply words. Words can be powerful tools, but there are no magic words – not even Abracadabra – that in themselves can change reality. Words are not deeds. It follows that offensive speech should not be policed as if it were a criminal offence.

It is true that 'words can be weapons' in a battle of ideas, or even just in a slanging match. But however sharp or pointed they might be, words cannot be knives. However blunt words are, they are not baseball bats. No matter how loaded they are or how fast you fire them off, words are not guns.

Yet all too often today we see words treated as if they were physical weapons. People in the UK are imprisoned for tweeting insults, as if they had handed out a bodily beating. Outraged online mobs pursue 'rape deniers' or other speech deviants across social media much as the London mob pursued the misogynist murderer Bill Sykes through the Dickensian city. Politicians and public figures in the US or UK are forced to apologise for having caused unintentional offence with some words, as if they had unintentionally caused a war (which is something they would never apologise for, of course).

This confusion of words and deeds is even written into UK law, with the Public Order Act used to imprison thousands of people each year for 'threatening, abusive or insulting words *or* behaviour' (my italics), blurring the distinction between what people say and what they do, as if abusive language really was the equivalent of physical abuse.

Words can hurt but they are not physical weapons. And an argument or opinion, however aggressive or offensive it might seem, is not a physical assault. The difference is far more than semantic. There are and should be laws against assault and threats of violence. There often are but should not be laws or rules against words used to express opinions, however violently one might disagree with them. The right response to violent assault is to end it, as forcibly as necessary, and possibly to lock up the perpetrator. The answer to bad words is not to end speech or lock up the speaker. It is more speech – to resist or simply to rubbish the words objected to.

But should all speech really be free? Is it really possible to draw such a firm distinction between offensive words and criminal offences? The answer is yes, once we are clear what we mean by free speech as encompassing all forms of expression from ideas and opinions, through invective and insults, to jokes or mindless jabber.

There are other types of speech that the most liberal-minded among us have long considered to be indefensible: direct threats of violence or blackmail, for example, or malicious defamation of individuals, or illegal obscenity such as child pornography. Even the US First Amendment has not protected these forms of words, and the US Supreme Court takes a dim view of what it calls 'fighting words' and incitement, both of which are intended and likely to cause violence or other unlawful action.

But these are not really arguments against free speech. In properly distinguishing between words and deeds, we need to make a distinction between words that are simply speech – the expression of something – and words that instead become part of an action – the execution of something. For instance there is a big difference, recognised by US Supreme Court cases as we shall see, between expressing a general violent hatred of the government or minority groups, and deliberately inciting, provoking or organising specific acts of violence against particular institutions, individuals or groups. The first category is speech, to be tolerated, like it or not (but challenged as you see fit). The second is something other than free expression, and we do not have to put up with it.

Of course many serious crimes will involve some sort of speech, whether that means people conspiring to murder or planning a robbery. Nobody imagines that a criminal haggling over the price of a gun on the black market, or demanding money at the point of that weapon, is exercising his free-speech rights, and there will be few 'I am Charlie' banners on parade if Charlie the armed mugger gets his comeuppance.

Those who support free speech have long sought to distinguish words from deeds and to have legal exceptions to the principle overturned or at least defined as narrowly as possible. In the US the

Supreme Court responded by, for example, narrowing the grounds on which speech can be deemed to be 'fighting words' and so not protected by the First Amendment. When that category of speech was first defined, in a 1942 Supreme Court case, a Jehovah's Witness was found guilty of using 'fighting words' simply for calling a town marshal who was attempting to prevent him preaching a 'God-damned racketeer' and 'a damned fascist'. By contrast in 1969, the Supreme Court justices overturned a New York law against abusing or burning the American flag, on the ground that 'mere offensiveness does not qualify as fighting words'. In the early Seventies, in a near-reversal of the original 1942 judgement, they also overturned the 'fighting words' convictions of individuals found guilty of cursing at police officers.[4]

The trouble is, however, that in wider discussion in the Anglo-American world today, things are moving in the opposite direction. The tendency now in politics, the media and academia seems always to try to broaden, rather than narrow, the grounds on which words should arguably be kicked out from under the free-speech umbrella.

As we shall see, the insistence that 'This is not a free-speech issue' has become a staple expression of the free-speech fraudsters, as a way of maintaining their alleged support for the principle whilst shafting it in practice. Once, the phrase 'This is not a free-speech issue' might justifiably be heard only in response to something as serious as a direct threat to kill – or just something as trivial as a request to make less noise in a bar or on the bus. Now we hear it used promiscuously in response to all manner of questions that obviously *should* be 'free-speech issues', from demands for new laws against nasty internet 'trolls' to bans imposed on controversial political speakers or comedians on campus. It can seem as if some would like to turn the exception to free speech into the rule.

In this spirit there has been a remarkable inflation of the meaning attached to 'harm' everywhere from academic philosophy circles to the UK courts, so that it now includes not only physical harm inflicted by force but also mental or emotional harm said to be inflicted by speech. It might once have been considered straightforward, for example, that the offence of 'actual bodily harm' would involve some actual harm to the body. No longer; for the past two decades, UK courts have ruled that ABH could include 'psychiatric injury'.

Faced with these attempts to impose new restrictions by narrowing the scope of free speech and broadening the exclusions, it is all the more important that we come out fighting for freedom of expression and holding the line between words and deeds.

But what about incitement? Inciting somebody to commit an offence is a crime. Offering an offensive opinion or inflammatory argument should not be. In a sense all arguments are 'inciting' – as in urging or provoking – somebody to do something, whether that means to change their opinion or the brand of coffee they drink. Those on the receiving end are still normally free to decide whether to do it. We should be very wary of criminalising speech so long as all that is being chucked about are words.

And what about offensive and hateful speech? These issues are addressed at length in this book. To begin with let us simply remember that in Western societies it is usually only those consensus-busting opinions branded offensive or unpalatable that need defending on the grounds of free speech. Nobody ever tries to ban speech for being too mundane. This is not a question of celebrating extremism or obnoxiousness. It is simply a matter of recognising that, when it comes to upholding the principle of free speech in practice, if we look after those opinions branded extreme, then the mainstream will look after itself.

Free speech is more important than hurt feelings. It is a sorry sign of the times that such a statement might seem outlandish to some. As recently as 1999 David Baugh, a leading black American civil liberties lawyer, defended a Ku Klux Klan leader who had been charged after a cross-burning, gun-toting rally. The attorney assured the jury that he was well aware that his client and the KKK hated black men like him. But that, Baugh argued, did not alter the racist's free-speech rights: 'In America, we have the right to hate. And we have the right to discuss it.'[5]

Baugh lost that cross-burning case on a point of law. Today he might be widely considered to have lost his mind. Yet he was right. In a civilised society, if we are talking about thoughts and words – however vitriolic – rather than violent deeds, all must be free to hate what or who they like, whether that means Muslims, Christians, bankers or Bono. To seek to ban the right to hate should be seen as no less an outrageous interference in the freedom to think for ourselves than a tyrant banning the right to love. The best way to counter hatreds and ideas we despise is not to try to bury them alive, but to drag them out into the light of day and debate them to the bitter end.

There is a good reason why it's important to remember the meaning of both Free and Speech, however uncomfortable they might make us. Because the third thing we tend to forget about free speech is that it is the most important expression in the English language. Free speech is a key to unlock the door to much that we hold dear.

To borrow a phrase from the techies, free speech might be called the 'killer app' of civilisation, the core value on which the success of the whole system depends. It is worth reminding ourselves of what makes free speech so all-fired important that every other right or claim should have to get in line behind it.

Freedom of thought and of speech is part of what makes us unique as modern humans. The ability consciously to formulate and communicate ideas is one of the things that separates us above all from the animal kingdom. Free speech is the link connecting the individual and society. The essence of our modern humanity is to be able to think freely and rationally, but also to say what you think, to engage with and try to persuade (or be persuaded by) other people.

Free speech is the voice of the morally autonomous individual, nobody's slave or puppet, who is free to make his or her own choices. It is the spirit of the age of modernity on full volume, first captured more than 350 years ago by the likes of Spinoza, the great Dutchman of the Enlightenment, who challenged the political and religious intolerance that dominated the old Europe and set the standard for a new world by declaring that 'In a free state, every man may think what he likes and say what he thinks.'[6]

Free speech is not just about individual self-expression. It is the collective tool which humanity uses to develop its knowledge and understanding, to debate and decide on the truth of any scientific or cultural issue. Free speech is also the means by which we can bring democracy to life and fight over the future of society, through political engagement and the battle of ideas.

Free speech is not just a nice-sounding but impracticable idea, like 'free love'. It has been an instrumental tool in the advance of humanity from the caves to something approaching civilisation. It is through the exercise of free speech and open debate that individuals and societies have been able to gain an understanding of where they want to go and why. The open expression of ideas and criticism has often proved the catalyst to the blossoming of creativity.

That's why history often suggests that the freer speech a society has allowed, the more likely it is to have a climate where culture and science could flourish. Even before the modern age of Enlightenment, those past civilisations that we identify with an early flowering of the arts, science and philosophy had a disposition towards freedom of thought and speech that set them apart.

Ancient Greece, which laid foundations of civilisation in everything from architecture and theatre to mathematics and medicine, was the society where philosophers such as Socrates, Plato and Aristotle lit up the Athenian practice of free speech, or *parrhesia*. (Though even in democratic Athens, as we shall discuss later, Socrates was ultimately executed for taking free speech 'too far'.)

Several hundred years later the era now thought of as the Golden Age of Islamic civilisation, in the Middle East and Spain, was marked by important advances in the arts, education and science. Contrary to the image we might have of an Islamic caliphate today, many of those gains were made possible by a more tolerant attitude towards alternative ideas and foreign philosophies than prevailed under the conformism of the Christian empires of the Middle Ages.

The advance of free speech has been key to the creation of the freer nations of the modern world. Every movement struggling for more democracy and social change recognised the importance of public freedom of speech and of the press for articulating their aims and advancing their cause.

In 1649, at the time of the English Revolution and the execution of King Charles I, the radical Leveller movement petitioned parliament to end all state licensing of the press and allow everybody freedom to publish. Not because John Lilburne and the Levellers thought it would be a nice idea, but because these pioneers of the modern struggle for democracy understood the importance of press freedom and free speech to furthering the people's fight for liberty. As the Levellers' petition declared, 'the liberty [of the press] appears so essential unto Freedom, as that without it, it's impossible to preserve any Nation from being liable to the worst of bondage. For what may not be done to that people who may not speak or write, but at the pleasure of licensers?'[7]

Those fighting for American independence from British colonial rule in the eighteenth century also grasped that their democratic revolution required freedom of speech and debate to succeed. The wild pamphleteering and speech-making of the era played a central role in spreading ideas and information, in the forming of American revolutionary associations and forging of a new nation. In 1775, in one of the most famous speeches of the revolutionary era, Patrick Henry called upon his fellow delegates to the Virginia Convention to forget about going cap-in-hand to the Crown and instead stand and fight their oppressors – 'Give me liberty or give me death!' Henry spelled out the need for free speech to lay bare the truth of what was at stake, even if it risked offending or outraging his more moderate peers: 'I consider it as nothing less than a question of freedom or slavery; and in proportion to the magnitude of the subject ought to be the freedom of the debate. It is only in this way that we can hope to arrive at truth, and fulfill the great responsibility which we hold to God and our country. Should I keep back my opinions at such a time, through fear of giving offence, I should consider myself as guilty of treason toward my country, and of an act of disloyalty toward the majesty of heaven, which I revere above all earthly kings.'[8]

One sure sign of the historic importance of free speech to liberation struggles is the instinctive way that tyrants have understood the need to control it to preserve their power. Thus during the struggle over slavery in America in the nineteenth century, the slave-owning classes did all they could to suppress any public discussion of slavery as a means of keeping control. Southern states outlawed criticism of slavery and used gag rules to prevent the US Congress in Washington even discussing anti-slavery petitions. The Alabama slave code of 1833 decreed that no black person was to 'preach to, exhort or harangue any slave or slaves or free persons of color, unless in the presence of five respectable slave-holders'. The punishment for speaking publicly without supervision was thirty-nine lashes for a first offence, and fifty lashes for each offence thereafter.[9] As the anti-slavery campaigner (and former slave) Frederick Douglass said in 'A Plea for Free Speech in Boston', after an 1860 meeting to discuss the abolition of slavery was attacked by supposed gentlemen in that civilised northern city, 'Liberty is meaningless where the right to utter one's thoughts and opinions has ceased to exist. That, of all rights, is the dread of tyrants. It is the right which they first of all strike down. They know its power … Slavery cannot tolerate free speech. Five years of its exercise would banish the auction block and break every chain in the South.'[10]

Those striving for freedom and democracy more than 150 years later still understand the centrality of free speech to their struggles. Charter 08, a modestly framed call for political reform in China signed by more than 300 Chinese intellectuals and 'prominent citizens' in 2008, recognises that its proposals for more legislative democracy and greater human rights must rest on 'Freedom of Expression': 'We should make freedom of speech, freedom of the press, and academic freedom universal, thereby guaranteeing that citizens can be informed and can exercise their right of political supervision.' It calls for the abolition of 'political restrictions on the press' (shades of the Levellers) and of 'the crime of incitement to subvert state power' and concludes: 'We should end the practice of viewing words as crimes.'[11] In recognition of the Charter having hit an authoritarian sore spot, the Chinese authorities duly locked up its author.

All of these and many more history-making movements and individuals have demonstrated that if not for the fight for free speech, other freedoms would not be possible. Without the ability to argue your cause there would be no way to clarify your aspirations, make clear your demands, or debate how best to strive for them.

More recent struggles for freedom and equality in Western societies were just as intimately bound up with freedom of speech. The demand for free speech, for the right for their voices to be heard, has proved central to the struggles for women's emancipation, gay liberation and racial equality in the UK and US. There is a grim irony in the fashion, examined in the next chapter, for feminist, trans or anti-racist activists today to demand restrictions on free speech as a means of protecting the rights of the identity groups they claim to represent. Without the efforts of those who fought for more free speech in the past, these illiberal activists would not be free to stand up and call for less of it in the present.

We should remind ourselves, not only of why free speech has been so important to humanity, but of what it has meant in practice. Free speech at its best has involved the freedom to challenge the most ardent orthodox beliefs of the day, regardless of whose toes that might tread on. That is why the essence of free speech is always the right to be offensive. Those who would deny the right of others to break taboos, offend against the consensus and go against the grain of accepted opinion would do well to remember where we might be without it.

Look at how the likes of Bruno and Galileo were persecuted by the Inquisition in the sixteenth and seventeenth centuries for offering and endorsing scientific insights that we take for granted today. Anybody suggesting now that the Sun circles the Earth would be accused of insulting our intelligence. Yet even four centuries ago, the notion of God's Earth orbiting the Sun as a mere satellite and acolyte was among the most offensive ideas possible to Europe's ruling religious and political powers, and they condemned those who suggested it as heretics. It would be hard to imagine anything more offensive in twenty-first-century Western society than trying to deny votes to women or demanding the reintroduction of legalised slavery. Yet not so very long ago those who opposed such oppression were being arrested and worse for offending against the state or nature in our Anglo-American civilisation.

Let's be clear on what we are talking about here. The right to be offensive is not about the freedom to fart in a restaurant, or to yell drunken abuse in the street, or to direct personal insults at the Pope's or anybody else's mother. We should be wary of self-centred souls who wish to turn petty matters of personal interaction into major issues of political debate. They bring to mind the exchange in *The Big Lebowski*, where serial offender Walter Sobchak, having been asked to be quiet at the coffee house, responds in high dudgeon: 'Excuse me, dear? The Supreme Court has roundly rejected prior restraint!' However, Walter's companion The Dude puts him straight: 'This isn't a First Amendment issue, man.'[12] Good manners generally cost nothing in terms of free speech either – although we should resist demands to tone down an argument in the name of civility. Heat and passion are important. Being honest and above all clear in what you say, however, is usually more important than just being loud or lairy. Being passionate about your argument need not necessarily involve being profanely rude to the other side (although it might).

But the right to be offensive is really about what you say rather than the way you say it. It is about having the liberty to question everything; to accept no conventional wisdom at face value; to challenge, criticise, rubbish or ridicule anybody else's opinion or beliefs (in the certain knowledge that they have the right to return the compliment to you).

This is what makes the right to be offensive so invaluable. It is why it has been key to human progress and the advance of our collective culture and society through modern history. We would do well to remember that it is the cutting edge, the beating heart, of freedom of speech and of the press. What, after all, would be the point of those freedoms if you were only at liberty to say what somebody else might like? How could it be a right if it was withdrawn the moment you choose to use it to say what others consider wrong?

Thus has free speech become the voice of individual choice, scientific truth, and political progress. If we forget why free speech matters so much to our society, and allow its standing to be sunk in a deluge of ifs and buts and not-too-fars, we risk undermining those foundations of civilisation and ruining any prospects of building on them further.

Remembering why free speech matters so much should lead us to demand more of it rather than less. Even before concerns about free speech were brought to a head by the *Charlie Hebdo* massacre and the Copenhagen shooting, the truth is that there was not enough freedom of speech in the UK, US or Europe. And things have been getting worse.

In recent years it has been easy for civil liberties lobbyists in the UK and Europe to appear rather smug about free speech on the home front. They could go about banging the drum on behalf of free-speech martyrs in China or Iran, whilst pointing out that, in our societies, freedom of expression had been made safe by the European Convention on Human Rights (ECHR), incorporated into UK law under Tony Blair's New Labour government by the 1998 Human Rights Act, which enshrines the right to freedom of expression.

In fact the ECHR and the Human Rights Act embody the attitude of 'free speech, but ...'. As the leading UK textbook on civil liberties and human rights says, the legal conventions 'recognise that the exercise of these freedoms comes with special responsibilities, and so may be subject to restriction for specified purposes'.[13] As soon as you attach legal responsibilities, never mind special ones, a freedom ceases to be a right.

That problem is spelt out by a glance down the list of the 'specified purposes' for which the ECHR, supposed stone tablet of European liberalism, concedes that freedom of expression can legitimately be restricted:

> The exercise of these freedoms, since it carries with it duties and responsibilities, may be subject to such formalities, conditions, restrictions or penalties as are prescribed by law and are necessary in a democratic society, in the interests of national security, territorial integrity or public safety, for the prevention of disorder or crime, for the protection of health or morals, for the protection of the reputation or rights of others, for preventing the disclosure of information received in confidence, or for maintaining the authority and impartiality of the judiciary.[14]

It is enough to make you wonder what might escape such a broad net of 'conditions, restrictions or penalties'. The 'public safety' and the 'protection of health and morals', for example, sound like the sort of catch-all excuses for restricting free speech beloved of dictators down the decades. Once a formal commitment to freedom of expression is hedged around by so many caveats, it appears as a triumph for the alleged responsibilities over the actual right. It is the restriction of speech in the name of freedom. And it is ultimately up to the learned judges of the UK and European courts, of course, to decide just how much liberty to allow.

In the US, the First Amendment to the Constitution sets out a far clearer commitment to free speech, stating baldly that 'Congress shall make no law ... abridging the freedom of speech, or of the press'. Those fourteen words set a global gold standard for free-speech law that has still to be equalled anywhere in the world more than 200 years later.

Some of us in the UK get called 'First Amendment fundamentalists' for arguing that we could do with a First Amendment-style hands-off attitude to free speech over here. It is not meant to be a compliment, but to imply that there is something of the dangerous extremist about embracing the spirit of the First Amendment. That is a sign of the times.

Yet from the point of view of this free-speech fundamentalist it is arguable that even the First Amendment does not take us far enough. Even in its own legalistic terms, it leaves the interpretation of freedom for the whole of American society in the hands of the nine Supreme Court justices. It is for them alone to judge, for example, whether what somebody says crosses the line from protected speech to 'fighting words' which are granted lower protection. As that same authoritative legal textbook observes with lawyerly understatement, this 'still leaves the right to free speech somewhat exposed'.[15] As we shall see, there have been times in not-so-distant history, such as around the First World War and during the Cold War, when the Supreme Court generally took a dim view of the free-speech rights of any radical political views and dismissed those it deemed to pose a 'clear and present danger' to the status quo.

Once you step outside the legal confines of the courtroom, the power of the First Amendment to protect free speech in America is severely limited. The constitutional ban on legal censorship by the state has not prevented the proliferation of informal censorship and bans across US college campuses, for example.

Those who imagine the US safe from all this behind the all-important First Amendment forget that, even in America, the cultural tide appears to be turning against free speech. We might all do well to recall the words of the US judge Learned Hand who, speaking in 1944 at a wartime rally for liberty in New York's Central Park, warned against investing 'false hopes' in the paper constitution and the courts to protect freedom: 'Liberty lies in the hearts of men and women; when it dies there, no constitution, no law, no court can save it.'[16]

Free speech may not have died in the hearts of the men and women of the West, but it is ailing badly. The combination of official censorship, unofficial censorship and self-censorship is reducing the scope for debate, creating a climate of stultifying conformism and the fear of straying from the straight and ever more narrow. Free speech is left looking like that 'free-range' chicken, fenced in and approaching its use-by date. If we want to live in a truly tolerant world we should reject every demand to cage, censor, parole or punish speech. No matter how sympathetic a case the censors make, and however much you might abhor the words others use.

Behind the universal lip service paid to the principle, if we forget the true meaning of free speech the losers will not only be those relatively few who find themselves banned or prosecuted for 'speech crimes'. We will all be the poorer for allowing the creation of a culture in which people become scared to say what they mean, development of knowledge is stifled, political debates effectively suspended, and where, as the chapters in this section show, from the university campus to the internet we are living with a bland, 'safe' environment in which anodyne becomes the new normal.

It's time to expose the free-speech fraud of those who claim they support it in principle yet dump on it in practice, and to take a stand for unfettered free speech. That will involve a considerable leap in imagination from where we are. Our society has forgotten why free speech should count above other concerns. Such is the lack of faith in freedom that it is not unusual to hear free speech talked about as some kind of trick, something that people 'hide behind' to pursue a different agenda. It is now considered almost unimaginable that anybody could support free speech without a long list of exceptions.

As the political director of Huffington Post UK stated in matter-of-fact style in the aftermath of *Charlie Hebdo*, 'None of us believes in an untrammelled right to free speech. We all agree there are always going to be lines that, for the purposes of law and order, cannot be crossed; or for the purposes of taste and decency, should not be crossed. We differ only on where those lines should be drawn.' Unfortunately his presumption was pretty well justified.[17]

Some of us do, however, believe in 'an untrammelled right to free speech' where opinions and ideas are concerned, regardless of whether or not they might be to our or somebody else's taste. Much of this book is devoted to challenging the arguments for drawing more sweeping lines through free speech for the alleged purposes either of law and order or of 'taste and decency'.

To turn things around means dealing with new opponents of free speech today. The next chapter examines the creeping problem of the silent war on free speech – a war fought by those who claim to support free speech, but … The battlegrounds are many in this war. It is primarily a fight, not just against censorship, but conformism; not just to end restrictive laws, but to free the mind of society.

As the Victorian genius J. S. Mill says, in his landmark essay *On Liberty*, 'Protection, therefore, against the tyranny of the magistrate is not enough; there needs protection also against the tyranny of the prevailing opinion and feeling; against the tendency of society to impose, by other means than civil penalties, its own ideas and practices as rules of conduct on those who dissent from them'.[18] The consequence of what we have forgotten about free speech has been to give a free hand to those who wish to impose conformist ideas as 'rules of conduct on those who dissent from them'. However it is presented and excused, the result of infringing on free speech is always to close down discussion and bland everything out in a world of grey conformism.

No doubt the awful truth is that a world in which we enjoy free speech will contain ugly, difficult and hurtful ideas as well as good and inspiring ones. But the alternative to free speech is inevitably worse. That is why free speech is always a price worth paying, and much too important to pay mere lip service to.

2

The age of the
reverse-Voltaires

I believe in free speech. You believe in free speech. Everybody with
more than two free brain cells to rub together in the free world
believes in freedom of speech. Or so they say.

'Blasphemers' can be sentenced to death in Islamist states. The
internet might be censored to near-death in Communist China. In
our civilised Western universe, however, we still enjoy freedom of
expression. Or think we do.

Ignoring the disaffected online fans of the 'Islamic State', who
tend to favour censoring the press by decapitating journalists, it
would be hard to find serious voices in the Anglo-American world
who publicly reject the principle of free speech as a Good Thing.
Any takers out there for the opposing principle of 'enslaved
speech'?

Strange, then, that so many now choose to exercise their freedom of speech in order to tell the rest of us what we can't say.

This is the dirty secret of the great free-speech fraud. Our politicians and public figures stage displays of support for free speech in
principle. Yet in practice they will trash it. When they say they
support free speech 'in principle' they apparently mean on another
planet, rather than in the real world.

Back here on Earth meanwhile the fashion is to support something called 'free speech-but', as in: 'I believe in free speech-but there are limits/-but not for hate speech/-but you cannot offend or insult or upset other people.' And the buts are getting bigger and wider all the time. As one US commentator had it in the wake of the *Charlie Hebdo* massacre, 'The "but" in the phrase "I believe in free speech but" is bigger than Kim Kardashian's [and] has more wiggle-room than Jennifer Lopez's.'[1] Those remarks would probably get him banned from speaking on several campuses for offensive 'fat-shaming'.

To say that you believe in free speech 'but' is not simply to qualify your support, but to dissolve it altogether. Free speech is not something you can sort-of believe in on a scale of 1 to 10.

To imagine that you could believe in free speech 'but' not for certain opinions is rather like saying 'I believe in scientific proof, but that's no reason to rule out Father Christmas and fairies at the bottom of the garden'; or 'I believe in the equality of the sexes, but equal pay for women is going too far'; or 'I believe in same-sex marriage, but not for lesbians'. The b-word does not 'clarify' your stated belief, but effectively buts it out of existence.

The predominance of the 'but' lobby reflects the underlying ambivalent attitude towards free speech in Anglo-American society. The right to free speech is not only written into the First Amendment to the US Constitution and (with more umming and ahhing) the European Convention on Human Rights, but also apparently into the hearts of the people. In 2014, while the UK's political elites indulged in another round of breast-beating about 'British values', ComRes pollsters asked the British public what they thought the most precious of those values might be. The runaway winner of this popularity contest was old-fashioned red-blooded free speech, with 48 per cent of the vote.[2]

Yet behind the headline support for the principle of free speech, the UK seems not so sure in practice; one major 2007 survey found that a larger section of the British public (64 per cent) supported the right of people 'not to be exposed to offensive views' than supported the right for people to 'say what they think' (54 per cent).[3] Perhaps more surprisingly, polls suggest that many Americans, too, might not be as certain about free speech as they once were. Washington's prestigious Newseum Institute conducts an annual survey on attitudes to the First Amendment, which alongside other liberties enshrines freedom of speech and of the press in the US Constitution. Asked whether they think the First Amendment goes 'too far' in upholding those freedoms, in 2014 38 per cent of Americans answered 'yes' – an increase from 34 per cent in 2013, and a big jump from the mere 13 per cent who said yes in 2012.[4]

Despite enjoying widespread support in principle, in practice free speech is on the endangered list. Freedom of expression today is like one of those exotic animals that everybody says they love, but that still appear to be heading inexorably towards extinction. The difference is that if we continue to lose the habitat where free speech can flourish, the truly endangered species will be humanity as the free and civilised creation we know, love and sometimes hate.

Yes, we all believe in free speech. And yet … everywhere from the internet to the universities, from the sports stadium to the theatrical stage, from out on the streets to inside our own minds, we are allowing the right to freedom of expression to be reined in and undermined. Free speech is seen as a Good Thing gone bad, increasingly regarded with suspicion if not outright hostility. The freedom that, as the next chapter outlines, was so hard won through history is now in danger of being given away without a fight, or even offered up willingly for sacrifice.

Barely a day seems to pass without news of another knock-back for free speech: a proposed British law against the wrong type of political ideas, another US or UK university ban on the wrong types of joke, pop song or speaker on campus, yet another Twitter shitstorm descending on the head of somebody foolish enough to express the wrong 140-character opinion about rape or abortion law, Islam or immigration, Scots or gay adoption.

A steady drip of outrage is eroding the rock of free speech. The response is even worse. On any day when cartoonists are not being murdered in Europe, few voices are raised to speak up for freedom. We seem to spend far more time discussing the problem with free speech and how to curb it than how to defend, never mind extend it. That's why the 'Je Suis Charlie' placards had not even been cleared from the streets before the discussion turned to the importance of avoiding further offence to anybody. And every little extra curb on one sort of speech encourages mission-creep towards censoring another.

The freedom to think what you like and say what you think has become another empty ritual to which we just pay lip service. Even the lip service stops when somebody dares to think it is real and says something beyond the pale or the bland. People might oppose outright censorship, but a self-censoring muted conformism is the order of the day.

What's going on? There is nothing new about free speech being threatened. The modern right to freedom of speech has been under threat since the moment it was first won. It would always be true to say that 'free speech is in danger'. But there is something different happening today.

The danger to free speech in the West now comes not only from such traditional enemies as the little Hitlers and aspiring ayatollahs who disdain to conceal their contempt for liberty. More important today is the challenge from those who claim to support that freedom, yet seek to restrict it in practice. This is the new threat: the silent war on free speech.

It is a silent war, but not because its proponents are quiet – they are anything but. This is a silent war because nobody who expects to be taken seriously will admit that they are fundamentally against the right to free speech. To oppose freedom of expression has historically meant being in favour of fascism, totalitarianism and the burning of heretical books if not of actual heretics. Few want to be seen goose-stepping out in such company today.

Instead we have a silent war on free speech; a war that will not speak its name, fought by wannabe censors who claim that they are nothing of the sort. The result is not violent repression and brute censorship, but the demonising of dissident opinions in a crusade for conformism.

The silent war is not ostensibly aimed against free speech at all. It is posed instead as a worthy assault on the evils of hate speech and incitement. It is presented, not as a blow against liberty, but as a defence of rights: the right to protection from offensive and hateful words and images; freedom from media harassment and internet 'trolling'; the right of students to feel 'comfortable' on campus.

In order to confront these new lines of attack on free speech, it is necessary first to crack the code that is being used to infiltrate our lines. You will rarely hear anybody admit that they hate free speech. Instead the crusaders come up with a coded way to get that message across, and their codes can change as fast as if controlled by an Enigma machine (rather than by a student union committee meeting). You might be accused of hate speech, or told to go and 'check your privilege' (e.g. make sure you are not a white person talking about racism); or you could be accused of 'mansplaining' an issue to women, or of committing 'micro-aggressions' in your speech. All very confusing no doubt, and easy for even a sympathetic speaker to get caught out and left behind the fast-changing tide.

But whatever coded form of words they deploy, the crusaders are really saying one of two things: either 'You-Can't-Say-THAT!', if you're attacked for what is said; or 'YOU-Can't-Say-That!' if the attack is on who said it. Or possibly, both.

But no, no, we must understand, those demanding restrictions on what others can say today are not against free speech. They are simply in favour of freedom from words that may upset or do harm. Who could disagree with such humane sentiments or fail to empathise with those facing what they deem offensive, harmful speech?

You don't have to be a Bambi-shooting bigot to defend unfettered free speech. Quite the opposite. Free speech is the lifeblood of any modern, liberal-minded society. It follows that any attempt to restrict free speech, however worthy the case might sound, imperils a liberty that has helped to make all our other rights possible.

In today's intellectual climate it can sometimes seem as if offending others is the worst offence of all. What are presented as progressive attempts to protect people from harmful words have become coded ways to insist that there is too much freedom of expression. It might sound a nice idea to live in a warm, womblike world of inoffensive insipidity. The problem is that to demand the right not to be offended is to deny everybody's freedom to offend against the accepted ethics and opinions of the age. And without that subversive freedom to question the unquestionable – the right to be offensive – society might never have advanced to a point where anti-racism or LGBT rights became acceptable subjects for public debate in the first place.

Never mind the lip service paid to it 'in principle' by the free-speech fraudsters today. Underlying attitudes to that freedom have not simply altered in recent times. They have been turned on their head.

We are living in the age of the reverse-Voltaires. The revolutionary writer François-Marie Arouet, known by his pen name Voltaire, was a pioneer of free speech in eighteenth-century Enlightenment France. Voltaire is credited with one of the great historical sayings on the subject: 'I disapprove of what you say, but I will defend to the death your right to say it.' (In fact those words that resound down the years were not written by Voltaire, but by his biographer, Evelyn Beatrice Hall. More than a century after his death, she pithily captured the spirit of his writings for an English-speaking audience.)[5]

Voltaire's principle is a clear statement of the attitude to tolerance and free speech that characterised the Enlightenment. Some might prefer the updated version credited to Oscar Wilde – 'I may not agree with you, but I will defend to the death your right to make an ass of yourself' – though the spirit remains much the same. It recognises that free speech is something more than a personal possession, something bigger than a personal opinion. Free speech is too important to be restricted, however it might be used and abused. It is a test of any free society that, with Voltaire, we allow open debate and freedom for the thought that we disagree with or even detest.

Now, however, we have the rise of the reverse-Voltaires. The *cri de coeur* of today's hardcore offence-takers turns his principle inside out: 'I know I'll detest and be offended by what you say, and I will defend to the end of free speech my right to stop you saying it.' The reverse-Voltaires do not wish to dispute ideas or arguments that offend them. They would deny the other person's right to say it in the first place.*

For the reverse-Voltaires, nothing can be more important than their personal emotions, nothing is bigger than their ego or identity. The only test of whether something should be allowed is how it makes them feel (and most important, how it makes them feel about themselves). Reverse-Voltaires cannot tolerate having their opinions challenged, prejudices questioned, self-image disre-

---

* The idea of reversing Voltaire's principle was first publicly championed fifty years ago by the composer Igor Stravinsky. Asked in an American interview why he made such an issue of unfavourable reviews by critics 'of such slight importance', the great man replied: 'I agree that what a reviewer says may be inconsequential, even in the short run. What I protest is his right to say it – Voltaire in reverse.' An attitude that was once the preserve of a few cultural elitists now characterises the outlook of a mob of online crusaders. A classical snob such as Stravinsky would no doubt be horrified. *New York Review of Books*, 3 June 1965.

spected or toes stepped on. The result is a demand to limit free speech in the name of their right to be protected from words.

The reverse-Voltaires are as intolerant of dissent as any old-time religionists. But where the priests of yore based their intolerance on the supposedly objective authority of a supreme God above, today's would-be censors base theirs on the subjective wishes of their personal idol within. They are often self-regarding narcissists; except that where Narcissus fell in love with his placidly beautiful image reflected in a pool of water, they are in love with their angry image of permanently outraged self-righteousness, reflected in the murky pool of social media.

The champion of free speech Voltaire said (in his own words this time): 'Think for yourself and let others enjoy the privilege of doing so too.' The mantra of the reverse-Voltaires is more like: 'Think *of* yourself and don't let others enjoy the privilege of thinking any differently.'

The rise of the reverse-Voltaires, who insist on their right to stop the speech of others, marks a counter-revolution in Western attitudes to free speech.

In the next chapter, we take a whistle-stop tour of the history of how free speech was won in the West. Until a few hundred years ago intolerance was the accepted orthodoxy of the ruling elites in a straitjacketed European society. The belief in free speech first emerged in modern Europe and then America not as an abstract ideal, but as the expression of a newly envisioned freedom in society.

Freedom of speech was conceived as a way for individuals, groups and entire nations to defend their interests against overbearing political or religious authority. It was not only about people having the right to express themselves. It was also about exposing the use and abuse of power, and holding the powerful to account.

That was why the demand for free speech and a free press was at the heart of the movements for democratic government first in

England, then in America, then continental Europe. It was why free speech was spoken of in terms of a battlefield defence – as a 'bulwark' or a 'fortress' in the fight against tyranny. Free speech became the weapon that men (and later, women) would wield to defy and even to help defeat the authoritarian power of states.

That was then. This is now – a time when, rather than embracing the demand for free speech as a defence against the power of the state, many demand that the authorities use their powers to suppress the 'offensive' or 'harmful' speech of other people. Voltaire the free-speaking revolutionary has been replaced by reverse-Voltaire, the radical crusader against excess of freedom. Where once the danger was seen as the state's control of speech, now free speech running wild is the threat proclaimed.

How have we come to this? It is not that free speech has really declined in importance. Freedom of expression remains the most important of freedoms, the voice of a free society.

The real change is one of perceptions. Not just in what we think of words, but in what we think of one another. Attitudes to free speech almost always reflect our attitudes to people, and how much freedom we believe they should have. The growing mistrust of free speech partly reflects the declining faith we hold in humanity. The existentialist philosopher Jean-Paul Sartre suggested that hell is other people. To update Sartre for today, some fashionably misanthropic philosopher might declare that hell is other people's opinions.

These changes in attitude towards words and one another are underpinned by wider cultural shifts that are beyond the scope of an argument about free speech. The consequences, however, should be clear enough. In Anglo-American society today a therapeutic concern with protecting emotions is often seen as more important than a clash of ideas. People are perceived and often perceive themselves as vulnerable, capable of being either harmed or incited to harm others by words alone. The view of humanity as vulnerable, thin-skinned and ultra-sensitive makes free speech appear more dangerous today. In the twenty-first century you can draw moral authority from your status not only as an old-fashioned warrior or a leader, but more often from claiming public recognition as a victim. That elevation of vulnerability into a virtue has clear implications for attitudes towards the liberty of others to indulge in offensive speech.

As people become more wary of one another, free speech has become something to fear, an unpredictable spark that could start a conflagration. The worries about too many words roaming around freely without constraint is really a fear of people being allowed to say and hear what they choose without the guiding hand of a parental figure or policeman.

The reverse-Voltaires are demanding the right to be cocooned against the discomfort caused by other people's words running riot. And they are quite prepared to use official or unofficial forms of censorship to get their way.

We might think that we live in an age when, at least in Western societies, there is less repressive government censorship than at any time in recent memory. Yet as one critic, Philip Johnston, notes, the reality is that in the non-censoring UK, 'more people are being jailed or arrested in Britain today for what they think, believe and say than at any time since the eighteenth century'.[6]

How can there simultaneously be both less censorship and more punishment of words? Because, the UK authorities will insist, the legal crackdown on what people say, especially online, is not state censorship of free speech at all. It is simply a positive attempt to protect people from harmful and offensive words. For example, official figures suggest that on average there are 25,000 proceedings in the UK each year for speech offences under Section 5 of the Public Order Act 1986 alone, with around half ending in convictions. But in the eyes of officialdom that's not censorship, since those arrests were for using words or behaviour the courts considered threatening or abusive.[7]

Laws That Make Offensive Speech a Criminal Offence
Despite the UK's proud boast to be the historic home of freedom since the Magna Carta, dozens of laws impinge on our right to free speech. Here are just a few of the more recent ones that can criminalise speech which some might find offensive.

- Sections 4A and 5 of the Public Order Act (POA) 1986 make it an offence to use threatening, abusive or insulting words or behaviour that causes, or is likely to cause, another person harassment, alarm or distress. This means it can be a crime to say something which *might* upset a hypothetical other, *if* they were to hear it. The scope of the law is further broadened by equating 'words or behaviour', as if words were the same as deeds. (The word 'insulting' has now been removed from Section 5, but only after police and prosecutors assured the politicians that they could arrest and prosecute the same people for using 'abusive' words anyway.)
- Section 127 of the Communications Act 2003 makes it an offence to send a message by means of a public electronic communications network that is grossly offensive, or of an indecent, obscene or menacing character. This is a remarkably sweeping offence – who is to say what is or is not 'grossly offensive'? It has been used to prosecute and imprison people for the crime of making bad jokes and tasteless remarks on social media, or swapping online insults with other football fans.
- The 2006 Racial and Religious Hatred Act amended the Public Order Act to make it an offence punishable by up to seven years' imprisonment to use threatening words or behaviour intended to stir up religious hatred. The 2008

Criminal Justice and Immigration Act further amended the POA to add an offence of using threatening words or behaviour intended to stir up hatred on the grounds of sexual orientation. (Note the characteristic equation of 'words and behaviour'.) These are potentially wide-ranging laws given, for example, that a racist incident is now defined as 'any incident which is perceived to be racist by the victim or any other person'.

- The Terrorism Act 2006 criminalises 'encouragement of terrorism', punishable by up to seven years' imprisonment. The offence is defined so broadly that it includes making statements which are deemed to 'glorify' terrorism, even if that was not the intention of those making the statement. The sweeping law could be used to prosecute not just supporters of Islamic State, but also of, say, Kurdish groups fighting against IS.
- The Offensive Behaviour at Football and Threatening Communications (Scotland) Act 2012 creates two new offences specifically aimed at football fans, at matches and online. The law makes it a crime to use words and gestures around football that would be legal elsewhere. It has been used to arrest, prosecute and even imprison fans for singing offensive football songs – an extraordinary act of authoritarian control in an allegedly free society.

None of these laws would last long if passed by American politicians, since the First Amendment to the US Constitution enshrines the rule that 'Congress shall make no law abridging the freedom of speech, or of the press'.

Source of legal facts: Liberty

In the USA, we are assured, there can be no state censorship of speech, thanks to the protection given by the First Amendment. But that does not stop the politicians trying, in the cause of protecting citizens from harmful words. In May 2014 the New York court of appeals finally struck down as unconstitutional the state's 1965 'aggravated harassment' statute, which made speech deemed 'annoying and alarming' a criminal offence. Weeks later, however, New York state's highest court had to strike down a remarkably far-reaching new law on cyberbullying passed by Albany County, which sought to criminalise any electronic communication posted 'with the intent to harass, annoy, threaten, abuse, taunt, intimidate, torment, humiliate, or otherwise inflict significant emotional harm on another person'. The notion that it could be an offence not simply to threaten but to 'annoy' somebody online was judged to infringe the First Amendment protection of free speech.[8] Yet other US districts still enforce apparently constitutional laws against 'annoying' people with words.

No politician or official in the West, it seems, is publicly in favour of censorship today. A ban, however, by any other name still smells the same. The way that state curbs on speech can now be presented as positive, even liberating, measures is a sign of changing times. But it should not alter our attitude to censorship.

In the UK, once we had to deal with an authoritative nation state that might rarely but unashamedly impose political censorship in the name of defending the 'national interest'. Now we have something more like the 'indignation state', which promiscuously bans words and punishes speakers as a form of therapy, to protect individuals from offensive and outrageous speech. Official censorship today presents a far softer, more people-friendly face. But it is none the better for that.

The UK state now lacks the authority boldly to censor in its own name, using the traditional excuse of 'national security'. When it tries to do so, as with the recent attempts to outlaw 'extremism', it runs into trouble and opposition. More often today the authorities claim to issue bans and pass laws on behalf of others. They insist that they are not attacking free speech, but simply protecting the vulnerable from harmful words. The state censors reluctantly, not because it hates freedom, but only because it is outraged by what it deems offensive hate speech. As Boris Johnson, the Conservative Mayor of London, declared when banning a ridiculous Christian advert about 'curing' homosexuality from the capital's buses, we must be 'intolerant of intolerance'.[9] But then we end up with the even more ridiculous notion of banning the expression of opinions in the cause of freedom.

In the USA the indignation state might be frustrated in its desire to pass laws against offensive hate speech by the pesky First Amendment (although polls claim growing support among Americans for anti-hate-speech legislation). But the US authorities are prepared to go down the route of informal censorship to achieve the same ends. In 2011, as the fifty-six Muslim states of the Organization of the Islamic Conference pushed for an international law prohibiting blasphemy, US Secretary of State Hillary Clinton sought to reassure them that the Obama administration was onside. Clinton told the OIC that, although the First Amendment meant Washington could not ban anti-Islamic speech, rather than stand up for free speech the administration could still apply 'some old-fashioned techniques of peer pressure and shaming so that people don't feel they have the support to do what we abhor.'[10] Arm-twisting and embarrassment, the 'old-fashioned techniques' of the school playground, appear to be the US state's preferred methods to stop the naughty citizens talking out of turn. Where could these Islamists have got the idea that it was legitimate to force blasphemers into silence?

Yet the official censors of our Western governments and courts are rarely the driving force behind censorship today. The authorities more often take their lead from the army of unofficial censors demanding action against allegedly dangerous speech.

These lobby groups, individual politicians, media figures and student activists are the leading reverse-Voltaires of public life. They are often full-time offence-takers, whose default emotion (and emotions count more than ideas now) is outrage. Theirs is a free-floating sense of outrage which, while apparently reflecting a deeply held moral conviction about an issue, can quickly detach itself and move on to the next free-speech scandal.

Among the preferred tools of these crusading reverse-Voltaires are the online petition and the twitterstorm, which can create an instant impression of mass outrage with relatively little effort or substance. These unofficial measures are often sufficient to silence the targeted forms of speech. If not, their demands for official censorship will generally find a willing ear among the UK authorities.

So it was that in November 2014 the UK Home Office took the extraordinary step of barring somebody from entering the country solely because of his unpleasant views. Julien Blanc was not an Islamic extremist or a racist demagogue. He was a professional 'pick-up artist' who hoped to give young British men the benefit of his dodgy advice on how to seduce women. Stupid and sexist no doubt, but hardly subversive.

Yet for the reverse-Voltaires, this pathetic wordplay was not just objectionable, it was intolerable, and had to be stopped. Having successfully lobbied for Blanc to be denied entry to Australia, they turned their attention to the UK. An online petition demanding that his UK visa be blocked, backed by sound and fury on the twittersphere, effortlessly attracted 160,000 virtual signatures. That is the sort of language that the authorities understand, easily drowning out any talk of Blanc's right to free speech. The British government duly banned him. But, they insisted, barring somebody from the country on the basis of his idiotic ideas was not about censorship of opinions. It was because, Home Office minister Lynne Featherstone insisted, his advice on how to pick up women 'could have led to an increase in sexual violence and harassment'.

Alternatively of course, it could have led to nothing more than a few embarrassing moments in the singles bars of Britain. But the new rule is that it's better to be safe than sorry when policing free speech.[11]

The perma-outraged, professionally offended reverse-Voltaires are relatively few in number. Yet they punch well above their weight in terms of influencing public policy and debate – as symbolised by the disproportionate importance attached to their favourite playground, Twitter. They have helped to create an atmosphere in which standing up for a fundamental right – free speech – can be seen as extremism. It is not that most people are enthusiastic about official censorship, but many have internalised the idea that it is better not to offend than to express a controversial opinion. These are the self-censoring 'sorry majority', symbolised by politicians and public figures who will apologise and withdraw their remarks at the first sign of a wagging finger.

The lugubrious England football manager Roy Hodgson encapsulated the spirit of the sorry majority in November 2014, after he was informed that some England supporters at a match against Scotland in Glasgow had been singing anti-IRA songs. Hodgson assured the media that he had not heard the chants in question, but that did not matter: 'If anyone was offended,' declared the England manager, 'I'm sure the FA [English Football Association] would like to apologise to them.'[12] Police confirmed there had been no complaints about the chanting from offended members of the IRA or anybody else, but at the merest mention of the possibility that 'anyone was offended', a national figure who had heard nothing felt moved to issue an official apology to the imagined victims. Such is the effect of the silent war on free speech in creating the stultifying atmosphere in which we live and try to breathe today.

The reverse-Voltaires are seeking to overturn some long-established principles of free speech. Nadine Strossen, a professor at the New York Law School and former president of the American Civil Liberties Union, points out that there are two 'bedrock' principles of free-speech law in America. The first of these is 'content neutrality' or 'viewpoint neutrality': 'It holds that government may never limit speech just because any listener – or even, indeed, the majority of the community – disagrees with or is offended by its content or the viewpoint it conveys.' The second bedrock principle of US law holds that 'a restriction on speech can be justified only when necessary to prevent actual or imminent harm to an interest of "compelling" importance, such as violence or injury to others.'[13]

Twenty years ago, in a book entitled *Defending Pornography: Free Speech, Sex and the Fight for Women's Rights*, Strossen demonstrated how the radical feminist campaign for legal bans on pornography in America 'violates both of these principles', by demanding that a form of expression be restricted because of its offensive content; in order for that campaign to succeed, she wrote, 'the very foundation of our free speech structure would have to be torn up'.

The Nineties' would-be feminist censors might largely have failed. Two decades later, however, the reverse-Voltaires have had considerable success in tearing up the principle of 'content neutrality' and getting speech restricted on the ground that they find what it says offensive. They have not managed to rewrite the legal principles of the US First Amendment (not yet, anyway). But they have secured countless bans in practice on US and UK campuses, and shaped the British state's censoriously interventionist attitude towards offensive speech. As the British conservative commentator John O'Sullivan noted in a *Wall Street Journal* essay reviewing these changes in both the US and the UK, 'Today, content is increasingly the explicit justification for restricting speech. The argument used, especially in colleges, is that "words hurt" ... In the new climate, hurtful speech is much more likely to be political speech than obscene speech.'[14] The success of the reverse-Voltaires in chipping away at those bedrock principles is certainly hurting free speech.

* * *

The silent war on free speech often appears a remarkably one-sided affair. Where are those voices prepared to speak up for freedom against all the official and unofficial censorship, and wake the sorry majority from their self-censoring slumber? There are relatively few prominent figures today prepared to stand on the shoulders of the heroes of the historic fight for free speech. The Tom Paines, John Wilkeses and J. S. Mills of the twenty-first century are most often noticeable by their absence. The outburst of rhetorical support for free speech immediately after the *Charlie Hebdo* massacre was striking precisely because it was so out of kilter with what we (don't) hear the rest of the time.

What has happened to the West's liberal lobby in defence of free speech? They are still willing to speak up for the rights of repressed dissidents in far-flung places, yet when it comes to battles on the home front, many self-styled liberals have accepted the case for restricting the 'wrong' types of speech. It is not just that they are failing to resist the assault. Many have gone over to the other side in the free-speech wars.

This war is not led by the traditional enemies of free speech. It would be easier to defend freedom of expression against old-fashioned bigots and censors. But this silent war is more often prosecuted by liberal politicians, intellectuals, academics, writers, judges and suchlike. And those who might once have been in the front rank of the censorship lobby, from religious conservatives to cranky right-wing politicians, can now find themselves on the receiving end.

This turnaround has even helped to create a situation among progressive-minded students where censorship can appear cool. Once radical youth demanded 'Ban the Bomb'. Today's generation of student activists are often more likely to be demanding that the authorities ban the book, the bloke or the boobs.

A refined-looking liberal lobby of cultural high-flyers might seem to make an unlikely mob of book-burners. But consider if you will the strange case of Monty Python's Flying Circus, Her

Majesty's Most Honourable Privy Council, and the attempt to sanitise Britain's unruly press.

The issues of press freedom and regulation have been in the front line of the UK's free-speech wars in recent times.* In the summer of 2011 a scandal exploded over phone-hacking at Britain's bestselling Sunday tabloid, the *News of the World*. Revelations that journalists had been listening to the private voicemail messages of celebrities, public figures and high-profile crime victims caused a storm of public and political outrage. The turning point came when the *Guardian* reported that the *News of the World* had not only accessed the voicemail of Milly Dowler, a Surrey teenager who was kidnapped and murdered on her way home from school in 2002, but that the paper had also deleted 'key messages', thus giving the Dowlers 'false hope' that their missing daughter was still alive. This last allegation later turned out not to be true, but the damage was done. Rupert Murdoch's News Corp announced the closure of the *News of the World*, and prime minister David Cameron announced a major official inquiry to be headed by Lord Justice Leveson.

That was only the beginning, however. The indefensible hacking of Milly Dowler's messages and other tabloid transgressions were seized upon as the pretext for a broader campaign to purge the tabloid newspapers. Those in UK politics and the liberal media who view the 'popular' in popular press as a dirty word sought to use the sympathetic victims of phone hacking as human shields behind which to advance their campaign to tame the despised, dirt-digging tabloids. The Leveson Inquiry was given the power not just to probe the hacking scandal, but to take apart the entire 'culture, ethics and practice' of the British media and propose a tough new system of regulation to help sanitise what many in high places looked down upon as the gutter press.

---

* For a fuller analysis of and argument on these issues, see Mick Hume, *There Is No Such Thing as a Free Press – And We Need One More Than Ever*, Societas, 2012.

Lord Justice Leveson's final report in late 2012 called for (alongside other punitive measures) a new regulator backed by law to police the press. Shortly afterwards the leaders of Britain's major political parties stitched up a late-night deal over pizza with Hacked Off, the lobby group for state regulation fronted by celebrities such as Hugh Grant, to create a new system of press regulation. It would be underpinned by Royal Charter and overseen by Her Majesty's Most Honourable Privy Council, an ancient secretive group of senior politicians. This suitably medieval-sounding instrument was the first attempt at state-backed policing of press freedom in Britain since the Crown's licensing of all publications lapsed in 1695. The twenty-first-century press, unsurprisingly, failed meekly to line up to receive a right royal thrashing.

Regardless of their feelings about phone-hacking or tabloid journalism, anybody with a liberal mindset or a liberty-loving bone in their bodies should surely have risen up against this attempt to police what can be published and read, and declared that the freedom of the press is the pulse of a free society. Or as that old freedom-lover Karl Marx put it more than 150 years earlier, that 'The free press is the ubiquitous vigilant eye of a people's soul, the embodiment of a people's faith in itself'.[15] That was not quite what happened, however. Instead, many of the UK's most prominent liberals took up the cudgels in support of the Royal Charter and against excessive press freedom. The leading figure in the UK civil liberties lobby, Shami Chakrabarti of the lobby group Liberty, had sat in judgement on the tabloid press and found it guilty, as a select member of Lord Justice Leveson's panel at the inquiry that was effectively a show trial of tabloid journalism. Now the rest of the liberal elite demanded the sentence be carried out.

In the spring of 2014 Hacked Off issued a public demand for the press to bend the knee and submit to being regulated by Royal Charter. Rather more remarkably, Hacked Off was soon able to boast that this illiberal demand had been signed by more than 200 of the UK's 'leading cultural figures'.

The list of those 200-plus prominent signatories read like a who's who of the supposedly enlightened world of arts and culture, science and literature, even including some prominent journalists. It was as if the liberal UK had signed its own death warrant.[16]

One group of signatories which caught my eye included all of the surviving members of Monty Python, then preparing for their big live comeback shows on the London stage. This was a surreal turnaround of the type which bores of a certain age (my age, sadly) might once have called 'Pythonesque'.

Thirty-five years before, the Pythons had to resist a public crusade led by Mary Whitehouse – Britain's most prominent 1970s prude – Christian bishops and Tory councillors to have their movie masterwork, *Monty Python's Life of Brian*, banned from cinemas as blasphemous. Having seen off the old forces of censorship back then, the Pythons and their successors now appeared to have effectively switched sides and joined a secular crusade for less press freedom. The jokes and sketches in their revival show might have remained the same, but the world outside had clearly changed. The excoriatingly funny anti-censorship campaigners of yesteryear (and their younger duller imitators) have become the po-faced pro-regulation prigs of our times. It might seem reasonable to conclude that open-minded liberalism is a dead parrot – not just resting and definitely not 'pinin' for the fjords', and that a new breed of 'illiberal liberalism' now rules the roost.

Shortly after this another symbolic nail was apparently hammered into the coffin of the liberal UK when the actor and former funnyman Steve Coogan – a leading light in the press-bashing Hacked Off lobby, who had declared that 'press freedom is a lie' – was announced as a new patron of the charity Index on Censorship. Since the dark days of the Cold War, Index had campaigned for freedom of speech around the world. Lyudmila Alexeyeva, a leading Soviet-era dissident still campaigning for human rights in Russia at the age of eighty-six, reacted in horror to the news of Coogan's sign-up: 'Index on Censorship is a well-known organisation, and a very important one. There were just a few organisations in the Western world which supported us in Soviet times – and we appreciated it a lot. It is such a pity to hear what is going on with it now.' She added: 'Honestly, maybe I have been too idealistic about the situation with freedom of speech in Great Britain. I was always convinced that this was something immovable – and now we see that this is not so. If we do not have any freedom of speech here in Russia, we do want to see it solidly existing somewhere else in the world. And Britain has always been a citadel of media freedom.'[17] One might wonder for how much longer, if the illiberal liberals have their way.

In the name of protecting people against offensive and allegedly harmful words and images, we are now witnessing attacks on free speech that reactionary politicians might have baulked at in the past. It is not just that people pretend to support free speech in principle while undermining it in practice. In a sign of how far the free-speech fraud has gone, it has now become acceptable for protesters to demand censorship – and yet claim they are fighting for freedom.

A funny thing happened on the way to the theatre in September 2014. Punters arrived at a south London arts venue, The Vaults, expecting to see a new exhibition about the horrors of colonialism and slavery staged by the prestigious Barbican theatre. Instead they witnessed an exhibition of the horror with which some now behold artistic freedom of expression.

Brett Bailey's 'Exhibit B', based on the 'human zoos' that were popular in Europe and America in the age of empire, used black actors in cages to depict the dehumanising effects of racism. It had been exhibited in a dozen European cities before it came to London. But it was apparently deemed unfit to be seen by the public in Europe's greatest and most diverse cultural capital.

An online petition and protests led by black activists accused Exhibit B of racism and 'mental terrorism'. One organiser condemned it as 'in very, very bad taste to our community' and 'offensive to the memory of our ancestors'. Barbican management caved in to their stated demand that 'The Show Must Not Go On', and cancelled the much-anticipated performance. The demise of 'Exhibit B' became Exhibit A in a public showcase of the dangers of a culture that says anybody should have the right to suppress whatever they find offensive.

There could have been several nominations for Most Shocking Performance in this shameful little melodrama. Bad enough was the performance by the self-righteous protesters who took it upon themselves to play the role that had been performed until the 1960s by Britain's official censor, the Lord Chamberlain, and close a show that they decided, without bothering to see it, was 'in very, very bad taste'.[18]

Worse still perhaps was the pathetic performance from the invertebrate theatre authorities (backed by those subtle arbiters of public taste the Metropolitan Police), who effectively hung the white flag from the stage door and allowed the intolerant mob to decide what could be staged in London.

But the award ultimately went to those who argued, apparently with a straight face, that closing down the 'offensive' exhibition was actually a triumph over censorship and for free speech. Protest organiser Lee Jasper, a prominent black rights activist and former adviser to London Mayor Ken Livingstone, declared that the Barbican's attempt to stage 'Exhibit B' without consulting people like him symbolised 'the iniquitous power relations that renders black people [sic] voice inaudible in such debates'. However, Jasper said the protests demanding its closure had shown that they would 'remain muted and silenced' no longer. Thus demanding censorship becomes a blow for free speech.[19]

In February 2015, in England's leading university city of Oxford, protesters gathered to demand 'No Platform' for Marine Le Pen, leader of the right-wing French Front National, who was speaking at the Oxford Union. As masked protesters tried to get past the police and scale the walls, they chanted: 'This is free speech – that's a platform!' The clear implication being that free speech that night was the exclusive preserve of those demanding that the speaker with whom they disagreed be kicked off the public stage.

Such is the surreal atmosphere surrounding free speech today. A time when almost nobody admits to opposing free speech, and even pro-censorship campaigners can claim to be upholding it. The result, as with the closing of Exhibit B, is that explicit attacks on freedom of expression can go virtually unopposed. As Stella Odunlami, one of the black actors denied a chance to perform in the show, put it, 'The protesters have censored me and silenced me. The sense of irony here is heavy.'[20] It will not be the last time we feel the heavy weight of irony in seeing free speech attacked in the name of defending rights and freedoms.

There are other important barriers, too, now being scaled by the reverse-Voltaires in their silent war on free speech. One of the important gains of the Enlightenment was the drawing of a firm line between the private and public spheres of life. The newly independent autonomous individual would have a public voice, and a private space in which to think and speak, free from the watchful eye of any intolerant inquisitor.

That line is now being seriously blurred. There is no place to hide from the silent war on free speech on either side of the Atlantic – even, it seems, inside your own mind.

In the 2014 sporting year, three high-profile figures – two in the UK and one in the US – were pursued by angry mobs in the media and online, demanding that they be kicked out of their particular game. Nothing unusual about that, you might think, in the always over-emotional world of professional sports. Except that these three were not being hounded for anything that happened on the pitch or anywhere in public. They were nailed to the crossbar for words that they used in private phone calls, emails and text messages.

First up for a battering was Donald Sterling, billionaire owner of the LA Clippers basketball team. The US media got hold of a secretly recorded phone call, in which Sterling told a female friend: 'It bothers me a lot that you want to broadcast that you're associating with black people', after she had posted online a photo of herself posing with basketball legend Magic Johnson.[21] The nationwide 'secret racism' storm that followed blew Sterling out of the Clippers and the National Basketball Association.

Next up was Richard Scudamore, chief executive of the English Premier League and one of the most powerful administrators in football. Scudamore was very nearly knocked off his perch after his PA handed a newspaper private emails between him and a group of old friends and colleagues, in which they chatted among other things about somebody having sex with 'skinny big-titted broads' and shared juvenile golf club jokes about 'fending Edna off my graphite shaft'.[22] There followed a huge outcry and demands for Scudamore to be sacked; he survived, at least temporarily, after issuing grovelling public apologies.

Then it was the turn of Scottish football manager Malky Mackay, who had been sacked by Cardiff City. As part of that ongoing business dispute, Cardiff's owners obtained a court order empowering private investigators to raid the homes of Mackay and his former sidekick at the club, Ian Moody, and seize mobile phones and computers. They trawled through thousands of private text messages, a few of which were somehow leaked to the media, featuring such choice phrases as 'Fkin chinkys', 'He's a snake. A gay snake', 'Go on fat Phil. Nothing like a Jew who sees money slipping through his fingers', 'Not many white faces in that lot' and 'I bet you'd love a bounce on her falsies'.[23] Mackay and Moody were branded 'vile' sexists, racists and homophobes, threatened with being banned from football, and both lost their new jobs at another club. When Mackay was subsequently appointed to manage Wigan Athletic, it sparked a repeat row.

None of the words used by the three men were defensible. They were at best stupid and puerile, at worst racist. Yet they should never have had to defend them. None of those offensive words ought to have put Sterling, Scudamore or Mackay in the public stocks, because they were all spoken or written in private conversations.

It has long been accepted that there is a difference between what people think and say in private and their public statements. The notion of interrogating a person's private thoughts at the point of a hot poker went out with the Inquisition. As the seventeenth-century pioneer of English law Sir Edward Coke made clear, in modern civilised society: 'No man, ecclesiastical or temporal, should be examined upon the secret thoughts of his heart.'[24] And a good thing too. Many of us are quite capable of ranting or ridiculing away in private to an extent we would never dream of doing in public. As the English philosopher Thomas Hobbes understood, unlike our public speech, 'The secret thoughts of a man run over all things, holy, profane, clean, obscene, grave and light, without shame, or blame.'[25]

No longer, it seems. Shaming and blaming men for their 'secret thoughts' is now apparently back in style. In recent years the distinction between the public and the private has become as blurred as a muddy touchline. Our voyeuristic political and media class increasingly demands that we be made accountable for what we do in private. Meanwhile exhibitionist public figures have turned their private lives into a profession.

The result of fudging the line between private and public is disastrous for freedom of thought and speech, as one *Washington Post* columnist spelt out in response to the Donald Sterling scandal: 'If you don't want your words broadcast in the public sphere, don't say them … Such potential exposure forces us to more carefully select our words and edit our thoughts.'[26] We are now expected not simply to mind our language, but even to 'edit' our private thoughts to make sure they don't infringe a cultural etiquette.

That ought to be a frightening, unedited, thought. Yet things have now gone so far that there was hardly a word of protest raised against the monstering of those three stooges for their private words. The novelist Joyce Carol Oates felt moved to ask if she was 'the only person in the US surprised that a private conversation, no matter how ugly, can be the basis for such public recrimination?' against Sterling. (She wasn't quite the only one, but the minority was small.) In an article headed 'End of Free Speech in America', she asserted the basic truth that in a democratic society we should be free to 'say anything in private, no matter how stupid, cruel, self-serving or plain wrong, and not be criminalised'. It is a dark sign of the times that those sensible words could themselves now seem shocking to many.[27]

The implications of where this ends are starker still. *Spiked* editor Brendan O'Neill wrote of the 'new inquisition' into men's private thoughts mounted in these cases that: 'There is surely only one solution to the alleged scourge of people saying bad things in private – put a telescreen in every home to capture our banter and alert the morality police to the utterance of dark or daft thoughts.'[28]

The dangerous trend towards policing private words and thoughts brings to mind the all-seeing telescreens, Thought Police and thoughtcrime from George Orwell's *Nineteen Eighty-Four*. One element of Big Brother's system of surveillance is that people are encouraged to spy on one another and inform on what their colleagues, neighbours and even their parents say and do in private. That is echoed in the way that those who leak private information today – such as Sterling's former friend who taped and leaked their private phone conversation, and Scudamore's personal assistant who handed his personal emails to the press – can now be hailed as heroes.

The purpose of Orwell's Thought Police is not simply to punish those found guilty of mentally straying from the correct state diktat. It is also to encourage the rest to practise 'crimestop' – described by Big Brother's public enemy number one, Emmanuel

Goldstein, as 'the faculty of stopping short, as though by instinct, at the threshold of any dangerous thought ... Crimestop, in short, means protective stupidity.'[29]

Thanks, but some of us would rather take the risk of living in a relatively free world where there might be dodgy private texts lurking on somebody's smartphone, rather than one where everybody's unedited inner thoughts can be laid bare and we are kept safe in a blanket of collective 'protective stupidity'. The stymying of new ideas and stagnation of discussion and debates are just two casualties of the silent war on free speech.

We have arrived at a peculiar point in history where the danger is not only that the free-speech wars will be lost, but that it will no longer be considered worth fighting them. It is almost 350 years since Spinoza declared that 'In a free state, every man may think what he likes and say what he thinks.' In our twenty-first-century free states, many would find his straightforward case for freedom as unpalatable as did the Jewish elders of seventeenth-century Amsterdam, who banned him from the synagogue and cursed him to damnation as a heretic. As an online mob of heretic-hunters might tweet Spinoza today, 'Think what you like and say what you think? WTF? You-Can't-Say-THAT!'

To put these unprecedented developments in a bit of perspective, to help grasp what's at stake and how strange are these times, the next chapter runs through some highlights of the historic struggle for free speech. It is a bloody tale in which the forces for free speech are always struggling and often under threat. It makes the willingness and even enthusiasm of so many today to give it away without a fight seem all the more inexcusable.

3

A short history of free-speech heretics

In the beginning was the Word, and the Word was with God. And God gave the Word to be spoken only by Kings and Cardinals and Barons and Archbishops. And God saw that it was Good.*

Or at least, that's what the kings and the archbishops assured the peasants that He had told them. But God was wrong.

And so it came to pass that the people took the Word and made it their own. And they used the Word to tell the kings and the cardinals and the barons and archbishops where they could render their commandments. Thus did Man create free speech. The rulers of all faiths and none have been trying to take the word back from the ruled ever since.

Free speech was not a gift from the gods, an act of charity handed down by governments, or a natural right that grows on trees. Like any freedom worth having, it often had to be taken at the point of a sword as well as a pen, in the West as much as elsewhere.

Greek mythology has it that Prometheus stole fire from the gods on Mount Olympus for the good of humanity. In the non-mythol-

---

* With apologies to the King James Bible, St John 1:1.

ogised history of Western civilisation, real-life heroes had to seize free speech from earthly lords to enable humanity to light the fires of liberty and progress. In the process they also won the freedom to spread salacious gossip, fifty shades of guff and a billion selfies.

That those heroes of history won a degree of freedom not only to think in private but to speak as they saw fit is a victory still to be admired. But free speech is not a prize to be gained once and then taken for granted, a trophy stuck on a shelf gathering dust while we reminisce about the battles of yore. Down the centuries the right to freedom of expression has had to be defended, fought for and advanced over and again, against new enemies and fresh arguments. It is worthwhile reminding ourselves how hard-won the liberties we often take too lightly today were.

The hard history of the fight for free speech in the West – beginning in England before moving to America – is really the story of the painful birth and often-stunted growth of our modern democratic society. Free speech in the form that we know it is still a relatively new idea. The American Declaration of Independence, published in 1776, begins with the famous statement that: 'We hold these truths to be self-evident, that all men are created equal, that they are endowed by their Creator with certain unalienable Rights, that among these are Life, Liberty and the pursuit of Happiness.' Thomas Jefferson and the other authors of that historic cry for freedom might have considered rights and liberties self-evident, but until the age of Enlightenment in which they were writing, such 'truths' would have been evidently unimaginable to many.

There is not and never has been anything 'natural' about the right to freedom of speech. These liberties were man-made, hewn out of turning points in history. This point is of more than historical interest. If freedom of expression did not always exist and had to be created by humanity, it follows that that right need not automatically exist for ever. Free speech can also be destroyed or at least redefined out of existence if we allow it.

Free speech, understood as the ability to openly express an opinion, take part in public debate and criticise those in authority, is not nearly as old in the West as some might imagine. The year 2015 marks the 800th anniversary of the sealing of England's Magna Carta, an historic document through which a collection of barons and bishops forced King John to concede for the first time certain legal rights to 'free men', including the right to trial by a jury of their peers. For establishing the idea that there were limits to the power of the Crown, the Magna Carta should rightly be celebrated as creating a prototype for liberty in the Anglo-American world, laying what one legal authority called 'the foundation for the freedom of the individual against the arbitrary power of the despot'.[1] Yet the historic Magna Carta, which establishes such important foundations of our civilisation as the standard measure of a pint of ale, makes no mention of freedom of speech. That was hardly surprising. Such a concept would have been meaningless for the mass of people in the England of 1215, among the most advanced nations of its medieval age.

In feudal society the natural order of things, accepted as God-given, was that peasants were in bondage to the lords, and did their bidding. A serf owned 'only his belly', which might well be empty – all else was the property of the lord of the manor. One typical seventh-century oath of loyalty pledged that the Anglo-Saxon serf would follow his master's will 'according to the laws of God and the order of the world. Nor will I ever with will or action, through word or deed, do anything which is unpleasing to him, on condition that he will hold to me as I shall deserve it.'[2] A society in which the mass of people were sworn 'according to the laws of God and the order of the world' to do nothing 'unpleasing' to their lord 'through word or deed', on pain of harsh but 'deserved' punishment, was not one in which the idea of public free speech could even be articulated, never mind understood or accepted.

The one 'right' which mattered most until a few hundred years ago was the divine right of kings to rule. It was captured in the

English Crown's royal motto 'Dieu et Mon Droit' – old Norman French for 'God and My Right'. The double meaning of 'right' is deliberate. The king ruled in theory by divine right, having been placed on the throne by the grace of God. In practice, he ruled by the exercise of 'my right' – the power of his sword-wielding right arm and the forces it commanded. Anybody who challenged that right, by word or deed, could expect to feel the force of it. (The same royal motto of state power still adorns British courts and official buildings, in case any of us upstarts get ideas above our station and start to imagine we might be free citizens rather than subjects of the Crown.)

Matters of English state were legitimately to be discussed only by the king and his courtiers, quite possibly in Norman French. In 1275, sixty years after the original Magna Carta was first sealed, King Edward I could impose the law of *Scandalum Magnatum*, which made it a grave offence 'to tell or publish any false News or Tales' that might defame or cause disaffection towards the king 'or the Great Men of the Realm' – effectively outlawing much public criticism of Crown and government. Other laws enforced by the Crown and the Church ruled that matters of faith were officially to be read and spoken of only by the priesthood, in Latin. Anything else could be deemed heresy, potentially punishable by death. The political principle of free speech could not take hold in England or Europe until humanity moved history on, the notion of individual rights gained currency and people began to question the absolute power of Crown and Church.

There were some pre-Enlightenment attempts to give a voice to the lower orders and challenge the monopoly of the king and his Great Men over public affairs. During the Peasants' Revolt of 1381, for example, the radical priest John Ball – who had apparently been excommunicated by the Church for preaching to the people in the English vernacular – addressed the rebels at Blackheath in a famously subversive sermon. Ball posed the question, 'When Adam delved and Eve span, Who was then the gentleman?', exhorted the peasants to 'consider that now the time is come, appointed to us by God, in which ye may (if ye will) cast off the yoke of bondage, and recover liberty' and ended by recommending 'first killing the great lords of the realm, then slaying the lawyers, justices and jurors'. But the revolt failed, and Ball was hanged, drawn and quartered for his words, his head stuck on a pike on London Bridge as a warning to anybody else tempted to speak out against the 'great lords of the realm'.[3]

Those in authority did all they could to preserve their public monopoly on the Word. The first printing press was introduced to England by William Caxton in 1476. The response of successive English monarchs to this miracle of the modern age (apart from an impulse to smash the infernal machine) was to control it. They imposed a system of Crown licensing under which nothing could legally be published except with the permission of the Star Chamber, a secret court of privy councillors and judges, and any criticism of the Crown could be branded treason or seditious libel. The stone walls of the Tower of London still bear graffiti scratched by men imprisoned there because their loose words offended the Crown.

In 1579, the Puritan John Stubbs had his writing hand publicly severed with a cleaver in Westminster marketplace for publishing a pamphlet criticising the proposed marriage of Queen Elizabeth I to a French Catholic duke. In 1637 another Puritan author, William Prynne, had his ears cut off for writing pamphlets attacking the religious policies of King Charles I's regime; Prynne was also branded on both cheeks with 'SL' for Seditious Libeller. Even as late as 1663 John Twyn was hanged, drawn and quartered at Tyburn in London – now Marble Arch – under the recently restored King Charles II, having been found guilty of high treason for printing – not writing – a 'seditious, poisonous and scandalous book' justifying the people's right to rebel against injustice.[4]

Intolerance remained a core 'value' of Western culture until the dawn of modernity. As late as 1691, the French Catholic theologian Jacques-Bénigne Bossuet could boast that: 'I have the right to persecute you because I am right and you are wrong.'[5] No nonsense about everybody being 'entitled to their opinion' there. With the ruling elites declaring their 'right to persecute' anybody whose beliefs strayed from the official line, notions of free speech were not to be tolerated.

The phrase 'freedom of speech' first appeared in English writing just less than 400 years ago, coined by the famous jurist Sir Edward Coke in his *Institutes of the Lawes of England* (first published in 1628), which laid the foundations of England's common law. It was in the seventeenth-century age of Enlightenment that the growing belief in the freedom of the individual made free speech both necessary and desirable. Even then King James I was at pains to make clear to members of parliament that 'freedome of speech ... are no Theames, or subjects fit for vulgar persons' such as MPs 'or common meetings' such as the House of Commons.[6]

Not too long after that, however, freedom of speech and of the press burst out as a burning political issue in the struggles between king, Church and parliament in the run-up to the English Revolution (often called the civil war, sometimes by those who still wish to pretend that respectable old England could never have had a bloody revolution or beheaded the king). That fire was to burn across the Atlantic, where the demand for freedom of speech and of the press would be at the heart of the American Revolution and the constitution of the new republic.

But what about the ancient Greeks? Surely they are famous for practising free speech in their assemblies and auditoriums, a couple of thousand years before Sir Edward Coke came up with the phrase in English or the Founding Fathers wrote the First Amendment? A glance back at the Greek experience throws some revealing light on free speech in the modern age.

Freedom of speech did prevail in the civilised society of ancient Athens – at least for the privileged minority of full male citizens, if not for their slaves and certainly not for their womenfolk. Like much else discovered or invented by ancient civilisations, from science to sewers, the concept of free speech in society disappeared in Europe's Dark Ages before being reinvented once more in the modern world.

When free speech and the freedom of the printing press became a burning issue in seventeenth-century England, its new champions looked back to the ancient Athenian tradition for support. In 1644 the poet John Milton published his classic pamphlet arguing for the freedom of the press – 'the liberty of unlicensed printing' – in the middle of the English civil war. Milton named it *Areopagitica*, after a speech given by the Greek philosopher Isocrates in the fourth century BC. The founding fathers of the American republic also liked to see themselves standing in the classical tradition of Athenian free speech.

Yet free speech – or *parrhesia* as they called it – meant something different to the ancient Greeks than to Milton or Jefferson or indeed to us. Athenian democracy was based on the idea of all citizens being of equal standing and merit. The offices of state could be filled by any of them, chosen at random through a lottery rather than a contested election. Free speech represented this equality of merit. It was not supposed to be about freedom from overbearing government, which is what Milton and later James Madison wanted. As an expert study says, the ancient Athenians 'lived in a city where there was no external government – no other – with the potential to oppress them. Freedom of speech was the tool of self-government, not a bulwark [against tyranny].'[7]

The Athens experience did help to mark out the field for the conflicts over free speech in the modern era. Most notably with the trial and execution of the greatest of philosophers, Socrates, who was put to death at the age of seventy for talking out of turn. Scholars have long asked how the pure democracy of Greece, founded upon a commitment to free speech among its citizens, could have executed the wisest of men as a criminal purely for what he thought and said.

The short answer is apparently that Socrates 'just went too far' in exercising his freedom of speech.[8] He was the philosopher who questioned everything, often to the discomfort of his fellow citizens, and refused to be bound by the sacred traditions or deities of Athens society. The formal charges against Socrates accused him of 'not believing in the gods that the city believes in' – heresy. Nor did Socrates believe in restraining his speech in line with the Athenian tradition of Aidos – respect, modesty or shame. He was, literally, shameless, even stripping naked to speak before his accusers to symbolise that everything must be out in the open. And the naked philosopher made clear to the Athenian court that even if they voted to spare him, he would not change, but would continue saying the unsayable and asking the forbidden questions. The jurors in the tribunal voted 280–221 for his conviction.

The trial and execution of Socrates shows that free speech can always be a dangerous and contentious thing. Even in a society of equals with a commitment to open discussion, many who think they believe absolutely in that principle will recoil when confronted with free speech bare-arsed and red in tooth and claw. So it could be that, in the end, '[w]hen Socrates practises *parrhesia* as the Athenians understood it, the bold affirmation and shameless articulation of what one believes to be true, the Athenians vote to execute him'.[9] How much more horrifying real free speech must seem to many who claim to support it in our timid society today.

Socrates posed the question that, for all the changes down the centuries, still stands as a central issue in the free-speech wars: should there be a right to be a heretic? Heresy is often at the heart of struggles over free speech. What changes is what society might consider to be heresy at different stages in history.

Heresy is defined as a belief contrary to orthodox religious opinion; or in non-religious terms, an opinion profoundly at odds with what is generally accepted. To be a heretic is not a self-defined label like Socialist, Conservative, Republican, Democrat or Klingon. Heresy is always a label stuck on you by somebody else, to define your opposition to the prevailing orthodoxy.

The origins of heresy are revealing. It comes, like many of the best words, from the ancient Greek. An early Christian leader defined his own views as 'orthodox', from the Greek for 'right belief'. The views of his opponents he branded as heresy – from the Greek for 'choice of belief'.

The thing that has always got you branded a heretic is making an intellectual choice. Heresy is the desire to choose what you believe in and to dissent from the authoritative dogma of the day. What better case for freedom of speech could there be than that?

Those called heretics of one stripe or another have often been the heroes, the whipping boys and the *causes célèbres* in the historic struggle for freedom of speech. From the trial of Socrates to today, the big battles have been about the right to go against the grain, dissent from respectable opinion and question the unquestionable. What we might call the Right to be Offensive.

The rest of this chapter is by no means intended as a comprehensive history of the modern struggle for free speech, but just a few highlights of moments when religious, political, cultural and sexual heretics have fought for the right to dissent. It is a story that begins in England and moves on to America to set the new standard for liberty.

In the first wave of the modern free-speech wars in England, those demanding free speech were religious heretics. The Puritans and other advocates of the new Protestant thought wanted the right to break ranks with the ruling Church of Rome and to preach and worship in their own way. At the heart of their heretical demand was the wish to have a Bible printed in their own English language. The punishment for such heresy was for not only the book, but also the printer, to be burned at the stake. Despite the ban, William Tyndale famously printed an English version of the New Testament in Germany in 1526 and smuggled it into England. Tyndale was eventually executed by strangulation and then burned at the stake for the crime of heresy in 1536. Just three years after he was executed, Henry VIII – having by now split from Rome and founded the Church of England – gave approval for an English text, the Great Bible, based on Tyndale's translation, to be printed and made available to every church. Yesterday's blasphemous heresy had become today's orthodox religious belief.

The role of religious heretics in demanding free speech is worth remembering, when religion is often seen purely as a force for reaction and repression. Since these religious heretics came up against the censorious power of the central authority, their demands soon melded into a rising political clamour for the freedom of the press.

As the English civil war broke out between the king and parliament, John Milton published his plea for unlicensed printing in 1644, the *Areopagitica*, asking parliament to 'Give me the liberty to know, to utter, and to argue freely according to conscience, above all liberties.'[10] Milton was equally adamant that those who published blasphemy should still be punished after the event. Nor did he wish the liberty to 'utter and argue freely' to be extended to those devilish Papists or non-believers. Tolerance has always been a difficult principle to uphold in practice.

The turmoil of the English Revolution, when the king was overthrown and executed in 1649 and the 'order of the world' turned on its head, brought new voices from below into public life for the first time. The radical Levellers movement formulated its own demands for more far-reaching changes in society, not least in relation to freedom of speech and of the press. Leveller John Lilburne called for an end to state licensing of the press as 'expressly opposed and dangerous to the liberties of the people'. They met with Oliver Cromwell's parliamentary leaders in the Putney Debates of 1647, unprecedented meetings where ordinary soldiers and peasants argued with commanders and aristocrats. The Levellers were soon betrayed and crushed, but the Putney Debates left the legacy of the voice of the people 'speaking truth to power' for possibly the first time, as in Leveller sympathiser Sir Thomas Rainsborough's statement that 'the poorest he that is in England hath a life to live as the greatest he … and I do think that the poorest man in England is not at all bound in a strict sense to that Government that he hath not had a voice to put himself under'.[11]

The English monarchy was restored in 1660, and whatever gains for free speech had been made were soon buried again under a new system of Crown licensing of the printing press. But as the 'Glorious Revolution' replaced the autocratic Catholic King James II with the Protestant William and Mary, parliament passed a Bill of Rights in 1689. This wrote freedom of speech and debate into English law, at least for those 'vulgar persons' the members of parliament and their 'common meetings' in Westminster. It was a sign of how important the rise of free speech would be in the emerging struggle for democracy on both sides of the Atlantic that free speech should first be enshrined in law in relation to parliament – however limited both that freedom and democratic government were at first. By 1695, the system of Crown licensing of the press finally ended, and the news-sheet-reading society of the London coffee houses started to develop more liberal attitudes. The fight for freedom of speech and of the press, however, was just beginning.

It was in that same era of England's Glorious Revolution that John Locke, philosopher and physician, took society another step forward towards enlightenment. In 1689 Locke's *A Letter Concerning Toleration* appeared (actually a private letter to a friend, who promptly published it). The letter established the classical liberal case for freedom of conscience – the precursor of public freedom of speech. Locke's message was a direct challenge to the intolerance of the old order, which had deployed Inquisitions and blasphemy laws to try to force heretics to change their minds and submit to the religious orthodoxy of the times. That, argued Locke, was both wrong in principle and useless in practice. Instead, he insisted, 'the care of each man's salvation belongs only to himself', since 'faith is not faith without believing'. Anybody forced outwardly to follow a religious creed in which they did not inwardly believe was not being saved, but was putting their salvation at risk. Therefore governments should stick to 'civil interests', protecting people's 'life, liberty, health ... and the possession of outward things, such as money, lands, houses, furniture, and the like'.

But the state had no business interfering in matters of conscience or faith: 'The business of laws is not to provide for the truth of opinions, but for the safety and security of the commonwealth and of every particular man's goods and person.' More than three centuries later that is a message we might think our rulers would do well to take on board today, when many governments seem to think that testing 'the truth of opinions' and failing those they disapprove of is very much the business of laws. In his own time, Locke's argument for toleration and freedom of conscience marked an important transition in the developing case for freedom of speech.[12]

In the 1760s, the English free-speech wars were carried forward by one of my favourite heretical heroes, John Wilkes – maverick journalist, printer, member of parliament and Lord Mayor of London, and a pioneer of the fight for liberty and democracy. At a time when any criticism of the Crown and its ministers could still get you locked up for seditious libel, Wilkes published a scandal-mongering newspaper, *The North Briton*, that ridiculed the royal court and its pet politicians – often suggesting, for example, that the king's mother was intimate with the prime minister – and declared on its front page that 'the liberty of the press' was 'the birthright of every Briton'.

For publishing what the authorities deemed heresy, Wilkes was convicted of both seditious libel and blasphemous libel, sent to the Tower of London, imprisoned for almost two years, declared an outlaw, expelled from parliament and then barred from returning, despite winning four elections. In the course of these personal struggles Wilkes helped win hard-fought victories for liberty. He effectively ended the British state's use of arbitrary 'general warrants' to arrest political opponents, established the right of English electors to choose their MP, and won the vital freedom of newspapers to report what the country's rulers said and did behind the doors of parliament.

Wilkes the Georgian gentleman heretic was one of the earliest examples of a people's champion, a popular figure in a way that writers or politicians could only dream of being today. The cry of 'Wilkes and Liberty!' resounded through the streets of London, often accompanied by the sounds of that pre-democratic expression of the people's will, the riot. When the fight for the right to report what was said in parliament reached its climax in 1771, and Wilkes's allies arrived at Westminster to be sent to the Tower, a reported 50,000 Londoners laid siege to parliament in their defence and came close to lynching the prime minister, Lord North. As the *Middlesex Journal* reported these riotous scenes: 'Lord North's chariot glasses were broken to pieces, as was the carriage soon afterwards, by which he received a wound, and was exceedingly terrified. The populace also took off his hat and cut it into pieces, and he narrowly escaped with his life.'[13]

The Wilkes riots left the British ruling class exceedingly terrified of a populace now demanding liberty and the freedom of the press. Yet the figure at the centre of this crisis was hardly a righteous crusader for high principles or squeaky-clean campaigner for human rights. John Wilkes was no Angelina Jolie. He was a notorious rake, a scoundrel, a womanising drunkard, gambler and debtor. He once described his journalistic method thus: 'Give me a grain of truth and I will mix it up with a great mass of falsehood so that no chemist will ever be able to separate them.'[14] His publications which became *causes célèbres* in the fight for press freedom mixed scurrilous scandal with downright filth. At the same time as

Wilkes was convicted of seditious libel by the House of Commons for criticising the king, he was also found guilty of obscene libel by the House of Lords for publishing pornographic poetry.

Yet Wilkes the heretic and his ignoble publications helped to change the course of political history and struck a major blow for press freedom. To my mind John Wilkes the scoundrel and publisher of porn was far more of a moral force for good than any high-handed attempt to limit people's freedom of speech 'for their own good'. His story is a reminder that in the real world, freedom is less an abstract principle than a messy and sometimes bloody business, and that high-minded notions of liberty can be deployed for base aims, too. That does not alter the need to defend the principle of free speech, regardless of what we might think of its specific content, and the rights of the heretical heroes who fight for it, even if, like Wilkes, they have feet caked in clay.

The ideas of liberty pioneered by English radicals and revolutionaries such as Milton, Wilkes, Tom Paine and the two newspaper essayists who wrote as 'Cato' helped to inspire the revolutions that swept first America and then France at the end of the eighteenth century. These republican uprisings were to take the concept of free speech some way beyond its English origins.

The American settlement had famously been founded by religious heretics from England – the Pilgrim Fathers – seeking space to replace the ruling orthodoxy with one of their own. When the colonies came under control of the Crown, the authorities quickly found that their American subjects had minds of their own and were willing to speak them. One study suggests that more than 1,200 prosecutions for seditious speech took place in the sparsely populated British American colonies in the seventeenth century. While few of these concerned printed words, as there were only a handful of printing presses in America, 'the massive number tells us that people had things to say that government and church officials did not like'.[15]

In the eighteenth century Americans proved to have many things to say that the colonial authorities did not like. By the 1770s, heretics who rejected the divine right of the English king to control their lives became the leaders of the American Revolution. Their success in mobilising support was due in no small part to the radical pamphlets and newspapers they had fought for the freedom to publish. Looking back on these momentous events later, the second US president John Adams reflected that the war for American independence which started in 1775 was not the real revolution. That, said Adams, had been the earlier revolution in the hearts and minds of the people, the spark for which had been the pamphlets and newspapers 'by which the public opinion was enlightened and informed'.[16] Freedom of expression had proved the catalyst for the creation of a free nation.

Little wonder, then, that after independence was won the First Amendment enshrined that freedom in the new US Constitution in 1791, establishing that: 'Congress shall make no law respecting an establishment of religion, or prohibiting the free exercise thereof; or abridging the freedom of speech, or of the press; or the right of the people peaceably to assemble, and to petition the Government for a redress of grievances.' Two years earlier, in 1789, the revolutionary French National Assembly had passed the declaration that: 'The free communication of thought and opinion is one of the most precious rights of man; every citizen may therefore speak, write and print freely' in the new French republic.

It might seem that the fight for freedom of speech as a universal right had been won in parts of the West, the issue settled. But history suggests that is never true – even in America. A few years after the First Amendment was passed, it was effectively bypassed by laws that sought to criminalise criticism of the US government.

The commitment of the Founding Fathers to freedom of speech was not necessarily as deep or as wide as might be assumed. When they were drafting and arguing over America's Bill of Rights, the principle gained the iconic status of First Amendment almost by accident; freedom of speech and of the press had actually been the fourth article presented by James Madison to the first session of the US Congress in 1789. Thomas Jefferson and the other Founding Fathers took their lead from the restricted form of free speech written into English law; they had, says one critical historian, 'an unbridled passion for a bridled liberty of speech'.[17]

The question of how tight that bridle should fit was soon tested, with the passage of the Aliens and Sedition laws in 1798. Not for the last time, the US government used a foreign threat, real or imagined, to justify restricting liberties at home: in this case the threat from 'Wild Irishmen' and French 'Jacobins'. The Sedition Act made it a serious offence, punishable by fines, prison and even deportation, to utter or write words which might 'defame' the US president, government or Congress, bring them into 'contempt or disrepute', or 'excite against them … the hatred of the good people of the United States'. In short, it potentially became a crime to criticise the American government. The oppressive old English laws of seditious libel had effectively been transported to the new America, the First Amendment notwithstanding.

It was when faced with the threat of being branded seditious – that is, being cast in the role of heretics – that the opposition became First Amendment fundamentalists. James Madison now argued that the American system of government was different from the British, resting as it did on the sovereignty of the people rather than of parliament. Therefore 'a different degree of freedom in the use of the press' was required. That freedom must be extended beyond 'an exemption from previous restraint, to an exemption from subsequent penalties also'.[18] In other words Americans must have the right not only to speak and publish freely, but to be free from the threat of being punished by the government afterwards. The Sedition Act lapsed, Madison was elected fourth president of the United States in 1809, and free speech took another unsteady step forward.

The story of the First Amendment and the Sedition Act is a tale that reveals how even in the heart of the land of the free, public freedom of speech has never been a right that can safely be taken for granted for long.

Back in Britain in the early nineteenth century, freedom of speech and of the press became central issues for the Chartists and others campaigning for a democratic system of government and the extension of the vote.

Even after state licensing of the press had ended, governments imposed a stamp tax on newspapers to try to price the growing radical press out of the reach of working people. These penalties were increased after the infamous 1819 Peterloo Massacre in Manchester, when cavalry troops charged a mass rally for parliamentary reform (the booming industrial city still had no MPs to represent it), leaving an estimated 15 dead and up to 500 injured.

The government of Lord Castlereagh moved quickly, not to reform the system but to repress the protest movement and the free press. One new law increased the maximum penalty for writing or publishing 'blasphemous and seditious libels' against the religious and political authorities to fourteen years' transportation – banishment from Britain to a penal colony. Another extended the stamp tax for the first time to publications carrying political opinions. This became known contemptuously as the 'tax on knowledge'. Many radicals refused to pay it and went to jail for editing, writing or simply selling heretical newspapers. These heretics played a key role in forcing greater democracy on the 'Mother of Parliaments'.

Elsewhere in Europe, too, the radical movements that ignited the democratic revolutions of 1848 across the continent put their right to speak out against the status quo at the forefront of their demands. Karl Marx, revolutionary author of the *Communist Manifesto* and *Capital*, is often thought of as an enemy of freedom, thanks to the association of his name with the repressive system of the Stalinist Soviet Union. Less well known is that the first articles the young Marx published in a German newspaper in 1842 were a series of essays 'On Freedom of the Press', fiercely attacking Prussian state censorship and insisting that 'lack of freedom is the real mortal danger for mankind'.[19]

The nineteenth-century case for free speech took another leap forward with the publication of John Stuart Mill's *On Liberty* in 1859. Mill made an uncompromising case for individual freedom of speech as a social good, and the importance of allowing the heretical voice to test the accepted truths and values of society:

> If all mankind minus one were of one opinion, and only one person were of the contrary opinion, mankind would be no more justified in silencing that one person, than he, if he had the power, would be justified in silencing mankind …
> If the opinion is right, they are deprived of the opportunity of exchanging error for truth; if wrong, they lose, what is almost as great a benefit, the clearer perception and livelier impression of truth, produced by its collision with error.[20]

Mill's message was far from universally accepted, however, even in the high seats of English learning. In that same year of 1859, Charles Darwin finally published his masterwork outlining the theory of evolution, *On the Origin of Species*. The blasphemous book was soon banned from the library of Trinity College, Cambridge, the university where Darwin had been a student.

In mid-nineteenth-century America, too, free speech was still a battleground, nowhere more so than in the struggle over slavery. Pro-slavery forces outlawed criticism of slavery in southern states, and passed 'gag rules' at federal level to prevent anti-slavery petitions being discussed in Congress, creating what one study calls 'the Southern blockade against free speech about slavery'. These bans and restrictions went unchallenged by the US Supreme Court, which did not consider free speech in the states to be its business until well into the twentieth century.[21]

By the twentieth century, one might imagine that the idea of heretic-hunting and damning blasphemers was well past its use-by date in the democratic West. Yet there were still new challenges to face and battles to be fought for free speech – and not just against Nazi Germany or Stalin's Soviet Union, either. In the 'American century', it is no surprise that the US should have become a key battleground in the free-speech wars. Time and again, it was those seeking to change society who found themselves cast in the role of heretic and witch-hunted for their views.

For example, in the years just before the First World War the revolutionary syndicalists of the Industrial Workers of the World – better known as the IWW, or Wobblies – fought (both politically and physically) to organise impoverished and unemployed American workers in a militant trade union. Some of the Wobblies' fiercest battles became known as the 'Free Speech Fights'. Whenever the local authorities threw IWW organisers in jail simply for making public recruitment speeches, large numbers of Wobblies would descend on the town to demand their release and the right to free speech.

As the best-known radical history of the Wobblies says of the San Diego Free Speech Fight in 1912, 'The word spread in the hobo jungles that "Out there in San Diego/Where the western breakers beat/They're jailing men and women/For speaking on the street."'[22] The Wobblies' Free Speech Fights were in the best American tradition of resolutely demanding that paper rights be made real. As the radical critic Courtenay Lemon wrote, these political heretics had 'kept alight the fires of freedom, like some outcast vestal of human liberty. That the defence of traditional rights to which this government is supposed to be dedicated should devolve upon an organisation so often denounced as "unpatriotic" and "un-American" is but the usual, the unfailing irony of history.'[23]

Between the two world wars the US Supreme Court became the scene of several major cases – remarkably, the first ones it had ever heard concerning the First Amendment – that set new benchmarks in the legal battle to defend and extend free speech. We need not wade through the legal details here. Some cases were won, some lost, notably during the 'Red Scare' crackdown on political radicals after the First World War (the Supreme Court's famous ruling regarding shouting fire in a theatre is discussed in a later chapter). But they helped eventually to broaden the legal definition of free speech under the First Amendment. And none of those court cases was a narrow legal affair. Most were about political heretics engaged in political struggle in wider American society, attempting to challenge the mainstream consensus and force the state to acknowledge their free-speech rights, be they anti-war agitators, religious pacifists, anarchists, socialists, anti-Semites or Communists.

In the Cold War decades after the Second World War, an icy front of anti-Communist laws sought to freeze free speech in America, with the complicity of the Supreme Court. During the era of the McCarthyite witch-hunts in the 1950s, the Supreme Court refused to uphold the First Amendment rights of the black-listed movie screenwriters, directors and producers known as the Hollywood Ten. Then, in the liberalising atmosphere of the 1960s, two challenges from heretical views at either end of the political spectrum finally broke further new ground in building the 'bulwark' of free speech in America.

In the 1964 case of *New York Times Co v. Sullivan*, the Supreme Court found for the newspaper against L. B. Sullivan, the public safety commissioner in Montgomery, who claimed that he had been libelled in an advertisement placed by the black civil rights movement. Sullivan had been awarded half a million dollars by state courts. The US Supreme Court judges ruled, however, that the First Amendment meant it should not be an offence to criticise or defame public officials, even if the criticism contained honest mistakes, unless publication was motivated by malice. As the ruling put it: '[D]ebate on public issues should be uninhibited, robust and wide open', which 'may well include vehement, caustic, and sometimes unpleasantly sharp attacks on government and public officials'.

Recognising that the advert did get some facts wrong, the justices nonetheless declared that 'erroneous statement is inevitable in free debate, and ... it must be protected if the freedoms of expression are to have the "breathing space" that they need to survive'. This 1964 decision, legal observers have since noted, finally removed the ancient threat of being prosecuted for 'seditious libel' from over the heads of US heretics who criticised the authorities.[24]

Five years later in 1969, a political heretic from the other end of the spectrum helped push back the barriers further still. In *Brandenburg v. Ohio* the Supreme Court reversed the conviction of a Ku Klux Klan leader who had denounced Jews and black people at a rally. The judges ruled that simply holding or expressing hateful or inflammatory views would no longer be sufficient to break the law. Instead, under the First Amendment, a speaker would be protected except if his words were intended towards 'inciting or producing imminent lawless action' and also 'likely to produce such action'.[25] Establishing the right of the KKK to spout its bile may not seem like a particularly famous victory for freedom today, but in drawing a firm line between hateful words and deeds, and affirming that the holding of views that many found repugnant could not in itself be considered a crime, it laid a firmer foundation for free speech in America as an indivisible and universal right.

One more case from the civil rights era is worth a mention, especially since it echoes the debates about the right to protest against military conscription and war, which the Supreme Court came down so hard on in the First Amendment cases of the early twentieth century. In this case, anti-Vietnam war activist Paul Robert Cohen had been convicted by a Los Angeles municipal court for protesting outside a county courthouse while wearing a jacket that read 'Fuck the Draft!' Cohen's case reached the Supreme Court for judgement in 1971. The justices ruled that free expression was 'powerful medicine in a society as diverse and populous as ours' and was generally not to be tampered with by government. Instead, the 'decision as to what views shall be voiced' had been 'largely put into the hands of each of us … in the belief that no other approach would comport with the premise of individual dignity and choice upon which our political system rests.'

The fact that the opinion expressed might be offensive to many was no reason for punishing it. Instead the state could only 'shut off discourse solely to protect others from hearing' if 'substantial privacy interests are being invaded in an essentially intolerable manner'. Whether or not American citizens had the right to shout fire in a theatre, they certainly now had the right to exclaim 'Fuck the Draft!' on the steps of a public building, whether others liked it or not.[26]

Back in the slightly more stultified British society, meanwhile, the post-war era was also marked by some set-piece legal battles over freedom of expression between the conventional forces of reaction and the new cultural heretics.

In 1960 the failed prosecution of Penguin Books under new obscenity laws, for publishing D. H. Lawrence's sexually explicit novel *Lady Chatterley's Lover*, ushered in an era of more liberalised publishing. In 1971, however, three editors of the 'alternative' magazine *Oz* who had wrongly assumed that the battle was over were found guilty of obscenity for their infamous Schoolkids edition, which included a cartoon of Rupert the Bear having sex. For this blasphemy against St Rupert of Nutwood, they were sentenced to up to fifteen months in prison, though the convictions were quashed on appeal.

Then in 1977, Christian censorship crusader Mary Whitehouse successfully brought a private prosecution for blasphemy against *Gay News*, over a poem in which a Roman centurion describes having sex with a gay Jesus after his crucifixion. *Gay News* was fined £1,000, which increased to £10,000 with court costs, and its publisher, Denis Lemon, was given a suspended jail sentence.

These were the last throws of the old censorious order. There would be no more trials for obscene publications or blasphemous libels in Britain. The offences of blasphemy and blasphemous libel were finally abolished by the New Labour government in 2008. It seemed that the West's cultural heretics, like the political ones before them, had come in from the cold.

That was only the end of the fight for free speech against its old enemies. New ones would soon emerge. In recent times the offences of heresy and blasphemy have simply been redefined again in Anglo-American culture and society. Now we have new heretics, new blasphemies and new orthodoxies.

Hate-speech laws in the UK have even reintroduced a form of blasphemy-lite onto the statute books, effectively making crimes of racial and religious hatred and homophobia. And there are many new informal rules about things that cannot be said, heresies that should not be spread. The fact that the proponents of the old orthodoxies can now find themselves in the dock – like the Christian and Muslim preachers convicted in UK courts for preaching words deemed homophobic – might raise a wry smile in some quarters. But heresy-hunting is still a threat to free speech, no matter who is on the receiving end, be they religious bigot or cartoon bear-baiter.

Just a week after blasphemy was finally abolished in Britain in 2008, an advert was banned – on the basis that it offended Christians. The coincidence captured the shift from the old moral order of supposedly objective crimes against the teachings of God, to the new censorship based on subjective offence-taking by groups and individuals.

Today the biggest threat comes not from official bans and censorship imposed in the name of central authority and intolerance, but from unofficial censorship and an atmosphere of conformism justified in the language of protecting rights and diversity. That often makes the danger more covert and trickier to oppose. But the lesson of history is that defending free speech means standing up for the rights of heretics, no matter what we might think of them or how hard that might seem in the here and now.

The next chapters identify just some of the new battlefields where the free-speech wars are being fought today.

4

The Internet Front: hunting for trolls down 'memory holes'

The internet ought to be the best piece of kit to happen to free speech since the printing press, 500 years ago. If only they could invent a smart online printer that worked, it would be better still. The wonders of the worldwide web have shrunk the globe to the size of a smartphone screen and blown up the prospects for global communication. The traditional motto of the British Broadcasting Corporation expresses the admirable ambition that 'Nation Shall Speak Peace Unto Nation', preferably in the modulated tones of the BBC World Service. The internet and social media make it possible not only for that to happen but for person to speak, skype, email or tweet words and cat videos unto person, nerd unto nerd, 'civilian' unto celebrity and all the rest.

The possibilities have never been greater for reinventing the traditional media, creating new media and giving voice to once-silent majorities and minorities. Never mind Chairman Mao's (short-lived) exhortation to 'Let a hundred flowers blossom and a hundred schools of thought contend!' There is scope for a million to blossom across the web, whether they be thought-inspiring blooms or choking weeds.

This sounds like much too much freedom for the liking of some, for whom words such as 'net' and 'web' still evoke thoughts of capture and containment rather than liberation. China is far from the only state to try to tame the 'wild west' web with conventional weapons of censorship and control. Some democratic governments have also gone down the authoritarian route. Enraged by online allegations about corruption and the abuse of power that stoked street protests against his government, Turkey's then prime minister Recep Tayyip Erdogan declared in June 2013 that: 'This thing called social media is currently the worst menace to society' (quite a claim given the bloody wars raging along Turkey's borders with Syria and Iraq). The Turkish authorities rounded up dissident tweeters and tried to close down Twitter, before attempting to turn off Facebook and YouTube, too, as if the internet were an old-fashioned radio and parents could just pull the plug to stop the children hearing rude words.[1]

We may not have to contend with such explicit petty authoritarianism in the Western corner of the internet, but the web is subject to the same baleful pressures as the real world. It has become a major front in the silent war on free speech. In the West the arguments are not about defending our unpopular governments against online abuse – who would sign up to that? Instead the free-speech frauds pose their case for taming the internet in terms of protecting the vulnerable against harmful and hateful words.

There are more ways to try to control what is said online than crude top-down government censorship. The impetus for action often comes from those campaigning against 'hate speech', as Twitter mobs and social media lobbies demand that something be done to stop them being offended or harassed online. But whatever the pretext, the net effect is always the same: to reduce the scope for unfettered free speech online, and waste the extraordinary opportunities offered by the internet for advancing freedom and open discussion.

Two examples of recent controversies serve to illustrate the way free speech is being driven off course online: the rows over internet trolls, and the Right to Be Forgotten. Fear of trolls disappeared from European culture sometime in the Middle Ages. It reappeared in the West in the twenty-first century. In old Norse mythology and Viking folklore, trolls were vaguely characterised supernatural beings dangerous to humanity. One modern expert describes the troll as an 'all-purpose otherworldly being' that could be adapted to suit any legend or horror story of the times.[2]

The same could be said of the modern troll, apparent scourge of the internet and social media. Nobody seems certain how to define a troll, yet everybody apparently agrees that something must be done about them. This fashion for troll-hunting provides an all-purpose, all-seasons licence to police what is said on the internet.

In the US, where reverse-Voltaires still find the official channels blocked by that tiresome First Amendment, the troll-hunters have to seek more informal means to silence their apparently fearsome prey. Opinion appears divided over whether to mob and drown the trolls or to snub them. But the vanguard of reverse-Voltaires agree that they are a growing American problem.

One large US survey in October 2014 found that: 'Although only 45 per cent of adults have heard of the term troll, 28 per cent of Americans admitted malicious online activity directed at somebody they didn't know.'[3] That was enough for one columnist to dub America 'a nation of online trolls'. He was being ironic about the over-use of the term 'troll' by those who wish to 'criminalise opinions that they personally find offensive'.[4] Others however seem deadly serious about doing just that.

Some on the US web have been busy inventing new forms of unofficial censorship to spike the trolls. For example, former Google, YouTube and AOL Video executive Karen Cahn was hailed as 'the equivalent of a modern troll-slayer' in November 2014 after setting up a 'troll-proof website for women to discuss everything from politics to their sex lives, all without fear of garnering online abuse'.

Cahn explained that 'Our definition of "troll" is all about rude, hateful, mean, and unproductive comments' – an impressively broad target for a censor's blue pencil. Then she spelt out her four lines of defence against such wide-ranging 'trollish comments': a database that 'can determine whether a comment is intended to be disruptive', filters to 'catch words and phrases that are against our community guidelines', keen-eyed editors 'making sure the dialogue is one that is productive' and troll icons throughout the website so that whenever 'someone is being hateful or disrespect-ful, users can report the troll'.[5] Such closely policed 'troll-proof' websites sound more like opinion-proof bastions of conventional dullness. But prudery can be sold as something progressive in the name of slaying trolls.

With troll fever rising amid more tales of female public figures in particular being subjected to abuse online, even Twitter itself vowed to join the hunt. In February 2015, in a leaked internal memo to Twitter staff, CEO Dick Costolo declared himself 'embarrassed' at the US company's failure to censor trolls and swore to 'start kicking these people off' Twitter: 'We suck at dealing with abuse and trolls on the platform and we've sucked at it for years. It's no secret and the rest of the world talks about it every day. We lose core user after core user by not addressing simple trolling issues ... We're going to start kicking these people off right and left and making sure that when they issue their ridiculous attacks, nobody hears them.'[6]

It is a sign of our troll-obsessed times that discussion of what to do next with the innovative, culture-changing platforms of twenty-first-century technology should be all about narrowing the rules, closing doors and 'kicking people off right and left'. Haven't we got better things to talk about? Rather than 'making sure when [trolls] issue their ridiculous attacks, nobody hears them', how about just agreeing not to listen to them, and getting on with making more of the internet's opportunities for expanding debate?

It is in the UK that the law has been able to join the national troll-hunt and the dangers of trying to police Thoughtcrime on the internet have become starkly clearer. In March 2012 the UK general manager of Twitter, the 'real-time information network' and social media phenomenon, told a London media conference that his company tried 'to remain neutral' on whatever content users chose to post in their 140-character tweets. This was because Twitter, Tony Wang declared, liked to see itself as 'the free speech wing of the free speech party'.[7]

Months earlier the UK's Lord Chief Justice, the nominative determinist Lord Justice Judge, had granted a search order against Twitter in order to track down people who allegedly used the San Francisco-based microblogging site to 'spread lies on the internet'. Lord Judge announced in exasperation that the case proved 'modern technology was out of control'.[8] Or at least, out of control of the courts and the other official keepers of The Truth. And we can't have that, can we?

Fast-forward to September 2014, when a 33-year-old man from Bristol in England became the latest to be found guilty of being an internet troll and sent to prison for something he said online. Peter Nunn was given an eighteen-week jail sentence for sending 'a barrage' of highly offensive tweets to a Labour member of parliament, Stella Creasy, including retweeting a threat to rape her from another troll. Nunn's 'campaign of hatred', it turned out in court, had amounted to six messages. That worked out at three weeks in jail for each 140-character tweet.

Some of us might think such sentences draconian. Others deemed them soft. In October 2014 a UK government minister announced that jail terms for online 'trolling' would increase fourfold, from a maximum sentence of six months to two years. Tory Justice secretary Chris Grayling declared: 'These internet trolls are cowards who are poisoning our national life. No one would permit such venom in person, so there should be no place for it on social media.'[9]

The UK government's uncharacteristically fast and firm action came in response to the case of Chloe Madeley, the daughter of two television personalities. Madeley had received what she called 'extremely chilling and cowardly' rape threats on Twitter after defending her mother, Judy Finnigan (who in turn had been abused for daring to suggest on TV that a footballer convicted of rape and recently released from prison had now 'served his time' and should be allowed to resume his career). Ms Madeley told the media that: 'It needs to be accepted that physical threats should not fall under the "freedom of speech" umbrella. It should be seen as online terrorism and it should be illegal.'[10]

So the UK government believes that 'internet trolls' are 'poisoning' our way of life, and victims accuse them of 'online terrorism'. This is the sort of talk that normally presages air-strikes and Special Forces raids. Only one small detail remained to be clarified before all-out www-war could be declared and won against these vile men and women of online violence.

Exactly what is a troll, anyway?

As the Wikipedia page devoted to the subject puts it with uncharacteristic understatement: 'Application of the term troll is subjective.' Internet users have been branded as trolls for 'offences' ranging from expressing unpopular political opinions or provocatively winding up opposition fans in a football forum to hurling insults around about celebrities or issuing wild threats of sexual assault and violence. By no stretch of even the most febrile imagination could those be considered 'all the same thing'.

To label somebody a troll is no more precise than calling them a twit or a tosspot. That's fine if you just want a catch-all term of counter-abuse for tweeters you don't like, but as the basis for government policy, online codes, censorship and legal crackdowns, such a loose and moveable definition of the offence provides a dangerously open invitation to intervene.

That UK government minister responsible made a firm pledge to jail 'internet trolls' for up to two years. Yet nobody is certain what 'trolling' does or does not mean. As the journalist Grace Dent observed, the really scary thing should surely have been the sight of a government minister promising to quadruple jail sentences for offences dealing with the written word, based on his shaky grasp of 'the hazy, ever-mutating, inflammatory definition of the term "troll"'.[11] That sounds like a recipe for chaos, and an invitation to every offence-seeker and amateur thought-policeman online to demand action against their pet trolls. It also risks having a considerable chilling effect on free speech for anybody fearful of being accused of being a witch/troll and burnt at the stake/on Facebook/ in court.

Whatever any minister or maligned individual might say, and no matter how often they keep saying it, so-called internet trolls *do* 'fall under the freedom of speech umbrella'. Those dubbed trolls should have as much right as Mother Teresa to say what somebody else does not like. They do not, however, have any more right than me, you or the next tweeter to be listened to or taken seriously. Online ranters and wind-up merchants ought to be protected under that umbrella from persecution or prosecution, but then, like the stranger shouting at himself under the bus shelter, they can be safely ignored (the favoured solution of most sensible Americans in that big poll, by the way).

But that's outrageous, protest the dedicated troll-hunters. This is not about free speech, they say. It is about explicit threats, often involving sexual violence, made against public figures on social media websites. 'There is no "right" to tell anybody you intend to rape them!'

That's true, of course. The threat of violence is already a criminal offence, and has been since the days when the only troll anybody in Britain or America had heard of was the one under the bridge in the fairy tale about the Three Billy Goats Gruff.

There is no shortage of laws against real threats of rape, murder or assault, and no need for new measures to make such 'trolling' a crime. So what is this troll panic really all about? The headline focus might be on threats of violence, but that has been used to excuse a broader crusade, involving both the UK state and twitch-hunting twitter mobs, to curtail freedom of expression online.

It would be difficult to prove that any message posted on social media websites amounted to a credible threat of what UK law calls 'immediate unlawful violence'. If everybody using an everyday phrase such as 'I'll kill you!' or 'You're dead!' online was to be locked up, the authorities might need to open special internet internment camps. It is hard to prove that even a more specific-sounding threat online poses a credible and immediate prospect of violence. For instance, the six messages which the convicted Peter Nunn sent to Stella Creasy MP via Twitter included a retweet of a message from somebody else which reportedly read: 'You better watch your back, I'm going to rape your arse at 8pm and put the video all over.' A repulsive threat from an unknown individual. But did anybody seriously expect that stranger from somewhere in cyberspace to turn up for the 8 p.m. appointment with the MP at an unspecified location, armed with a camcorder?

Behind the horrified headlines, the UK authorities have apparently been aware of the problem of proving a credible threat. Guidelines issued by the UK Director of Public Prosecutions in December 2012 make clear that somebody should face prosecution if they post – or repost – a message online that 'clearly amounts to a credible threat of violence'. But they also acknowledged that online posts deemed 'grossly offensive, indecent, obscene or false' would be much harder to prosecute.

In practice, however, the police and prosecutors – informed and egged on by an online crowd of reverse-Voltaires – have fudged that distinction. The scare stories about online threats of violence have been used to justify cracking down precisely on those 'grossly offensive, indecent, obscene or false' posts that were meant to be kept out of court.

The imprisoned UK internet trolls have not been sent down for sending credible threats of violence. Instead they have been convicted of being grossly offensive. For example the three sad tweeters jailed for targeting Stella Creasy and the feminist campaigner Caroline Criado-Perez in 2013 were convicted, not under the Offences Against the Person Act 1861, which criminalises actual threats of violence, but instead under the Malicious Communications Act 1988, which makes it a crime to send 'any article which is indecent or grossly offensive, or which conveys a threat, or which is false, provided there is an intent to cause distress or anxiety to the recipient'. Like the term 'troll' itself, it is a loose and subjectively interpreted phrase that allows the authorities to target whoever they see fit, and has been deployed to prosecute people who post nasty jokes and crude insults. That is, to punish them for expressing offensive opinions.

These troll-hunts and prosecutions are about freedom of expression. They blur the line between abuse and assault, between threatening behaviour and offensive words, in order to excuse restricting free speech online. They should not be allowed to get away with rewriting the law and the meaning of the English language so easily. When a troll like Nunn posts a message to a female MP on Twitter, asking: 'If you can't threaten to rape a celebrity, what is the point in having them?', it's not funny, big or clever. It is puerile and stupid and offensive. But contrary to the oft-repeated claims, it is not the same as physically 'threatening to rape a celebrity' in the street. And nobody should be sent to jail for being an offensive arsehole.

There is a little-known case from America that might have some lessons here. During a civil rights rally against police brutality at the Washington Monument in 1966, an eighteen-year-old man called Robert Watts addressed the crowd. Informing them that he had received his draft classification for being conscripted into the US Army to fight in Vietnam, and told to report for his physical, Watts announced: 'I am not going. If they ever make me carry a rifle the first man I want to get in my sights is L.B.J.' – meaning US President Lyndon B. Johnson. In response, the crowd laughed.

Watts was convicted of threatening to kill the president, but when his case reached the Supreme Court in 1969, the justices threw out the conviction. They ruled that the defendant had not made a true threat because his statement was political hyperbole. Rather than constituting a threat, his words were merely a 'crude' way of expressing 'political opposition to the President'. The Supreme Court thus found that not words alone, but the context in which they were used, should determine whether they amounted to a true threat – including whether the statement was conditional on an event that was unlikely to occur. From this sober perspective, the 'trolling' of those UK politicians and feminist campaigners might look more like abusive hyperbole and crude political opposition than true physical threats. That might not make them any less offensive. It surely should stop them being treated as criminal offences.[12]

There is a further aspect of this free-speech war that is too rarely talked about. The organised forces of the troll-hunters are a bigger problem for a free society than the sporadic abuse from pathetic trolls.

There are individuals and groups on both sides of the Atlantic now who act as professional offence-seekers, searching the web for something to take umbrage at, waiting to be outraged by some passing troll. In the Dark Ages, people did not go about volunteering to be attacked or eaten by the dreaded inhuman trolls. Even the Three Billy Goats Gruff, who had to cross the troll's bridge to reach the grassy meadow, met such monsters only out of necessity. By contrast, today's online offence-takers would go out of their way to cross that bridge as noisily as possible, wake the troll, drown him and video it for YouTube – not to reach any green meadow, but as a self-satisfying end in itself.

To claim that you have been 'trolled' has become a sign of virtue through victimhood. To be outraged by trolls offers those attacked confirmation that they are in the right. In the process, the true balance of power is somehow reversed. The few pathetic and inadequate trolls (and a glance at most of the individuals dragged through the UK courts would confirm that view) are somehow turned into what that Tory government minister called a powerful menace 'poisoning our national life'. Meanwhile the influential twitter mob of reverse-Voltaires, backed by the UK state, are able to pose as hapless victims.

The truth about all this was better revealed in the sad case of Brenda Leyland, a British woman who is believed to have taken her life in October 2014 after being exposed in the media as @sweepy-face, a vociferous online critic of the parents of Madeleine McCann, the young British girl who became a global phenomenon after she went missing from her family's holiday apartment in Portugal in 2007.

Leyland had posted many acid messages, hiding under the cloak of anonymity, attacking the McCanns and their explanation of Madeleine's disappearance, but she had not threatened them and was never charged with any offence. Nevertheless she was branded a troll after appearing on a list of McCann-baiting tweeters handed to the police by troll-hunters. In response, Gerry McCann declared that more of these people should be prosecuted. Brenda Leyland was then 'outed' as @sweepyface and paraded across the British media as an evil troll. A TV news reporter confronted the church-going 63-year-old mother of two on the doorstep of her Leicestershire home. Shortly afterwards, she was found dead.

Leyland's posts would not make pleasant reading, particularly for the McCanns. Example: 'Kate and Gerry – you will be hated by millions for the rest of your miserable, evil, conniving lives, have a nice day!' However, since they insist that they never read online messages and don't have a Twitter account, it is questionable to what extent she could be said to have harassed them, never mind made a credible threat. What she was guilty of was expressing an opinion, an interpretation of events, deemed unacceptable in the climate of the time. Brenda Leyland was no Socrates, but she was, in her own disreputable way, found guilty of saying the unsayable.

When the reporter and camera crew knocked on her door and accused Leyland of posting offensive messages about the McCanns, her recorded response was: 'Yes, I am entitled to do that.' Well, wasn't she? Of course, others on the web and in the media can also claim they were entitled to criticise her. Whether that 'entitled' them to report her and other posters to the police for expressing the wrong opinions, and launch a nationwide witch-hunt to nail her as an evil troll, is another question.[13]

No musician likes bad reviews. Some complain about them to the publication concerned. But it was surely a first in October 2014 when the pianist Dejan Lazic wrote to the *Washington Post* demanding that the newspaper remove a three-year-old critical review from its website – and insisting that it was legally required to do as he said. The European Court's 'right to be forgotten' ruling, claimed Lazic, gave him and anybody else the right to control 'the truth' about his personal image online. The pianist's request was misdirected – the Euro-court's ruling applies to search engines, not publishers. Nevertheless, the *Post*'s writer Caitlin Dewey said: 'its implications are kind of terrifying. We ought to live in a world, Lazic argues, where everyone – not only artists and performers but also politicians and public officials – should be able to edit the record according to their personal opinions and tastes.' In that, Lazic could be said to have followed the spirit, if not the letter, of the new European law.[14]

The concept of 'memory holes', down which inconvenient truths of history can be dropped and forgotten, was introduced into fiction by George Orwell in 1949, in his classic dystopian novel *Nineteen Eighty-Four*. It look a little longer, but memory holes were eventually opened up in the real world (or at least, the internet) by the Orwellian powers of the European Court of Justice in 2014.

On the internet, 'anything goes' and nothing can be hidden, right? Not quite. In its landmark ruling of May 2014, the European Court of Justice upheld the so-called 'right to be forgotten' by ordering Google to remove a link to a Spanish newspaper article. The case involved a Spaniard, Mario Costeja Gonzalez, who wanted to bury an old notice from 1998 reporting that his house was to be auctioned off to pay his debts. Señor Gonzalez complained that, anytime anybody Googled him online, this embarrassing reminder of his past financial difficulties was still prominent among the search results. He not only wanted to forget about that episode, but wanted to force everybody else to forget about it too, by effectively purging it from the internet.

That might seem fair enough. What harm could it do to allow anybody to draw an online veil over their past indiscretions? And what does gawping at other people's embarrassments have to do with free speech, anyway? In fact the EU's 'right to be forgotten' ruling has far-reaching implications for freedom of expression online, potentially stretching over the Atlantic and right around the worldwide web. The new European law gives individuals and institutions the right to demand that search engines such as Google must de-list postings containing 'outdated' or 'irrelevant' information. Although the ruling was made by the EU's top court, the implications do not end at Europe's borders. The court rejected Google's argument that, as a US-based internet company, it was not really publishing anything in Europe. The judges made clear that wherever a search engine might be hosted, it would still be subject to this prohibitive Euro law.

The Euro authorities insist that this cannot be construed as censorship, since the material in question will not actually be removed from the internet – it will simply not be linked to by Google and Co anymore. When plans for these regulations were first announced in 2012, the European Commission's vice-president said: 'It is clear that the right to be forgotten cannot amount to a right of the total erasure of history.'[15] That sounds like rewriting history, too. The fact is that if material is not listed by search engines, it is effectively invisible to most of us online and ceases to exist as public information.

No, no, say the authorities, of course we are not banning this controversial book! We are simply ordering all libraries and bookshops to remove it from their shelves and websites forthwith. You will still be at liberty to read it – if you can find a copy anywhere that is, or even spot a reference to its existence …

It was no surprise that the European Court's ruling was followed by a flood of requests to remove search-engine links to stories on Wikipedia, Facebook, YouTube and many newspaper websites. By October 2014, just five months after the landmark case established the 'right to be forgotten', Google reported that it had removed 498,737 links for search results. And those half-million 'disappeared' pages were only the beginning.

The people who requested the removal of those links, and supporters of the right to be forgotten, will insist, like the troll-hunters, that 'this is not a free-speech issue'. At first sight they might appear to have a point. The right to be forgotten is presented as more about upholding the right to privacy and data protection. The outraged pianist Lazic failed to impress with his claim to the *Washington Post* that removing an article criticising his performance from 2010 'has absolutely nothing to do with censorship or with closing down our access to information'. Some of the examples cited in support of the new rules might seem to be more sympathetic, however. We have been asked to consider the plight of somebody with a criminal record in their past, but whose minor convictions are now 'spent', meaning they no longer need to be revealed to officials or prospective employers. Yet anybody could still Google the individuals and unearth their long-forgotten offences. Or what about all the young people who have allowed photographs of their drunken exploits and other student-style indiscretions to be plastered across social media websites? Should their future prospects of finding a job or a partner really be at the mercy of a quick search via Google?

Champions of the EU's new rules will insist that the right to be forgotten is intended simply to defend the privacy and personal data of people like this, not to encroach on anybody else's freedom. But that's typical of how the free-speech frauds fight their silent war, in code. Nobody ever admits that they are attacking freedom of expression. They are only ever upholding the inalienable rights of some victims – even if it is, in this case, the hitherto unheard-of 'right' to be forgotten and erased from the internet. The right to be forgotten is a free-speech issue. It strikes at both the historic freedom to report the truth – and the liberty to read it, and to remember.

The right to report events and put history on the record has long been a central part of the struggle for freedom of expression and of the press. One of the first great fights for that freedom in Britain was the eighteenth-century campaign fought by John Wilkes and other heroes for the liberty to publish reports of what politicians said in parliament. That battle was eventually won, after Wilkes and his allies had been imprisoned, sent to the Tower of London and outlawed, and 50,000 Londoners had rioted outside parliament in their support. Until then, it was illegal for anybody to expose what His Majesty's Government and His Loyal Opposition MPs were up to behind the walls of the Palace of Westminster. Britain's rulers ruled in effective secrecy – and were determined to retain their right to be hidden from history, or at least to write their history only as they saw fit.

The right to record and to remember what has happened, and who did what to whom, is a crucial component of the freedom of expression. And there is a flipside to freedom of speech that is far too often forgotten. That is the right of the reader, listener and viewer to access all of the facts and every side of an argument, and then to judge for themselves what they believe to be true.

The ability of the reader to act as a morally autonomous adult is as vital a freedom as the liberty to speak. It means making choices and decisions on the basis of all the available information and ideas, without any intervention from the European courts or any other parental figure saying You-Can't-Read-That. When some of us defend free speech for right-wing demagogues, it is not because we are enthusiastic about upholding 'rights for racists', but we believe in the freedom of the audience to decide what is true, not to be deafened and blindfolded like those two wise monkeys. So the 'right to be forgotten' undermines both sides of the free-speech principle – the right to tell and record the truth as you understand it, and the freedom to think and to judge everything for yourself.

Defenders of the Euro law might argue that the court set up this right to protect the vulnerable, and made clear that it would be harder for a public or powerful figure to have his history erased than for a private individual. But such lines are easily blurred these days, when few seem certain where the private ends and the public begins and public figures are keen to claim the right to privacy in order to censor their critics.

Google reported in October 2014 on some of the requests to remove links that it had rejected. Those from the UK included a 'public official' who wanted them to erase the link to a student petition demanding his removal; a former clergyman who wished to remove two links to newspaper articles about sexual abuse allegations; a doctor who hoped to remove links to fifty web pages that reported a botched medical procedure; and a prominent 'media professional' who requested Google effectively to erase four articles reporting 'embarrassing content he posted to the internet'. All of these are matters of public interest and record which quite rightly should remain available in the public domain.[16]

What about those cases where it really is a private individual trying to forget their past peccadilloes and embarrassments? It might be easier to feel some sympathy here, but that is no reason for allowing the creation of a right to be forgotten that could have wider damaging consequences. Everybody has things in their past they would rather erase from memory. That's life, and it can be tough. It is bad enough that many seem to want to wrap us in cotton wool to protect us from words in the present. Now they also want to protect people from their own words and deeds in the past. The right to be forgotten is far too high a price to pay for retrospectively trying to protect somebody's feelings.

Such an attempt at mass memory-erasure once more echoes George Orwell's classic *Nineteen Eighty-Four*. In Orwell's novel, Big Brother's system of authoritarian control was brutal. As O'Brien of the Thought Police tells the protagonist, Winston Smith, 'If you want a vision of the future, imagine a boot stamping on a human face – forever.' But it is not just about brutality. It also involves thought control and the manipulation of history. One of the ruling Party's slogans is 'Who controls the past controls the future: who controls the present controls the past'.[17]

To that end, Winston Smith's job at the Ministry of Truth involves continually rewriting and deleting articles from past editions of the official newspaper, *The Times*, so that the historical record will suit the regime's current political needs. The fact that today's mortal enemies had been yesterday's close allies can be conveniently removed from the records; and a former leading Party member who has fallen from favour can have his past achievements erased from official history overnight. The slots into which these excised stories are stuffed are nicknamed 'memory holes':

> When one knew that any document was due for destruction, or even when one saw a scrap of waste paper lying about, it was an automatic action to lift the flap of the nearest memory hole and drop it in, whereupon it would be whirled away on a current of warm air to the enormous furnaces which were hidden somewhere in the recesses of the building.[18]

Later, when O'Brien tortures Smith, the member of the Thought Police produces a photograph that Smith knows is evidence of a cover-up by the Party. Then O'Brien stuffs the evidence into a memory hole, and denies that it ever existed or that he has any memory of having seen or destroyed it. 'Ashes,' he said. 'Not even identifiable ashes. Dust. It does not exist. It never existed.'[19] Ring

116

any bells? True, the EU court has not ordered any torture or sanctioned any stamping of boots on human faces, either temporarily or for ever. Europe's highest court has, however, brought to life something that Orwell could only fictionalise, and in the heart of the democratic West. Its legal endorsement of the 'right to be forgotten' risks creating huge memory holes at the heart of the internet, into which people can cast all manner of unwanted memories and facts from the past.

At a London conference in August 2014, Wikipedia founder Jimmy Wales and the Wikimedia Foundation's chief executive Lila Tretikov spoke out about the threat that the right to be forgotten poses to their project. The danger now, observed Tretikov, is that the web becomes 'riddled with Orwell's memory holes – places where inconvenient information simply disappears'.[20] Who needs Big Brother if the civilised judges of the European Court of Justice are prepared to dig memory holes in the name of protection and harm-prevention?

We should remember (if we are still permitted to) that the internet has been such a boon to writers and readers partly because it made it so much easier to research and recall what has been said and done. The old cliché about today's newspapers being tomorrow's fish and chip wrappers is no longer true – what is written or reported in the press and elsewhere can now be there for good, for all to see, paywalls allowing. Some are obviously uncomfortable about this. But that's no reason to allow them to use the modern language of exaggerated 'rights' to turn recent history into today's disposable fast-food wrappers.

5

The University Front: students fight for 'freedom *from* speech'

The college year of 2014 marked the fiftieth anniversary of the birth of the Free Speech Movement at the University of California, Berkeley – a turning point in students' fighting for civil rights in the 1960s. How did today's Berkeley student activists celebrate this historic anniversary? By campaigning to stop comedian and TV host Bill Maher speaking on campus, because they didn't like what he has to say. As Maher observed on his TV show, 'I guess they don't teach irony in college anymore.'[1]

Once upon a time, students were in the front rank of those fighting for free speech. In 1964 students at the University of California, Berkeley, rebelled against management's attempts to ban political activity on campus and formed the Free Speech Movement (FSM). It was a broad coalition ranging from radical students campaigning for black civil rights to right-wing Republicans. They agreed that the one right that mattered above all was free speech. As FSM stalwart Steve Weissman recalls, 'We just expected that we should have the same rights on campus as we had off it, and the university shouldn't play parent.' Their protests, backed by an academics' strike, won the day for free speech on campus.

In 2014, Berkeley proudly celebrated the fiftieth anniversary of the Free Speech Movement. Sort of. Chancellor Nicholas Dirks praised the protesters of the past, before getting to his point: that free speech at university today must not go too far. 'We can only exercise our right to free speech insofar as we feel safe and respected in doing so,' he insisted, adding that free speech should be tempered by 'civility'. In response, FSM veterans sent the chancellor a letter pointing out the potentially dire consequences of his insistence on 'civility' for free speech. They quoted the lyrics of a song performed by then-Berkeley student Malvina Reynolds at the 1964 protests:

It isn't nice to block the doorway. It isn't nice to go to jail.
There are nicer ways to do it. But the nice ways always fail.
It isn't nice, it isn't nice.
You told us once. You told us twice.
But if that is freedom's price, we don't mind.[2]

Meanwhile, Berkeley students were busy putting their chancellor's words about 'feeling safe' into practice, burying the Free Speech Movement's legacy in the process. A petition and protests demanded that the university 'disinvite' comedian Bill Maher as the college's 2014 commencement ceremony speaker because of his 'blatantly bigoted and racist' routines about Islam. One of the organisers insisted, with the authentic voice of the free-speech fraud, that: 'It's not a matter of freedom of speech, it's a matter of campus climate.' He claimed that Maher's comedy and 'dangerous rhetoric' 'perpetuates a dangerous learning environment.'[3] So safety from dangerous rhetoric is apparently now more important than free speech on campus. It appears that today, student protesters *do* want the university to 'play parent' and protect them from the bogey man after all.

* * *

Around the same time, in the UK, the BBC splashed the headline news that students at the University of Nottingham had been fined £150 by college authorities for using 'sexist' words about 'violence and necrophilia'.[4] No, it was not a gang threatening to rape and murder. It was a group of male and female students from the college's Cavendish Hall residence, on a Fresher's Week booze-up, chanting an adaptation of an old rugby song which ended 'Now she's dead, but not forgotten, Dig her up and fuck her rotten. You wish, you wish, you wish you were in Cavendish.' Traditional boorish behaviour from the local 'rugger buggers', the nearest types in British universities to American college 'jocks', of the sort that has been commonplace since Fresher's Week immemorial. This time, though, the incident was filmed by a first-year student, broadcast by the student paper, investigated by the students' union, and officially cracked down upon by the college authorities, who issued the maximum fine for breaking their 'code of discipline'.

Puerile rugger-buggering about? Certainly. Deserving of official action, fines and a disciplinary record? Of course not.

Many of us would not wish we were in Cavendish with them, but neither should we be able to wish away the uncultured habits of those who do. The right to sing vulgar rugby songs might not sound like a high-minded free-speech issue, any more than the right to tell uncomfortable jokes about Islamists. But it should be, if we are serious about challenging the culture of conformism that wants all forms of expression and communication on campus filtered through a speech code. After all, if you can't say what you want during the supposed free-for-all of a college Fresher's Week, when can you?

What could be a more natural bastion of free thinking and free speech than universities and academia? As Benjamin Disraeli said in 1873, 'A university should be a place of light, of liberty, and of learning.'[5] If that was true in strait-laced Victorian England, how much more liberating and enlightened should Western seats of learning be in the twenty-first century?

Yet remarkably, the university campus has become a major new front in the silent war on free speech, on both sides of the Atlantic. What's remarkable is not that academic freedoms are under assault – they have been threatened by outside forces since the first European universities were established in the Middle Ages. What beggars belief is that it is now students and academics themselves who are joining campus authorities in trying to impose new limits on free speech and free thinking in UK and US universities. Far from being ivory-towered bastions of free thinking and speaking, our universities have come to see themselves more like a fortress to protect young people from the dangerous words and ideas running riot just outside the campus gates.

Students seem to be cast in two equally unattractive stereotypes. On one hand these young adults – in the USA, legally old enough to vote, fight and drive; in the UK, also to drink – are treated as children in need of swaddling in safety blankets. The impressionable infants at university therefore cannot be exposed to the sort of shocking or dangerous ideas that grown-ups might handle. At the same time, however, some students seem keen to adopt the caricatured attitude of senior citizens – set solid in their ways, and not open to fresh ideas or different experiences. Perhaps their slogan should be: 'You can't treat a young pup new tricks.'

The world has been turned upside down so that those who think of themselves as liberal- or even radical-minded are in the forefront of the attack on free speech in colleges. As elsewhere in the silent war, however, the crusade is not justified as an overt attack on freedom of expression. It is presented instead in code, as a defence of students from harmful or offensive words and images. As the slogan of the Berkeley students protesting against Bill Maher has it, they want 'Free Speech, Not Hate Speech'. They had failed to learn the hard fact that you cannot outlaw what some deem 'hate speech' – that is, ideas they find offensive or uncomfortable – without kicking the principle of free speech off campus at the same time.

It would take another book to detail all of the ways in which freedom of expression has been undermined in UK and US universities in recent times. To get a sense of the breadth and depth of the problem we will have to settle here for a brief bullet-point guide, of the sort you might cram on the way to that exam.

Let's start with the sorry tale of No Platform and Disinvitation Season. The policy of 'No Platform for Racists and Fascists' was adopted by the UK National Union of Students in 1974. Forty years later the NUS and local student unions at British universities have extended that stupid policy to something more like 'No Platform for racists, fascists, Tories, Islamists, Islamophobes, Christians, atheists, anti-abortionists, homophobes, Hegel, rugger buggers, page 3 pin-ups, Robin Thicke songs, Lads, Sexist Comedians, UKIP supporters, journalists called Julie (of whom more later) or Anything That Makes Anybody Uncomfortable'.

Even back in the Seventies and Eighties, some of us on the old UK left thought No Platform for fascists was nonsense. The notion that banning the enemy's ideas was the same thing as beating them made the proverbial ostrich with its head in the sand look far-sighted. Now, however, the No Platform culture beloved of student officials has evolved. It is no longer ostensibly about banning political ideas as too extreme and potentially provocative. It is more about banning any words and images that might emotionally offend or harm vulnerable students.

At the time of writing more than thirty UK student unions have banned the *Sun* newspaper because of its 'offensive' page 3 pin-ups of topless models, and more than twenty have banned Robin Thicke's international hit 'Blurred Lines' because its lyrics are deemed 'a bit rapey'. These officials hold their fellow students in such low esteem that it is assumed they either can't cope with pin-ups or sexualised song lyrics, or will be turned into potential sex criminals by them. It has been said that in Victorian times it was 'not done' in polite circles to mention trousers in front of a lady. Now it apparently is not done to mention nudity or hetero-sex in the company of delicate students.

Then there is the crackdown on rugby-style 'lad culture' that saw the Nottingham chanters fined and the London School of Economics rugby club banned for a year for putting out leaflets advising rugby lads to avoid 'mingers' and 'homosexual debauchery'. The club back-pedalled faster than a drunken scrum, publicly recanted its 'inexcusably offensive' behaviour and declared that its members have 'a lot to learn about the pernicious effects of banter' before packing the rugby players off to training – equality and diversity training, that is.[6]

Since the days when I was a revolting student, members of the rugby club have often been considered among the less charming blokes on campus. And don't get me started on the singing. But so what? Nobody else has to sing along. There is no reason why rugby boys should be made to sing from the same hymn sheet as the holier-than-thou campus word-watchers.

It becomes clear that this is really about banning ideas and opinions rather than dangerous behaviour when things move into the realm of political debate. In November 2014, a debate about abortion between two journalists at the historic Christ Church, Oxford was cancelled after furiously offended feminist students protested against it. One of the journalists, Brendan O'Neill, was 'pro-choice', the other, Tim Stanley, 'pro-life'. But both of them were male. The protesters said that people 'who do not have uteruses' should not talk about abortion. That seems a big step backwards from the days when feminists fought against women being defined by their biological functions. More insidiously, they objected that such a debate would endanger the 'mental safety' of Oxford students, demanded their right to feel 'comfortable' around college and threatened to protest at the meeting. The Christ Church authorities, coincidentally called the Censors, cancelled the debate, which they claimed raised 'security and welfare issues'.

The authorities at Oxford University, of all places, are now apparently so afraid of unorthodox ideas and a robust clash of opinions that they will give in to intolerance at the first mention of somebody feeling 'uncomfortable'. As Isabel Hardman of the *Spectator* pointed out:

> Where is the threat to mental safety in a debate, other than the danger that you might find the indelible lines you drew around an opinion are easier to wash away than you believed? … An opinion is not an irresistible force, it does not hurt you physically. It cannot stop you aborting a foetus or indeed force you to do so. It might upset you, enrage you, delight or convince you, but you don't even need to do something as terrifying as changing your mind after hearing it, if you choose.[7]

Things have reached the point with the free-speech fraud where well-educated students can seriously suggest that even the explicit censorship of political opinions is not really a free-speech issue. In November 2014, students at the University of East Anglia in Norwich successfully petitioned the student union to cancel a debate that was to feature a local parliamentary candidate from UKIP, the populist movement opposed to the European Union and immigration. Protest organiser Timea Suli's petition claimed innocently that: 'This is about ensuring UEA students are on a campus where they feel safe, secure and respected.' After the debate was cancelled, she insisted that: 'To call this an assault on freedom of speech is an error.' Call me an old-fashioned error-maker, but if censoring the expression of a political opinion is not an assault on freedom of speech on campus, what is?[8]

Irony alert: in November 2014, when the UK government announced new powers to 'order universities to ban extremist speakers from campuses' as part of its latest anti-terror package, student activists rightly protested about political censorship and free speech. Some of these were the same activists leading the campaign to ban 'Islamophobic' speakers, 'sexist' newspapers, 'rapey' pop songs and 'homophobic' rugby chants from campus. If you make free speech unwelcome at university, don't be surprised if you give the government ideas.

There have been similarly blatant displays of double standards among campaigning anti-Israeli academics on both sides of the Atlantic. They are understandably up in arms when one of their number loses his teaching job in America, apparently because of his views, or when a conference they have organised to question 'the legitimacy in international law of the Jewish state of Israel' is cancelled at Southampton University in England. Yet the campaigners' complaints about political censorship and the importance of free speech on campus might be slightly more convincing if they were not leading demands for an academic boycott of Israel, which would deny their Israeli counterparts the right to speak and be heard in the West.[9]

And then before you know it the No Platform policies start to eat themselves, with student activists who successfully demanded that the sexist comic character Dapper Laughs be banned from campuses astonished to find that feminist comedian Kate Smurthwaite's gig was cancelled soon afterwards amid confused reports that she had nonconformist views on trans issues and sex workers and fears that her 'Leftie Cock Womble' routine might infringe the Goldsmiths College safe-space policy. Those who live by the No Platform policy can perish by it too.[10]

The mission-creeping attitude of No Platform in UK universities might be better called No Arguments – a refusal to countenance any views other than your own. This is the opposite of the open-mindedness, experimentation and coping with new challenges that surely ought to characterise life at university. Those demanding more restrictions always express their outrage at the idea that expressions of sexism or other prejudices could just be 'banter'. No doubt that word is used to cover up all sorts of rubbish.

But surely young adults would be better off coping with a bit of adolescent lads' banter than living under the control of ban-happy old biddies (of any gender) in students' clothing.

In America too, student groups are well practised in removing opinions that they don't want to hear from campus, as if these ideas were illicit drugs or dangerous drunks. As with the comedian Bill Maher at Berkeley, there are frequent lobbies to prevent prestigious but disapproved-of public figures from speaking at university events. Greg Lukianoff of the Foundation for Individual Rights in Education (FIRE) describes this annual ritual as Disinvitation Season – a 'dark joke', he observes, which 'has grown less funny with each passing year'.

FIRE has uncovered 257 incidents between 2000 and 2014 where students and faculty demanded that speakers invited to campus be disinvited – more than half of them in the last five years. The more conservative the speaker's opinions, says Lukianoff, the less likely they are to be invited in the first place and the more likely to be the subject of disinvitation protests. It is as if, he concludes, 'we have come to accept an academic environment in which students crave freedom *from* speech and from speakers with whom they disagree. We can and should do better.'[11]

Those supposed liberals attempting to ban political and religious views they find offensive from universities on both sides of the Atlantic today might do well to recognise the historical company they are keeping. Two hundred years ago, fellows and students at Oxford University also took direct action to banish opinions they did not wish to hear or have heard, sweeping up and burning every available copy of a pamphlet that, says one account, had caused 'maximum offence'. Meanwhile the university authorities expelled the author from Oxford. He was the nineteen-year-old Percy Bysshe Shelley, and the Romantic poet's 'little tract' that caused such lofty outrage among Oxford's spires in 1811 was called *The Necessity of Atheism*. It would surely be better for today's protesting students to try to follow in the footsteps of the taboo-busting Shelley rather than those of the Oxford conservatives and censors who banished the offensive student and his opinions from university life.[12]

Among the many examples of misleading Newspeak in the silent war on free speech, few stand out as boldly as the welcoming-sounding policies creating 'Safe Spaces' and 'Free-Speech Zones' at universities. These apparently cuddly policies in fact deliver an underhand combination punch to free speech.

The idea of instituting a 'Safe Space' policy was initiated at North American colleges and has since been taken up by the National Union of Students and student bodies at UK universities. It sounds like an unopposable mom-and-apple-pie policy. After all, who could be in favour of making universities or anywhere else an 'unsafe zone'? The question to ask, however, is: Safety from what? These policies go far beyond obvious threats of violence or intimidation, to cover any sort of opinion or language that some students may not like. The 'principal values' of the national NUS policy on which other UK student union policies are modelled are apparently 'to ensure an accessible environment in which every student feels comfortable, safe and able to get involved in all aspects of the organisation, free from intimidation or judgement'.

The key factor in determining what is acceptable, it seems, is how an individual student 'feels'. Anything that makes him or her feel unsafe, or just uncomfortable, is out. Such a subjective test of 'safety' looks like a blank cheque for keeping student unions and debates free from any argument or expression that falls outside the bounds of the mainstream.

The way that the safe-spaces policies link in a single phrase 'intimidation or judgement' is telling. To be 'judged' – which can mean being told that you are an idiot or simply wrong just as much as being called a fat slag – is equated with being threatened. The key thing is that the student 'feels comfortable' at all times. But if that was really all young people wanted, they surely could have stayed home tucked up safe and warm with their mums and dads.

One of the best things for many students about university life is being exposed to new experiences and people outside their comfort zone. That includes serious debates where you are, yes, 'judged' on the strength of the arguments you can muster, as well as social situations where you have to learn to hold your own. Trying to restrict college life to an individual student's pre-set, safe comfort zone risks closing the door on the new – and worse, closing young minds.

Maybe the creation of Free-Speech Zones in universities could act as a counter to the censorious influence of Safe-Space policies? Or maybe not. The Free-Speech Zones pioneered in US universities are another Newspeak device for limiting free speech, all done in the name of defending rights.

A Free-Speech Zone is a specific space set aside for the expression of opinions and ideas, display of banners and issuing of leaflets on campus. It is basically a restricted area in which political and religious 'deviants' can gather to exchange their offensive banter without harming or offending ordinary, decent students. Everywhere else on campus, meanwhile, they must comply with the college's restrictive speech codes. In other words, these zones turn what ought to be the rule – the freedom of everybody to express him or herself – into the exception. A Free-Speech Zone is like a dirty little smokers' corner, where misfits who can't give it up can go to indulge the antisocial habit of speaking their mind that has been safely stubbed out elsewhere.

Even then they are hardly free. In October 2014, the Student Senate at Iowa State University rejected a referendum on expanding the free-speech zones on campus. But as the college paper pointed out, the problems with the free-speech zone went well beyond the space allocated:

[T]he troubles of free speech at Iowa State do not end when a Free Speech Zone starts. For an event to take place in the Edward S. Allen Area of Free Debate it must meet a list of requirements. If it does not, a request form must be submitted well in advance, 4–10 days, and can be approved or denied by the Student Activities Center and Facilities Planning and Management. Iowa State's free speech policies paired with the requirements of holding an event in a Free Speech Zone, make it difficult for ISU students or any individual or group to express themselves on campus.[13]

Around the same time, meanwhile, the university authorities at Iowa State were banning students on campus from wearing T-shirts calling for the legalisation of marijuana – a clear infringement of their First Amendment right to express a political opinion without legal restraint. The flipside of the restrictive free-speech zones is the intolerance of any controversial ideas elsewhere in the university. With freedom of expression officially treated as if it were a perverse aberration, it is little wonder that there were complaints of some students treating the Iowa Free-Speech Zone as a freak show where the weirdos could be mocked and photographed.

If this is the state of affairs at universities, what hope is there for freedom of expression in the world outside?

If there is one phenomenon which captures above all the mind-narrowing trends at universities, it is surely the onward march of Trigger Warnings.

A Trigger Warning is an advisory label stuck at the front of a book, article, film or whatever to warn students that this work involves words or images that may traumatise them in some way. They have grown more and more prevalent in major US colleges and British students are picking up on the idea.

Early in 2014, student leaders at the University of California, Santa Barbara, passed a resolution urging professors to introduce mandatory Trigger Warnings on syllabus readings, and to allow students who feared they would be adversely affected by what was being taught to skip classes. The college seemed keen to comply. The prestigious liberal arts college in Oberlin, Ohio had already published official guidance on Trigger Warnings, advising professors to 'be aware of racism, classism, sexism, heterosexism, cissexism, ableism, and other issues of privilege and oppression' and to 'strongly consider' making it optional for students to study 'triggering material'. It might be hard to imagine teaching any classical arts material that could not be accused of something on that sprawling list of possible triggers. The potential reach of these measures was highlighted when one student at Rutgers University made headlines by demanding that F. Scott Fitzgerald's classic novel *The Great Gatsby* should be branded with a Trigger Warning along the lines of 'TW: suicide, domestic abuse and graphic violence'.

And it goes further. What about law students who worry that they might be 'triggered' by discussion of traumatic legal cases? Are they to be excused studying those aspects of criminal law? In December 2014, Harvard law professor Jeannie Suk wrote in the *New Yorker* magazine about the increasing difficulty of teaching about the law on sexual violence in the age of Trigger Warnings:

> Student organizations representing women's interests now routinely advise students that they should not feel pressured to attend or participate in class sessions that focus on the law of sexual violence, and which might therefore be traumatic. These organizations also ask criminal-law teachers to warn their classes that the rape-law unit might 'trigger' traumatic memories. Individual students often ask teachers not to include the law of rape on exams for fear that the material would cause them to perform less well. One teacher I know was recently asked by a student not to use the word 'violate' in class – as in 'Does this conduct violate the law?' – because the word was triggering. Some

students have even suggested that rape law should not be taught because of its potential to cause distress.[14]

How long before sensitive medical students are asking to be excused classes involving bloodshed or physical trauma?

Outside the strictly academic sphere, meanwhile, Trigger Warnings have run riot across the internet. The writer Jenny Jarvie observed that, since 2012, TW alerts 'have been applied to topics as diverse as sex, pregnancy, addiction, bullying, suicide, sizeism, ableism, homophobia, transphobia, slut-shaming, victim-blaming, alcohol, blood, insects, small holes and animals in wigs. Some have called for Trigger Warnings for television shows such as *Scandal* and *Downton Abbey*.'[15]

Downton Abbey! Is nothing sacred? What's it all about?

Defenders of Trigger Warnings will argue that they amount to little more than a few words to help preserve students from harm. And where could the harm be in that? But the truth is that those few words speak volumes about the parlous state of freedom in the Western university. Trigger Warnings portray students, not as capable young adults, but as vulnerable victims who cannot be exposed to freedom of expression, even in classic works of literature, without suffering potential emotional and psychological damage.

The clue here lies in the origin of the concept. Trigger Warnings were not invented to apply to books on a college syllabus. They were initially conceived as an online therapeutic tool to help victims in discussion forums for sufferers from Post-Traumatic Stress Disorder (PTSD). If somebody posted about a particularly violent or distressing experience, others could be forewarned that reading such a post might 'trigger' a traumatic memory and reaction in them.

Even conceived in these narrow terms, however, the concept of Trigger Warnings appears unconvincing. Experts will point out that the 'trigger' for a bad episode among PTSD sufferers need not be so obvious. It could be anything from a shape to a smell, from a word to the weather. How is anybody supposed to formulate

Trigger Warnings to cope with such a random variety of everyday events? Maybe you could put a Trigger Warning by a PTSD sufferer's bed, warning them that each new day would contain unspecified hazards, but beyond that …

Extend the Trigger Warnings away from PTSD sufferers to books read by university students, however, and the whole thing becomes a nonsense. Post-Traumatic Stress Disorder was developed as a category to describe the psychological effects suffered by those exposed to the horrors of war, violence or other extreme experiences. What has that to do with students being made to feel uncomfortable by some 'naughty' references in literature?

This all goes back to the 'principal value' that ensuring that an individual student 'feels comfortable' on campus is now the most important thing. Their feelings are supposed to trump such other minor considerations as free speech for all, or academic freedom to teach as professors see fit. And protesting that their emotions might be 'triggered' if forced to study something has become a way for some young people to assert the importance of their own feelings over and above academia and literature.

The demand for Trigger Warnings has less to do with the traumatic contents of a book than with the inflated contents of a delicate student's ego. But while the causes might be slight, the consequences could be more serious in terms of the future of free speech and open discussion in our universities.

Where will it end? Once the notion of trauma is reduced to feeling emotionally uncomfortable, the sky is surely the limit for Trigger Warnings. Today we are advised that students should be allowed to opt out of those classes. Tomorrow the demand might be to stop teaching such 'triggering' texts altogether – and that list could stretch from Shakespeare to *Game of Thrones*, with much in between.

And why then should there not be more and more detailed Trigger Warnings on magazine or news articles (as there already are in the student press), TV broadcasts, and just about anything posted on YouTube? It is an open invitation to claim that what you do not like is dangerous, and then to question whether we should be allowed to read or watch it without warning signs. As wags have observed, why not put TWs on Trigger Warnings, to warn that they are about to mention sex or violence …?

Trigger Warnings are a model of how all the talk about harm and vulnerability and comfort can become a coded way of undermining both sides of free expression – the freedom to speak or write what you like, and the freedom to read or listen and judge for yourself. The sense of narrowing minds on campus is captured by the phenomenon of advising students that they may prefer to avoid reading or hearing something as too offensive or hurtful to their feelings. And like all of these episodes in the free-speech wars in universities, the repercussions go way beyond the campus.

As Jenny Jarvie says, 'what began as a way of moderating internet forums for the vulnerable and mentally ill now threatens to define public discussion online and off'. That should be the most serious warning of all to anybody who feels 'uncomfortable' at the undermining of freedom of speech.

A footnote. In April 2015, members of the Multicultural Affairs Advisory Board at New York's Columbia University protested that the Western canon of classical literature is full of 'triggering and offensive material', such as the rape of mythological characters in the Roman poet Ovid's epic, the *Metamorphoses* – inspiration of authors from Dante to Shakespeare. The advisory protestors wanted Trigger Warnings added to classic texts, a 'training program' to re-educate professors, and eventually the rewriting of Columbia's Core Curriculum, to make it feel 'welcoming and safe'. Columbia claims that its Core Curriculum for all students, a 'founding experiment in liberal higher education' remains both 'academically rigorous' and 'personally transformative' because it 'thrives on oral debate of the most difficult questions about human experience'. Not for much longer, if those critics dubbed the 'Trigger Warning Warriors' get their way. [16]

6

The Entertainment Front: football – kicking free speech with impunity; comedy – no laughing matter

Don't imagine that the silent war on free speech is confined to the frontiers of the internet or the ivory towers of university-world. It is being waged right across Western culture and in some unlikely places, such as British football (the one that's played with the feet), and the comedy scene on both sides of the Atlantic.

Those who campaign on free-speech issues often see them as rights to be defended for high-minded dissidents in faraway places. Chinese artists and Iranian poets are favourite objects of Anglo-American devotion. It would never occur to many of these lobbyists, however, to extend the same support to, say, uncouth working-class football supporters in the UK. The notion that vulgar crowds chanting deliberately offensive words at one another might be a free-speech issue fills the typical British civil liberties lobbyist (emphasis on 'civil', as in well-mannered) with horror.

That is why football has become a largely forgotten front in the new free-speech wars. Yet defending free speech for sports fans and players is every bit as important as it is for artists sitting sedately up in the higher tiers of the cultural arena. In sport the same rules have to be upheld for everybody, or nobody will be able to play the game properly. The same goes for free speech.

So brace yourselves. Like it or not, free speech is for (allegedly) fat and (mostly) white, male working-class football fans, too.

When did tweeting an obscure naughty word become a worse football offence than kicking an opposing player? When the powers-that-be lost their marbles and decided that the mad world of British football had to become a moral 'role model' for the rest of society.

In October 2014, former England and Manchester United captain Rio Ferdinand was suspended for three matches and fined £25,000 by a Football Association tribunal. A three-match ban is what a player gets after a referee shows him a straight red card and sends him off – typically for violent conduct on the pitch. An additional fine would mean that the authorities deem his offence worse than the average on-field assault.

But Ferdinand's extraordinary punishment was not imposed for breaking an opponent's leg. It was for cracking a schoolboy joke on a social networking website. He got that three-match ban and a £25,000 fine for posting a four-letter word – 'sket'.

A bantering fan had wound up the defender, who was then playing in London with Queen's Park Rangers, with the usual sort of taunt found on Twitter: 'Maybe QPR will sign a good CB [centre-back] they need one.' Ferdinand's razor-sharp riposte was also fairly typical of the Twitter playground: 'Get ya mum in, plays the field well son! #sket.'

It seems unlikely that the po-faced officials at the FA had ever heard that word before, let alone knew what it meant (no, me neither). Apparently it is shorthand for 'sketel', a Caribbean patois word for a promiscuous woman, or one who 'plays the field well son'. Having got their PA to Google its meaning, however, the Football Association suits moved with uncharacteristic speed to charge Ferdinand with making a comment that was 'abusive and/ or indecent and/or insulting and/or improper'. As if that charge wasn't catch-all enough, Ferdinand's offence was apparently 'aggravated' further still because it 'included a reference to gender'. Well, he did say 'mum' rather than 'parent'.

By sticking Ferdinand with a heavy ban and fine for this daft so-called offence, and ordering him 'to attend an education programme', the FA tribunal was making an example of the player. Not because of what he had done, but because of what they decided he was. As the tribunal statement on the punishment spelt out: 'With nearly six million followers, Mr Ferdinand is clearly an experienced Twitter user and should know better. He is, without doubt, a role model for many young people. His responsibility is therefore that much greater.'[1]

The notion that the number of Twitter followers reflects intelligence and judgement might raise the odd eyebrow, implying as it does that Justin Bieber and Kim Kardashian should surely rule the world. More relevantly, the dread words 'role model for many young people' should have aggravated us all. Apparently if Rio the role model uses an 'improper' word in a tweet, then millions of young lads will 'without doubt' all start treating women as whores and disrespecting their mums. And it will be his responsibility.

The notion that professional football, a game full of overgrown schoolboys, should be a 'role model' for our children and indeed society might be a lot funnier than Ferdinand's tweets, if the implications were not so serious. The ridiculous myth of the role model has been used as the pretext to restrict freedom of speech for football players and fans. Worse, this is based on the assumption that the masses are so gullible and gormless that we will emulate whatever our sporting heroes might put on offer, monkey-see-monkey-do style. So we cannot be allowed to read a footballer's tweet or hear a crowd's chant and judge for ourselves. The authorities have to step in as a referee, impose their rules, and give free speech the red card.

Ever since football became a mass spectator sport in Britain in the late nineteenth century, the authorities have been concerned about the riotous potential – and sometimes practice – of the unruly crowd. The panic about the threat of football hooliganism reached its peak in the 1970s and 1980s, when top English clubs installed steel cages to contain supporters inside the ground and police adopted paramilitary tactics outside stadiums to deal with away fans like prisoners of war. These two strands of footballing authoritarianism came together in Chelsea chairman Ken Bates's proposal to erect an electrified cattle fence around the Stamford Bridge pitch. The habit of treating fans as animals played no small part in the 1989 Hillsborough disaster, when 96 Liverpool supporters were crushed to death in cages while police were busy treating the tragedy as a public-order problem and pushing escaping fans back into the pens.[2]

How things have changed. The game dismissed by the *Sunday Times* in the mid-Eighties as 'A slum sport played in slum stadiums in front of slum people, who deter decent folk from turning up' is now hailed as 'the beautiful game' and played in the all-seater stadiums of the English Premier League in front of executive boxes full of prawn-sandwich-eating 'decent folk' and a global television audience of millions.[3]

The authorities are still preoccupied with controlling the ordinary fans, but that preoccupation too has changed. It is no longer primarily about policing crowd violence and battling hooliganism – those spectres have largely been laid to rest by comprehensive policing systems, CCTV, and high ticket prices that mean the average fan at a Premier League match is now a relatively sedate middle-aged bloke. The new aim of football's control-freaks is to police not just what the crowds do, but also what individual fans and players are allowed to say and sing and think about; not just in the all-seater, atmosphere-free, no-smoking/swearing/standing stadiums, but everywhere football is discussed from the pub to the internet.

There is a powerful new lobby that aims to sanitise football, to rid it of all the crude abuse, offensive songs and general naughtiness indulged in by those ugly proles who still insist on following 'the beautiful game' that has recently been colonised by the middle classes.

The crusade to tame the football beast and turn it into a 'soccer' kitten has been gathering strength over recent seasons. We have seen several simple-minded or simply legless British football 'trolls' prosecuted and jailed for posting idiotic abuse of their rivals online; Spurs supporters arrested on suspicion of racist abuse, for calling themselves the 'Yid Army' as a badge of pride; Gillingham Town fans nicked for a 'racially motivated public order offence' after calling the famously fat and Scottish manager of Rotherham United a 'fat Scottish wanker'.

As elsewhere in the free-speech wars, the law is not the half of it. There is also a wave of informal censorship and censoriousness across English football, backed by the FA, the clubs, crusading lobby groups and even supporters themselves. Those punished for posting offensive football-related messages online have generally been reported to the police by outraged fans. Meanwhile Liverpool FC have issued match-day stewards with a poisonous list of words that are now to be banned at their Anfield stadium, which includes not only the usual suspects such as the n-word, y-word etc, but also such outrageous expressions as 'man up' and 'playing like a girl'.

Nor have the players been spared in the crackdown. Rio Ferdinand is not the only one to be punished by the FA for using 'improper' words online. And as for policing speech on the pitch, the football authorities have sometimes proved willing to tackle 'offensive, abusive, improper' speech harder than the laws of the land might allow.

Another former England captain, John Terry of Chelsea, was at the centre of a notorious 2012 court case in which he was charged with a racially aggravated public-order offence for allegedly calling QPR's Anton Ferdinand (Rio's cousin) a 'fucking black cunt' (or 'FBC' as the key uncouth phrase became shortened to in the bizarre London court proceedings) during a Premier League match. Terry had been captured on TV apparently using those words, but insisted that it was only a sarcastic retort.

Finding Terry not guilty, Westminster's chief magistrate said that the player's explanation seemed 'unlikely'. But with the video evidence apparently inconclusive, contradictory accounts from lip-readers and no clear first-hand testimony, he concluded that there was too much reasonable doubt to convict safely. Fair enough. Terry walked free from court, essentially found to be obnoxious but innocent before the law. Cue howls of outrage from crusaders demanding that the FA ignore the verdict of the justice system, and make an example of Terry anyway. Despite the verdict, Terry – and football – were found guilty of racism and general repulsiveness and sentenced to be re-educated in the etiquette and speech codes of the FA's official 'Respect' campaign. Gordon Taylor, head of the Professional Footballers' Association, declared that: 'The players are role models whether they like it or not and they must behave accordingly.' Even such a serious player as the Labour Party rushed to join in the outrage against football, piously announcing that the language Terry used – which the court had ruled could not be proved was racist – 'has no place on any football pitch. The FA must restate its commitment to stamping out racism.'[4]

The authorities duly did as they were told; an FA commission ruled that Terry had racially abused Ferdinand, banned him for four games and fined him £220,000. Thus he joined the notorious OJ Simpson in that select team of sports stars cleared in court but found guilty outside of it anyway. It appears that the normal principle of innocent-until-proven-guilty can now be overridden in the UK by the new role-model rules.

The campaign to rid football of offensive, improper and abusive language marks an extraordinary turnaround. Football has gone from being one area ungoverned by the etiquette of everyday life, where it was accepted that people could let rip without following the rules of polite society, to being a 'role model' expected to set a high-minded example to the rest of society.

Football has long been a funny refuge from the stuffy real world, where fans can talk, sing, shout and behave in ways that they would not dream of doing elsewhere. The match is the home ground of what Sigmund Freud called 'the id' – the more emotional, irrational side of the human psyche. Fans generally accepted that abusing one another inside a stadium did not carry the same meaning as doing it in the street. Players too abided by the code that 'what happens on the pitch stays on the pitch', with winding up and abusing opponents just part of the game. Even the prosecutors in the John Terry trial conceded that if every player who used the c-word was sent off, no English Premier League game would be likely to last longer than ten minutes. Now it seems that many want to impose a sort of supper-party etiquette on football, and force fans and players to mind their language and gestures and behave as if they were all permanently in court or at an FA committee meeting.

The disdain with which the authorities view football's rough-and-ready idea of free expression was brought home in another court case in 2014, when former Blackburn striker Colin Kazim-Richards was found guilty of making an 'utterly disgusting' homophobic gesture at Brighton fans. The court proceedings revealed the problems of applying the blunt instrument of criminal law to people messing about at football, with leading lawyers and local magistrates earnestly debating the true meaning of Kazim-Richards making 'a masturbatory gesture next to his backside'. In his defence, Kazim-Richards admitted making a 'wanker gesture' to the crowd behind his back, to avoid being seen by the ref, but insisted it was only 'banter' with the Brighton fans and 'not intended to be homophobic or offensive'. He said he 'was getting called, excuse my language, you fat bastard', but claimed that he was 'not at all offended'. He was fined £750 plus costs.

The real punchline to this surreal carry-on came outside court, where the football liaison officer for Sussex police (good to know they have their priorities right) declared his satisfaction at the first-ever conviction of a footballer for homophobia, and issued a warning message to all football fans and players via the media: 'You wouldn't do it in an office, why do it on the terraces?'[5] A rhetorical question so smug and stupid, if you have to ask it you should be sentenced to stay in your nice quiet office and not allowed anywhere near the raucous carnival of a football match. Football is not played in an office, or a courtroom, or a police liaison officer's press conference. It is played on Planet Football, and they do things differently there. Players – and fans – will let rip in the heat of a match in a way they would not consider doing elsewhere. Of course this sounds shocking if repeated away from the match-day atmosphere – as when the chief magistrate in the Terry trial apparently used the word 'cunt' twenty-odd times in his summing up – but football is not played in a courtroom or at a supper party either. It involves unleashing passions and conflicts that can burst out in all kinds of unpredictable directions, yet can fade and disappear again just as quickly once the match is over.

The message that football has to sanitise its act has not only been endorsed by the police and the FA. It has also been internalised by many within the game, who have lined up to join the sorry majority in the free-speech wars. Thus at the start of the 2014–15 season one of English football's most famously outspoken characters, Ian 'Ollie' Holloway, suddenly turned gamekeeper and demanded supporters learn to button their collective lip. Now the manager of Millwall FC, a south-east London club with a tough reputation, Holloway turned on his own supporters after a home match against Leeds United, another tough club from Yorkshire. He condemned Millwall fans for chants linking Leeds supporters with the infamous Jimmy Savile, a native of their fair city. Holloway said such chanting was 'offensive, disrespectful. It goes against what football is about.'[6] To which some might respond that, for many fans, being 'disrespectful, offensive' is part of what following football is about. If it didn't wind up the other side, what would have been the point of singing it? A point which the allegedly 'disrespected' Leeds fans would surely have grasped far more readily than did the Millwall manager.

The reverse-Voltaires' attack has now reached the point where people can be afforded even less free speech as football fans than they would be elsewhere in life. The Scottish government has pioneered this tactic north of the border with its Offensive Behaviour at Football and Threatening Communications (Scotland) Act, aimed at curbing the sectarian passions of supporters of Glasgow's two big Old Firm clubs. The Act, described by the campaigning author Stuart Waiton as a 'snobs' law', has made it a crime to sing the 'wrong' song or wave the 'wrong' banner around football. It means that Celtic fans can be arrested and convicted for singing the sort of Irish republican dirges that can be heard in many Glasgow pubs. Meanwhile Rangers supporters could be prosecuted for offensively singing God Save the Queen – which, if the result of the Scottish independence referendum is to be believed, remains the national dirge of the United Kingdom.[7]

Things seem set to slide even further downhill for freedom in football north of the border. In December 2014, a Glasgow member of the Scottish parliament from the governing Scottish National Party (SNP) told the group Fans Against Criminalisation that Scotland's odious Offensive Behaviour at Football Act should be used against more supporters: not just Rangers and Celtic fans singing Loyalist or republican songs and waving offensive banners, but anybody displaying political opinions near a football ground, including Free Palestine T-shirts and ... 'Yes' badges supporting the SNP's own independence campaign. 'We should all know by now,' said MSP John Mason, 'that expressing political views is no longer acceptable at football matches.' Unless of course it is the highly acceptable political opinion that football fans are scum unfit for the same freedoms enjoyed by everybody else.[8]

What is this all about? Why have those who know little and care less about the 'slum game' gone to such lengths to try to wash football's loose mouth out with soap?

The battle over free speech at football confirms that the wish to control words is underpinned by a desperation to police people. The authorities still fear and loathe the unruly crowd. Yet they have also come to see football as a rare forum in which it might yet be possible for Britain's isolated elites to connect with the masses. These pressures have resulted in the crusade to 'clean up' football and teach the bad boy to behave like a role model.

In recent times most of the traditional institutions of the British Establishment, from the churches to the political parties and the police, have been relegated into the lower leagues of public respect. One response from the desperate UK political elite has been to turn to the popular institution of football. Every political leader, no matter how posh, now feels obliged to invent some affinity with the game. Meanwhile the football stadiums have largely replaced the cathedrals as the scene of Britain's national minute's silences.

A political creed has developed which I have described as 'Soccerism'. The Soccerists tend to view football in much the same way as Homer Simpson sees beer: as both the cause of, and the solution to, life's problems. No World Cup tournament is complete nowadays without inflated talk about how it can bring the world together, counter racism and speed development in South Africa and Brazil – or alternative and equally inflated claims of how it will lead to an increase in domestic violence in the West, or in people-trafficking for prostitution around the world. In 2014 the president of Brazil even declared the finals in his country to be 'the anti-racism World Cup', an irony which may not have been lost on the black Brazilian fans still stuck at the bottom of their society.

The aim of the Soccerists is to use football as an instrument of moral social engineering, to re-educate the vulgar masses around the match and to set an example for those following the game elsewhere. One clear consequence of this has been the drive to sanitise the 'ugly' side of the beautiful game and clean up what players and fans are permitted to sing, say or think.

None of this is presented as an attack on free speech. Instead it is done in the name of protecting the rights of others, by supposedly making football more 'family-friendly' and less off-putting to women or the LGBT community. The notion that all females or gay men must automatically be delicate petals who could not bear the 'industrial language' of the stands seems as unworldly as the idea that children do not enjoy witnessing adults behaving badly. But minority groups have provided convenient human shields for those Soccerist crusaders intent on making football follow their new speech codes.

The most commonly used excuse to justify crackdowns on free speech is the need to cleanse football of racism. Nobody could disagree with that aim, except that it has come about thirty years too late. The strange thing is, the less serious racism there is remaining in British football today, the more campaigns and crackdowns we seem to see against it.

Sport is something of a mirror of the society in which it takes place. British football was steeped in racism in the days when Britain was a deeply racist country. In a society where racial discrimination and even violence were considered normal, football was unlikely to provide an island of tolerance. That was then. But football has changed with UK society. The vast majority of fans and players would no longer tolerate explicit expressions of racism. Some crusaders might still like to highlight the famous photograph of Liverpool's black star John Barnes back-heeling away a banana tossed at him by Everton supporters. They seem to find it hard to accept that that picture was taken in the dark days of 1988, more than twenty-five years ago. The only British footballer to have a banana thrown at him in recent seasons was the white Welshman Gareth Bale.

Yet those zealots committed to turning football into a role model for society are still scouring every corner of the game in search of the spectre of racism, determined to find a wrong word to kick up a fuss about. The crusaders of the Football Association and its official Kick It Out campaign, backed by the police and courts, are on a mission to sanitise everything football-related, from chants and banners to players' tweets and managers' private text messages.

That is how we have ended up with a situation where in 2014 the 73-year-old chairman of Wigan Athletic, Dave Whelan, could be splashed across the media like a war criminal and effectively driven out of football after mistakenly assuming that the rest of the UK was in the same timewarp as Wigan and using outdated language about Jews and Chinese people. And where Kent police could arrest three Gillingham supporters 'on suspicion of a racially motivated public order offence' for (sensitive readers, look away now) calling Rotherham manager Steve Evans a 'fat Scottish wanker'.[9] How could even Kentish country coppers be moronic enough to consider taking a rise out of a football manager who's a Scot as a 'racially motivated public order offence'? Quite easily, as it happens, if they have managed to read current law books. Following the 1999 Macpherson Report into the murder of the black teenager Stephen Lawrence in south London, UK law now defines as a hate crime any incident 'which is perceived by the victim or any other person as being motivated by prejudice or hate'. So if the police or passing prigs think it's a race crime, it is.

But under the rules of Planet Football, it surely should not be a crime at all. The giving and getting of abuse is an integral part of what makes watching football entertainment. Football, as the sports columnist Duleep Allirajah defined it perfectly (after a storm over England fans booing Ashley Cole), is 'pantomime for grown-ups'.[10]

This sort of abusive badinage is the stuff of atmosphere and entertainment at football. It might be offensive to some, but it remains, in real terms, harmless. It should neither be considered as racist, nor as an offence in any sense that might apply if you shouted the same thing at somebody during, say, an FA inquiry hearing, or a court case.

Yet such is the determination to find modern football guilty of racism that some observers seemed keen to make a comparison between the Stephen Lawrence murder and the John Terry case, as rare examples of the racism they imagine to be endemic in the alien white working classes. One journalist noted the presence of Stephen Lawrence's mother, the now-ennobled Dame Doreen, in the court during Terry's trial for allegedly calling Anton Ferdinand an 'FBC', he presumed 'to see if another race-related crime had been committed'. As Adrian Hart, author of *That's Racist!*, notes, what is 'implicit in such genteel misrepresentations of the working class experience of football' is that 'the gap between offensive language and murder is not that great'.[11]

The official view is that it is no longer tolerable for football to play by different rules from the rest of society. Indeed if anything the authorities now demand that football must adopt higher ethical standards than the world outside, in order to set an example to us ignorant fans. The sterilisation campaign rolls on. Its effect is not only to infringe the traditions of free speech around football, but also to diminish the real meaning of racism, by putting a disputed stray word from an individual on a level playing pitch with real violence or discrimination meted out by powerful institutions.

In February 2015, football's reverse-Voltaire faction finally found what they had been searching for so hard – evidence that some supporters could still act like racist lowlifes. A smartphone video emerged of some Chelsea supporters in the doorway of a Paris Metro train (they were there for a Champions League match) refusing to allow a black Frenchman to enter their carriage while they chanted: 'We're racist, we're racist, and that's the way we like it!' The usual suspects fell upon this evidence of boorish behaviour not only in horror, but also with relish. This, the crusaders and their media supporters insisted, was proof at last of the 'hidden racism' that blights British football – so well hidden that they had previously failed to find it, despite their best efforts. Worse, they declared, this proved racism was on the rise. One *Daily Mail* columnist declared: 'There is a greater shame here because we foolishly, naively, believed the issue of racism among our football supporters was a thing of the past.' His counterpart in the *Guardian* announced that 'for decades this kind of thing has happened, continues to happen, and most troubling, appears to be happening a little more now'. Lord Ouseley, chairman of the official Kick It Out campaign, mounted his moral pedestal to inform the nation that: 'We know that prejudice is on the increase and that in itself leads to hateful attitudes and this sort of conduct.'[12]

How could one brief video clip of a few Chelsea boors in Paris prove that racism in English football is 'on the increase'? Only because so many reverse-Voltaires were predisposed to see it in that way. Some of us might have thought that, on the contrary, the real reason those pictures were so shocking was precisely because 'this kind of thing' does not normally happen around football. But that would not serve the purpose of providing a stick with which to beat up football and its fans for failing to fulfil their duties as national role models.

The forgotten front in the free-speech wars ought to bother even those who couldn't care less about football. The attempt to turn it into a sanitised role model for society is an insult to every principle of liberty, responsibility, autonomy, and preserving a space where you can think what you like and say what you think. Let's recall the words of the US basketball star Charles Barkley more than twenty years ago: 'I'm not a role model. Just because I dunk a basketball doesn't mean I should raise your kids.' Or as Barkley put it more bluntly in a Nike advert of the early Nineties: 'I'm not paid to be a role model. I'm paid to wreak havoc on the basketball court.'[13] We might do worse, too, than to take some inspiration from the words of those philosopher kings among football fans, Spurs' self-styled Yid Army, sung in response to the FA and police campaign against them: 'We're Tottenham Hotspur/ We sing what we want ...'

* * *

When Joan Rivers died aged eighty-one in September 2014, tributes poured in for the American comedy legend. To judge by events of the previous months, however, not everybody would have been quite so sad to hear of her passing. Shortly before she died Rivers had been bitterly attacked not only for her caustic and politically incorrect expressions of support for Israel's air-strikes on Gaza – 'If New Jersey was firing rockets into New York, we would wipe them out' – but also for telling the wrong kind of jokes involving race, sexuality and much else. (Asked whether she thought there would ever be a gay president, she told the TV reporter that there already was, since 'Michelle's a tranny'.) Worse, her offensive jokes tended to be funny.[14]

When Rivers criticised Justin Bieber's 'gangsta' dress sense on her TV show *Fashion Police* in August 2014, just a month before her death, it was hard to know which caused more outrage – what she said or the fact that others laughed out loud at it. 'That little bitch gets on my nerves,' Rivers said of Bieber. 'You are not a big black thug, you are just like your shoes – ordinary and completely white.' The reverse-Voltaires went quickly into action online, and Village People veteran Victor Willis made headlines by apparently tweeting for many: 'What Joan Rivers said is no laughing matter. It's Racist and she has a history of this. Time to shut her down. What say you?'[15] When death finally managed to shut her down just weeks later, there was much smug and charmless talk of 'karma' on social media sites.

What some of us say is that Joan Rivers's great quality was her insistence that nothing ought to be beyond a joke. In contrast to the 'shut-it-down' lobby, she believed that there was no such thing as 'no laughing matter'. In this she stood in the great tradition of subversive comedians. Unlike many alleged comedians who are coming after her, she also understood that simply trying to be offensive is not enough – you first have to be funny. And unlike many wannabe controversialists today, when what she said caused the expected outrage, she refused to withdraw or apologise. It was just a joke, after all. Rivers even dared to tell a Holocaust joke, saying of the model Heidi Klum's outfit at the 2013 Oscars ceremony that 'the last time a German looked this hot was when they were pushing Jews into ovens'. When that gag enlisted an army of critics, she would not back down or apologise. 'My husband lost the majority of his family at Auschwitz,' Rivers said, 'and I can assure you that I have always made it a point to remind people of the Holocaust through humour.' She also reminded them that humour was how Jewish people had coped with the horror.[16]

It is hard not to think that, when Joan Rivers died, a kind of comedy was shut down with her. As one obituarist asked, 'Who is going to slay all those sacred cows now?'[17]

Generally speaking, good jokes are in bad taste. They tend to mock the respectable rules and morals of society. By its nature comedy is always controversial, pushing as it must at the limits of what passes for taste and decency in any era. That is why there have long been attempts to control what is deemed 'acceptable' humour and to censor what is not. And why many writers and comedians have tried to subvert the rules.

However, as with other issues in the Anglo-American free-speech wars, the terrain has shifted. Once the complaints were about blasphemous and indecent comedy, and the censors were conservative politicians, policemen and priests. Now the protests are more often against comedians accused of breaking the new taboos – racism, sexism, homophobia, transphobia, Islamophobia, anti-Semitism and the other usual suspects. And the demands to shut them down tend to be led not by old-fashioned prudes but by radical online activists, the liberal media and even other comedians. Backed up, in the UK at least, by broadcast regulators, politicians and the newly PC police.

We have come a long way since the upsurge of modern radical comedy in the 1960s, when the Jewish comedian Lenny Bruce could be arrested in America and barred from Britain for using the word 'cocksucker' on stage. The political and social changes of that decade were paralleled by a sort of Western cultural revolution affecting music, theatre and comedy. The UK had the new satire movement led by Peter Cook. In the US, the new comedy and the counter-revolution against it initially focused on Lenny Bruce.

Bruce had been using comedy to upset the applecart since his days as a teenage sailor during the Second World War. In 1945 he entertained his shipmates aboard the USS *Brooklyn* with a comedy routine whilst dressed in drag – an episode which led to his discharge from the US Navy. But it was in the Sixties that the 'troubled' and drug-taking Bruce became infamous as the figurehead for a new kind of satirical and sexually explicit comedy. In October 1961 he was arrested for obscenity at the Jazz Workshop in San Francisco, after a routine involving the use of 'cocksucker' and some discussion of the expression 'to come'. The jury acquitted him, but the authorities had already found him guilty and several other arrests for onstage obscenity followed. In 1962 he was arrested in West Hollywood, Los Angeles, for using the word 'schmuck', which many might think simply means idiot, but originated as a Yiddish insult meaning a prick. Bruce wrote that he had been arrested 'by a Yiddish undercover agent who had been placed in the club several nights running to determine if my use of Yiddish terms was a cover for profanity'. He came to Britain and appeared at Peter Cook's Establishment Club, birthplace of modern British satire. But in 1963 the actual British Establishment, in the person of the Tory home secretary, barred him from coming back into the country, branding Bruce an 'undesirable alien' whose presence in the UK would not serve 'the public interest'.

Back in the States, the anti-Lenny Bruce show reached its climax in 1964, when he was arrested twice after leaving the stage at the Café Au Go Go in New York's Greenwich Village, where undercover cops had recorded his act. Bruce was found guilty of performing a routine that was 'obscene, indecent, immoral and impure', in which 'words such as "ass," "balls," "cock-sucker," "cunt," "fuck," "mother-fucker," "piss," "screw," "shit," and "tits" were used about one hundred times in utter obscenity'.[18] Three New York judges sentenced him, in what now sounds like a bad Dickensian joke, to four months in the workhouse. Bruce was released on bail pending appeals, but died before the legal process was complete. He was posthumously pardoned in 2003 by Republican New York Governor George Pataki, who acknowledged how far things had changed. Bruce's arrest for obscenity was now deemed a free-speech issue: 'Freedom of speech is one of the greatest American liberties,' Pataki said, 'and I hope this pardon serves as a reminder of the precious freedoms we are fighting to preserve.'[19]

These days Lenny Bruce is revered as a pioneering comedy hero. Yet if the young Lenny were magically to appear on the New York stage today, what reception might he get? His routine about a psychopathic rapist meeting up with a nymphomaniac after they each escape from their respective institutions, or suggestion that he enjoyed sex with a chicken, or description of his audience as 'seven niggers, six spics, five micks, four kykes, three guineas, and one wop' might not get him arrested for obscenity by the US state or barred from entering Britain, but it surely would see him accused of racism and sexism and possibly the abuse of animals and the mentally ill by the outraged illiberal liberals of the 'shut-it-down' lobby, who would try to have him banned from campuses. And Bruce's insistence that he used the n-word and other offensive epithets 'just to make a point', that 'it's the suppression of the word that gives it the power, the violence, the viciousness', would not wash with the new comedy censors, who claim the right to decide what jokes others should be allowed to tell or to laugh at, what points they should be permitted to make, all in the public interest of course.

The 'alternative' comedy scene of the 1980s in the UK and the US began partly as a punkish reaction against the older school of what was seen as one-note racist, sexist and homophobic humour.

These alternative comedians soon became the new establishment, creating an alternative comedic conformism of their own – not so much, as British tabloids might have claimed, 'political correctness gone mad', more PC gone mainstream. The fresh generation of comedians, including feminist stars, broke many old taboos in the way they talked about sex, sexuality or race. They were also, however, helping to create new taboos.

There is a powerful whiff of the reverse-Voltaire around the controversies about comedy today. The critics are not simply objecting to a comedian's shtick or saying that it's not funny – which anybody has the perfect right to do. They are denying the offensive performer's right to say it, demanding it is time to 'shut them down'. This sort of censoriousness can only have severe consequences both for comedy and wider issues of free speech.

Some of the targets of the reverse-Voltaires of comedy might seem unquestionably objectionable, but as with all forms of extreme speech, bans and proscriptions are not the answer. Take the example of the French comedian Dieudonné M'bala M'bala, who became infamous for his 'reverse Nazi salute', the so-called quenelle, has several convictions in France for anti-Semitic hate speech, and was convicted of encouraging terrorism for his remarks after the *Charlie Hebdo* massacre (see Prologue).

Early in 2014, the Socialist government in France, backed by the country's top court, banned Dieudonné from performing in public. Interior minister Manuel Valls, shortly to become prime minister, justified this act of official intolerance in the name of tolerance, declaring that: 'We cannot tolerate anti-semitism, historical revisionism and racism.'[20] Soon afterwards, the Conservative–Liberal Democrat coalition government in the UK gave in to pressure from the 'shut it down' lobby and banned Dieudonné from entering Britain. As with the arrests and bans used against the Jewish rebel Lenny Bruce, these measures are justified in the name of protecting the public good. Yet censoring comedy, trying to tell people what they may find funny, is never in the interests of a healthy public sphere. It is also counter-productive even in its own censorious terms. The disaffected young people in France and elsewhere attracted to Dieudonné by his apparently anti-Establishment stance are unlikely to be deterred by discovering that those same elites, on both sides of the Channel and both ends of the political spectrum, are trying to shut him up.

Other clashes in the new free-speech wars over comedy involve attempts to close down more mundane comedians who simply don't conform to the changed rules. One revealing episode in the UK was the strange case of Dapper Laughs. A London comedian called Daniel O'Reilly invented a character called Dapper Laughs on social media – a vulgar, laddish, sexist caricature who went on about women going 'proper moist' in his irresistible presence. The Dapper character – part send-up of himself, part reaction against the growing cultural dominance of feminism – proved quite popular among younger social media users. (Others had never heard of him until the backlash began.) In 2014 he was given his own television series, entitled *On the Pull*, on the UK terrestrial channel ITV 2.

This was unacceptable to the reverse-Voltaires, who launched a campaign to kill off Dapper with the message 'You can't laugh at that!' He was banned from university campuses while a wave of online petitions and postings and outraged media comment sought to wash the television airwaves clean of his seedy presence. This crusade was led not by old-fashioned censors or churchmen but by allegedly liberal publications and comedians themselves. Their complaint was not merely that there were no laughs in Dapper Laughs, but that he was dangerous. A po-faced magazine for comedians called *Chortle* branded Dapper's show as a 'rapist's almanac' which 'contributed to a prevalent predatory culture that reduces women to nothing more than a piece of cunt' (it now being acceptable to use the words that got Bruce arrested and banned, so long as you do so in support of PC censorship). *New Statesman* magazine, traditional house journal of the British left, instructed its readers to 'be worried about Dapper Laughs' because he was 'normalising sexual harassment'.[21]

How could a bad-taste joke told by an invented character seriously be accused of legitimising sexual harassment or even violence in the real world? Like all attempts to restrict free speech, it reflected a low view not just of the speaker, but of the audience.

What worried the comedy conformists was that Dapper was popular among an audience of young men or 'lads' who did not meet their standards of non-sexist behaviour. The criticism of Dapper Laughs seethed with contempt for working-class men who apparently look at every woman as a 'potential wank fantasy', as if that in itself was a sexual crime. *Chortle* described Dapper's young laddish followers as 'the unenlightened, the confused, the intellectually frightened ... a people shovelling themselves into the excrement of history'. *Vice* magazine, house journal of London hipsters, declared that Dapper came from and spoke to 'a universe that Vagenda [a feminist campaign group] seeks to destroy ... suburban white men with hairstyles and tattoos ... douchebags, basically'. However hateful an opinion the made-up character Dapper might have had of women, it was easily matched by the real-world fear and loathing with which these critics viewed his audience of working-class men. If these people were allowed to laugh as they saw fit, civilisation would surely be at risk. So their 'culture' must be not just derided, but 'destroyed'.[22]

The anti-Dapper crusade reached its nadir when almost fifty comedians signed an open letter demanding that ITV should follow the lead set by student unions and banish Dapper Laughs from its doorstep. The idea of liberal comedians stupidly cheerleading the censorship of comedy would be funny if it were not such a serious sign of illiberal times. The notion that no one must speak out of turn or laugh out of line is a far more dangerous threat to a free society than any sexist joke might ever be. But none of this, we were assured, had anything to do with freedom of speech.

Inevitably the liberal lynch mob succeeded in killing off Dapper Laughs. Having first offered the crusaders the sensible response that 'comedy is subjective', ITV bosses quickly caved in and cancelled *On the Pull*. The comedian behind the character then went on current affairs TV to apologise, cry, and swear that Dapper was now dead. It was enough to make anybody weep who cares about free speech, or just the right to have a laugh even if they didn't think Dapper provided many laughs.

The rise of the reverse-Voltaires has damaged comedy. On one hand it has created a stifling atmosphere of conformism and intolerance in which any humour that crosses the line must be not just ignored but 'shut down'. That in turn has given rise to a feeble backlash of comedians trying to be offensive for the sake of it.

Top American comedian Chris Rock, not noted for avoiding controversial issues, revealed in December 2014 that he no longer plays college venues, because the student audiences are 'too conservative'. 'Not in their political views – not like they're voting Republican – but in their social views and their willingness not to offend anybody,' Rock told *New York* magazine. 'You can't say "the black kid over there." No, it's "the guy with the red shoes." You can't even be offensive on your way to being inoffensive.'[23]

A similar atmosphere now appears to prevail even among some paying audience members in comedy clubs. The traditional art of heckling a performer you don't find funny is apparently outdated – now you hear tell of punters trying to shout down a comedian or flouncing out in outrage because they object to him or her breaking a taboo – say, by joking about gay marriage or police racism. Whether what they said was funny seems to miss the point for those who think a comedy set should be as orthodox as a sermon.

Inevitably, there has been an attempted backlash against these stultifying trends. We have witnessed the rise of comedians or just deliberate provocateurs whose aim is to appear as offensive as possible. This is the flipside of the attempt to sanitise humour. It leads unerringly to further attempts at ethical cleansing of the comedy cesspit. In spring 2015, when the South African comedian Trevor Noah was appointed to succeed John Stewart as host of *The Daily Show* on Comedy Central, online critics protested that Noah was an unsuitable choice due to his past record of tweeting 'controversial' jokes about women and Jewish people. One tweeter put this row in some welcome perspective: 'Trevor Noah doesn't offend me as a woman,' posted @helienne, 'he offends me because he's just not funny.'[24]

That is the question that appears to have been forgotten in all this: Is it funny? The attempt to impose codes of conduct on comedy reflects the idea that you can somehow apply a political and moral judgement to humour. That you can, in short, stop yourself laughing at something offensive or controversial. Good luck with that, and with preventing yourself sneezing at the same time.

The history of comedy surely shows that, as with old-time British comedians such as Bernard Manning, it is perfectly possible to talk like a bigot and yet be funny. That's life. Comedy is a messy business, and people can laugh at the most outrageous things. To attempt to impose order on it, by removing what is not to the taste of the moment, is to risk killing it. In the early 1990s, I recall, a young British comedian called John Thomson created a great send-up of the old-fashioned club comic, called Bernard Righton, who told impeccably politically correct gags such as: 'An Irishman, an Englishman and a Pakistani walked into a pub. What a wonderful example of a multicultural community!' The punchline, of course, was that Bernard Righton was not funny at all.

We are faced with a situation where what is considered acceptable in comedy could be every bit as one-note and conformist as in the bad old days, except that it now has to comply with different codes and taboos. Of course, nobody is against free speech for comedians. Until, that is, they decide somebody has gone too far in offending their own views and hurting their feelings.

In September 2014, while controversy raged about comedians accused of telling 'rape jokes', one UK feminist comedian made an appeal for a grown-up attitude to stand-up comedians talking about sex and sexuality. In the words of Katy Brand:

> Crass, misogynist, homophobic comedy has always been a part of the business, but surely we are all grown up enough to let the market decide, and those comedians who insist on telling crappy jokes about anything, let alone sex, are finding their audiences slowly ebbing away. So my motto for discussing sex in comedy is: say what you like, but stand up and take the consequences like a woman – if the late, great Joan Rivers has taught us anything, it's this.[25]

An admirable sentiment. Yet within weeks many of her fellow comedians were campaigning to censor the crass, misogynist, homophobic Dapper Laughs. The consequences those who transgress have to face today are likely to involve demands to 'shut them down'. Especially, it seems, when the market decides they are funny and the humorous heretics raise more laughs than the dour conformists. Unlike Joan Rivers, these days few comedians appear to have the balls to face down the shrill demands to apologise, conform or shut up.

As on other fronts in the silent war on free speech, the debate about taboos in comedy is marked by a straight-faced inconsistency. Whether it is left-wing comics protesting about sexism on ITV, or right-wing ones complaining that the lefties monopolise BBC panel shows, all sides will champion freedom – for the comedy which suits their own tastes. Whether anybody succeeds or fails as a comedian should not be judged by whether or not their jokes meet somebody else's political or ethical standards. It might be hard to get excited about defending free speech for those you consider sexist, Islamophobic or anti-Semitic comedians. There are few heroes in the battle for comedy's soul. Yet it remains as important to defend freedom of speech and thought here as in any other corner of Western culture.

It is a fact that the most bitter free-speech battles these days can often be fought in the muddy lowlands of sport or comedy, far from the cultural high ground. And the wish to dictate not just what jokes a comedian should tell, but also what we should laugh at, is the clearest conceivable attempt at thought control. What could be more intrusive than the attempt to police something as reflexive as a snort of laughter?

A bizarre and revealing crossover moment in the free speech wars surrounding football and comedy occurred in February 2012 when police took the unprecedented action of impounding *Red Issue*, the biggest and best Manchester United supporters' fanzine (for which I wrote), for publishing a 'potentially offensive' joke. Luis Suarez, the Uruguayan star of Liverpool FC – Manchester United's fiercest rivals – had been handed an eight-match ban and a big fine after being found guilty of racially abusing United's Patrice Evra during that season's match at Anfield. For the return game at Old Trafford, *Red Issue* printed a back cover ridiculing Suarez and Liverpool's support of their player – a spoof cut-out mask in the shape of a KKK hood, carrying the legend 'Suarez is Innocent'. When the magazine went on sale outside the stadium, Greater Manchester Police confiscated every copy on the ground that the Suarez cover was 'potentially offensive', and threatened to arrest *Red Issue* sellers for 'inciting racial hatred'. Thus did a (rather good) joke about racism in football somehow become the pretext for more 'anti-racist' censorship. The draconian and groundless police impounding of an entire magazine (no charges were ever brought) on the streets of a British city prompted few protests from the civil liberties lobby. Well, it's only football fans telling jokes, who cares about free speech for them?

The tortured efforts to patrol what is and is not acceptably funny have created a fraught situation where comedy is in danger of becoming a more staid and safe affair, certainly in the colleges and on TV. One side effect of this might be the recent elevation of old-fashioned uncontroversial one-line jokes at comedy festivals. Another is the upsurge of silly look-at-me acts where the main aim appears to be controversy rather than comedy.

The trends towards a more conformist and intolerant world of comedy put at risk one of the most important sorts of release we have left in a dour world. The pulling of comedy's teeth should be no laughing matter. The sight of outraged reverse-Voltaires rampaging across the comedy stage is also a dire warning for the wider free-speech wars. If comedians are not allowed to upset and offend, what chance have the rest of us got?

To quote another controversial line from the late, great, Joan Rivers, possibly channelling the long-gone great Lenny Bruce: 'Everybody just relax. Everybody's either a wop, a nigga, a kike, a chink, a fairy, a mick – everybody's something, so why don't we all just. Calm. Down.'[26] There seems little chance of that when comedy can be treated as a serious case for censorship.

Five good excuses for restricting free speech – and why they're all wrong

In the silent war on free speech, it is rare to hear anybody declare their outright hostility to freedom (that's what makes the war a silent one). Instead the free-speech fraudsters will typically nod to the importance of the principle, before spelling out the exceptions in practice. Usually introduced with the standard defence: 'This is not a free-speech issue/an attack on freedom of expression.'

The following chapters outline and take issue with some of the most common and strongest excuses offered for imposing restrictions on free speech. All of them have a point – words can indeed provoke or hurt, lies about the Holocaust really are despicable, the powerful get more say than the masses.

Yet in the end all of these objections point up the need for more speech rather than less, for open discussion and debate rather than bans and restrictions. The case for the prosecution of words can be turned into an argument for the unequivocal defence of free speech.

7

'There is no right to shout "Fire!" in a crowded theatre'

The prosecution alleges that some speech is simply too dangerous and inflammatory to be allowed to go free – even under a US-style First Amendment.

It was said that reactions to the massacre at the Paris offices of *Charlie Hebdo* magazine in January 2015 'left many questions unanswered'. Those confusing questions included: Exactly what does drawing a cartoon of the Prophet Muhammad have to do with shouting 'Fire!' in a theatre?

The online debates about free speech in the immediate aftermath of *Charlie Hebdo* sometimes read like a contest to see who could mention 'shouting fire in a theatre' first or loudest. Reacting against a *New York Times* article in defence of free speech, for example, one winning poster declared that: 'These *Charlie Hebdo* people just like poking a lion. Just stupid. Don't shout fire in the theater.' Elsewhere, supporting Catholic League president Bill Donohue's claim that the murders were the 'natural outcome' of cartoons drawn by 'pornographers disguised as satirists', another winner demanded of other posters: 'Ever hear of the SCOTUS [Supreme Court of the United States] decision from many years ago, RELATIVE TO FREE SPEECH, that said "Free Speech" does not give anyone the right to yell "FIRE!" in a CROWDED THEATER, just for the perverted fun of seeing people scream and scramble and fall over themselves running for safety.' The generous use of capitals here offers a clear indication that the statement is both IMPORTANT and TRUE.[1]

When was the last time anybody shouted 'Fire!' in a theatre? So why is it wheeled on as an apparently fireproof argument in every debate about the limits to free speech? What is this obsession with the hypothetical possibility of somebody having such perverted fun really all about?

There is today a flourishing market in fashionable short-hand rebukes and code words, deployed to tell somebody to shut up – 'I feel offended/That's hate speech/Check your privilege/Denier!' and so on. But the granddaddy of lines for dismissing a free-speech defence, which pre-dates those recent blow-ins and will probably still be around after they have been forgotten, is the shrill retort: 'There is no right to shout "Fire!" in a crowded theatre.'

Not many near-hundred-year-old US Supreme Court cases get cited in twenty-first-century arguments anywhere from the web to a bar or a TV studio or the UK parliament. In fact there is only one – the 1919 case where, it seems everybody knows, the Supreme Court justices ruled that there is no right to shout fire in a theatre. When it comes to finding a handy argument for restricting free speech in the present, apparently any of us can become an instant expert in American legal history.

Political allegiances count for nothing when it comes to the promiscuous deployment of the can't-shout-fire-in-a-theatre line. In recent times a UK Labour government used it to excuse banning an anti-Islamist speaker, a liberal US judge used it to suggest that the First Amendment should not allow bigots to burn the Koran, and Greens have deployed it to try to silence climate-change sceptics. But conservatives were just as quick and keen to wave the 'fire in a theatre' flag over the Wikileaks revelations of classified US information.

This mixed bag of prosecutors allege that some speech can simply be too dangerous to allow it to go unchecked. So they want to silence and punish those who use inflammatory language. Of course, they insist, this is not really an attack on free speech; incitement, threats, 'fighting words' and incendiary language have never been protected, even by the US First Amendment. Rather than an assault on the troublemakers' right to free speech, we are assured, proscribing such expressions is simply an attempt to protect people and society from the consequences of dangerous talk (or lion-poking cartoons).

The top authority cited for this case against unfettered free speech is Justice Oliver Wendell Holmes of the US Supreme Court. It was Holmes who, writing the unanimous judgement back in that 1919 case, ruled that: 'The most stringent protection of free speech would not protect a man in falsely shouting fire in a theater and causing a panic.' Justice Holmes's memorable metaphor is still cited as a supposedly unanswerable case for dousing inflammatory speech.

The fame which a 1919 Supreme Court case enjoys today in Anglo-US debate is remarkable. All the more so, since the judge who wrote that famous judgement later effectively abandoned his own words as too restrictive of speech, and the Supreme Court threw out the Holmes rule in 1969 – getting on for half a century ago.

So why is such an outdated court judgement still cited so often? Because it has become an all-purpose excuse for demanding limits on any speech considered inflammatory today. The abiding popularity of the fire-in-a-theatre metaphor reflects how we spend far more time discussing the need to rein in speech than to free it.

Here's the strange thing. The less relevant that legal ruling has become in US courts over the past half-century, the more it seems to be cited in public debate in the Anglo-American world outside. In overruling Holmes's old opinion, Supreme Court justices have further narrowed the criteria that can be used to restrict or punish

speech. Yet at the same time, politicians and crusaders have broadened the meaning of shouting-fire-in-a-theatre to apply to any
words they want us not to hear.

Does the prosecution case about shouting fire in theatres stand
up? Those of us appearing for the defence of free speech should
insist that, no, it does not; and we should be happy to shout that
from the rooftops, if not in a crowded theatre where it might spoil
the show.

It is worth looking a bit closer at this as a case study in how facts
can be twisted, arguments turned on their heads and history
rewritten, all to manufacture a legitimate-sounding excuse for
hobbling free speech. What did Holmes really say and why, and
what might it mean today? Any serious attempt to answer those
questions will find not only that Justice Holmes's judgement has
been repeatedly misquoted and distorted, but might also conclude
that his judgement was wrong in the first place and his case for
restricting speech should long since have been consigned to the
dustbin of history.

The Supreme Court case where all this began did not of course
have anything to do with shouting 'Fire!' in a theatre or anywhere
else. Lots of public figures might be keen to show off their knowledge of what Judge Wendell Holmes said. Rather fewer seem familiar with the words of Charles Schenck, the anti-war activist whom
the case was actually about.

In 1917, when the US joined the Allied side in the First World
War, Congress passed the Conscription Act and began drafting
men into the armed forces. Not for the first or last time, the draft
was criticised as disproportionately affecting the poor white and
black communities. Charles Schenck, secretary of the US Socialist
Party, mailed anti-conscription leaflets to several thousand potential draftees. The self-consciously moderate leaflets – originally
written in Yiddish, not English – began by citing the First
Amendment to the US Constitution, which protects freedom of

speech and of religion. It argued that the authorities 'violate the provisions of the United States Constitution, the Supreme Law of the Land, when they refuse to recognise your right to assert your opposition to the draft'. This infringed basic rights which 'it is the solemn duty of all citizens and residents of the United States to retain'. Schenck was charged and convicted under the wartime Espionage Act, which made it an offence to 'cause, or attempt to cause insubordination, disloyalty, mutiny, or refusal of duty, in the military or naval forces of the United States, or ... [to] willfully obstruct the recruiting or enlistment service of the United States'. Although the war ended in 1918, Schenck's fight to establish his First Amendment rights to express an opinion did not. In 1919 *Schenck v. United States* reached the US Supreme Court for final judgement.

The Supreme Court judges voted unanimously to uphold his conviction, and Justice Holmes wrote the official opinion or judgement on behalf of them all. Holmes's judgement dismissed the First Amendment defence in quite perfunctory fashion, briefly swatting it away as if it was unworthy of serious consideration. Yet in so doing, he set a benchmark for the limits of free speech under the US Constitution:

[The] question in every case is whether the words used are used in such circumstances and are of such a nature as to create a clear and present danger that they will bring about the substantive evils that Congress has a right to prevent ... We admit that in many places and in ordinary times the defendants in saying all that was said in the circular would have been within their constitutional rights. But the character of every act depends upon the circumstances in which it is done. The most stringent protection of free speech would not protect a man in falsely shouting fire in a theater and causing a panic.[2]

Holmes's objection was not to the language Schenck used or even the message his anti-conscription leaflet or 'circular' conveyed. For the judge the key question was: did the words present 'a clear and present danger' of creating 'substantive evils'? That could only be answered, he said, not by judging the words themselves but the context in which they were used. As he put it, 'the character of every act depends upon the circumstances in which it is done'. Holmes could concede that, in different circumstances, Schenck and his Socialist allies would have been within their rights to say what they did. But not when judged in the very particular context of national crisis and war. That was what his fire-in-a-theatre point was supposed to illustrate: that you could shout fire falsely to your heart's content in a field or on the beach, but it would have very different consequences in a theatre or, we might think, a modern nightclub.

Justice Holmes's judgement, then, was that speech could be criminalised only in very specific, narrowly defined circumstances where it posed a 'clear and present danger'. What's wrong with that reasonable-sounding argument, as a basis for restricting speech deemed dangerous or inflammatory in the US or the UK – or France – today?

Plenty. The old fire-in-a-theatre metaphor has been turned into a clear and present danger to freedom of speech in the here and now. Here are four reasons why it's time to put out the flame keeping that argument alive.

First, it has been distorted beyond recognition. For a typical top-level misuse and abuse of that old judgement to justify an attack on free speech, look to the UK. In 2009 the New Labour government moved to ban Geert Wilders, a controversial member of the Dutch parliament, from entering Britain to give public speeches, on the ground that his anti-Islamic views would prove too inflammatory. Foreign secretary David Miliband seemed convinced that barring a politician from speaking because you were worried about his opinions was not the same thing as attacking free speech. 'We have a profound commitment to freedom of speech,' declared the Labour government minister, 'but there is no freedom to cry "fire" in a crowded theatre and there is no freedom to stir up hate, religious and racial hatred, according to the laws of the land.'³ Miliband did not mention Justice Oliver Wendell Holmes by name, but he evidently felt the judge's ghostly hand on his shoulder. Whether Holmes would have approved is another matter.

This is a bad case of legal misrepresentation, m'lud. For one thing, there is the common misquotation. Holmes did not say there was 'no freedom to cry "fire" in a crowded theatre'. That would have been ridiculous. What is anybody supposed to do if they spot a fire in a theatre, just exit quietly and leave the rest of the audience to roast in peace?

What Holmes said was that there was no freedom 'falsely' to cry fire. That f-word matters. It raises the question: who is to decide if the argument put forward is 'false' or not? And how, unless they are allowed to hear it in the first place? Justice Holmes assumed the Supreme Court's right, not to prevent the Socialist Party's leaflet being published, but to punish Schenck after the event. The UK government went further and assumed the right to decide that, if he were allowed to set foot on British soil, the anti-Islamist Wilders was likely to go about falsely shouting fire. So they took pre-emptive action to prevent the British public hearing him and deciding for itself what might be true or false. That is prior constraint and state censorship of free speech, however you dress it up for an evening at the theatre.

This sort of misquoting of the fire-in-a-theatre is symptomatic of a wider misrepresentation. The crusaders have turned Justice Holmes's curt remark about the very specific circumstances in which he believed free speech could be limited despite the First Amendment, into a general excuse for trying to outlaw or control 'dangerous' words and opinions which they simply find objectionable.

What has Holmes's emphasis on the peculiar need for censorship during the First World War got to do with slapping a ban on a Dutch MP even entering the UK almost a century later, for fear that he might make an anti-Islamist speech of which the authorities disapproved? How does it justify implying that murdered Paris cartoonists were effectively asking for it because they drew pictures that a handful of homicidal fanatics objected to?

Other distortions of Holmes's meaning appear even more bizarre. Take, for example, an article published on the trendy website gawker.com in 2014, under the perfectly reasonable headline 'Arrest climate change deniers'. Never mind those who 'fuss and stomp' about free speech, wrote the author; to deny the scientific consensus on climate change should be a crime: 'First Amendment rights have never been absolute. You still can't yell "fire" in a crowded theater. You shouldn't be able to yell "balderdash" at 10,883 scientific journal articles a year, all saying the same thing'.[4]

It is quite a feat, pumping sufficient hot air into Holmes's strict rule about speech posing a 'clear and present danger' in the specific circumstances of a world war in order to make it justify a general law against climate-change 'denial'. It reveals the fear that the gullible public, on hearing a critique of climate-change orthodoxy, might mindlessly dash for the thermostat to turn up the heating and to the shops to run up the credit card bill, ignoring scientists and politicians telling us how to behave ourselves more 'sustainably'. The fire-in-a-theatre script can have no logical relevance to an argument questioning mainstream scientific views on climate change or anything else.

And it gets worse. Cracking jokes on TV can now, it seems, be seriously compared to shouting fire in a theatre. In 2014, as noted in the previous chapter, a campaign sprang up to have the comedy character Dapper Laughs barred from UK campuses and kicked off British TV for his sexist patter. The hapless comedian behind 'Dapper' insisted that his character was only engaging in harmless banter with women and his audience. This resort to the b-word provoked further fury, as if Dapper Laughs had incited or even committed a sexual assault. One contributor to an online discussion about banning the bantering comic spelt out the protesters' case: 'Banter basically is shouting "fire" in a crowded cinema. The fact that it is intended as a joke isn't sufficient excuse for the dangerous effect it has.'[5] We have come a long way from the reluctant acceptance of censoring anti-conscription activists during the First World War, to the enthusiastic demand to censor a sexist comedy character on television channel ITV2, all to be justified by citing the same portentous words.

The case against shouting-fire-in-a-theatre has been turned into a theatrical ticket for anybody who wants to impose a limit on dangerous ideas, which means ideas that they don't like. It has been twisted into an access-all-areas argument with which nobody can surely disagree. Except perhaps Justice Holmes, but fortunately for them he's not around to correct anybody.

Second, Holmes himself effectively abandoned his own words. Not everybody has a high opinion of Justice Oliver Wendell Holmes – one conservative free-speech advocate considers him to have been a 'eugenicist crackpot'. Yet those who wish to argue for limiting free speech appear to hang on his every venerated word. That begs the question: if all of our amateur law experts are apparently so interested in spreading the wise words of Justice Oliver Wendell Holmes, then why are these students of Supreme Court history so selective about which ones they highlight?

The danger test and the fire-in-a-theatre image Justice Holmes conjured up in his Schenck judgement stand out as the occasion when he displayed a notable nervousness about free speech. In later cases – where his judgement was more considered than the brush-off he gave Schenck – the judge seemed to take a different view. He came down firmly in favour of freedom of speech even when he strongly disapproved of the sentiments expressed. Yet for some reason we don't seem to hear much about these cases outside law school seminars.

Just a few months after the Schenck case, for example, in the October 1919 case of *Abrams v. United States*, a majority of Supreme Court judges voted to jail Russian immigrants who distributed leaflets attacking America's decision to send troops to invade Soviet Russia after the revolution there. The revolutionary leaflets were made of fierier stuff than the Socialist Party's anti-conscription efforts – 'Workers, our reply to the barbaric intervention has to be a general strike! An open challenge only will let the Government know that not only the Russian Worker fights for freedom, but also here in America lives the spirit of Revolution!' Despite that, however, this time Justice Holmes dissented from the court's decision to imprison them, on free-speech grounds, when he wrote:

> The ultimate good desired is better reached by free trade in ideas. The best test of truth is the power of the thought to get itself accepted in the competition of the market. We should be eternally vigilant against attempts to check the expression of opinions that we loathe and believe to be fraught with death, unless they so imminently threaten immediate interference with the lawful and pressing purposes of the law that an immediate check is required to save the country.

The 'eternal vigilance' Holmes calls for here is not against dangerous speech, but against attacks on free speech, aka 'attempts to check the expression of opinions that we loathe and believe to be fraught with death'.[6]

Ten years later, in the 1929 case of *United States v. Schwimmer*, Justice Holmes once more dissented from the Supreme Court's majority decision on free-speech grounds. Rosika Schwimmer was a refugee from repressive Hungary who applied to become a naturalised US citizen. In her application she admitted that, as a dedicated pacifist, she would be unable to take up arms to defend America. The majority of Supreme Court judges ruled that this meant she failed to meet the requirements of US citizenship (even though, as an elderly woman in a country that had never conscripted women or the elderly, it was an entirely hypothetical question). Writing a dissenting minority opinion on the case (which arguably reflected a majority of commentators' opinion outside the court), Justice Holmes observed that: 'Some of her answers might excite popular prejudice, but if there is any principle of the Constitution that more imperatively calls for attachment than any other it is the principle of free thought – not free thought for those who agree with us but freedom for the thought that we hate.'[7]

If you seek an historic monument to Holmes's views on freedom of expression, that is surely the line that stands the test of time. The clarion call to defend 'freedom for the thought that we hate' is crucial, not just for the US Constitution but for the foundations of any free and civilised society.

By contrast those who single out Holmes's earlier quote about shouting fire in a theatre want to pick and choose the thoughts for which they will defend that freedom. That is why they endlessly repeat his early statement, yet ignore or remain ignorant of all that he said afterwards. They take a selective attitude to his cases, because they want to take a selective approach to freedom of expression. Reciting the fire-in-a-theatre line has become another excuse for trying to cherry-pick who deserves to get freedom of speech, a denial of Holmes's own stated principle of 'freedom for the thought that we hate'.

Third, it has not been the law in the US for almost fifty years. Why do so many on both sides of the Atlantic seem keen to cite a Supreme Court case from 1919, rather than one from 1969 that superseded it? If they feel the need to rely on the authority of US constitutional law, one might expect them to look to the law as it currently exists, rather than as it was at the end of the First World War. Surely it's not because they simply want to grasp at some legal straw, no matter how outdated, to give an air of authority to their thoroughly modern wish to restrain free speech?

As noted in chapter 3 on the history of the heretics' fight for free speech, the Supreme Court redefined the possible limits of free speech more narrowly in the 1969 case of *US v. Brandenburg*. This case may have involved a racist Ku Klux Klan leader rather than a fighter for civil rights; nevertheless, as ever, the court was influenced by the climate in society outside – in this case the liberalising mood and movements of the 1960s, which demanded greater freedom.

The judgement in *Brandenburg* threw over the Holmes formulation from 1919 and replaced it with a freer one. From now on, in order to have your First Amendment rights restricted, it would no longer be enough for the courts to assert that your words posed a 'clear and present danger' that they might bring about 'substantive evils'. Instead the court would need to show that the words were intended to cause serious harm, and that there was an immediate prospect of them doing so. Simply holding or expressing a provocative opinion could no longer be considered a crime.

In the politically hot summer of 1964 Clarence Brandenburg, a KKK leader in rural Ohio, spoke at a rally where armed men in robes and hoods burned a cross and talked about 'revengeance' against 'niggers' and 'Jews' and their supporters. Brandenburg was arrested, charged and convicted with advocating violence under Ohio's sweeping criminal syndicalism law, which had been passed during the first anti-Communist Red Scare of 1919. He got a one- to ten-year prison sentence, and all of the Ohio courts dismissed his appeal out of hand.

However, when his case eventually made it to the US Supreme Court in 1969, the judges overturned Brandenburg's conviction. They held that it could not be a crime under the First Amendment to express a general opinion, however distasteful – even if that opinion included the 'mere Advocacy' of violence or lawbreaking. They replaced Justice Holmes's old 'clear and present danger' test with a new test, which said that the government could not punish inflammatory speech unless that speech was both deliberately intended to incite, and likely to incite, 'imminent lawless action'. That set a tougher test for the state to pass. It would no longer be enough simply to say that a speaker's inflammatory words were the equivalent of shouting fire in a theatre.[8] Holmes was officially legal history. Outside court, however, his fire-in-a-theatre formulation has remained very much in fashion as a modern argument for restricting free speech.

The Supreme Court judgement superseding Holmes was delivered, remember, more than forty-five years ago. In other words, his rule has not been part of US law for almost as long as it ever was. Yet Holmes's creaky line is still being quoted, perhaps more than ever, to demand and justify restrictions on free speech. It has been running for even longer than *The Mousetrap* on the London stage, and its fans seem determined to stick to their dusty old script whatever the weather outside.

Fourth and finally, in any case, the fire-in-a-theatre comparison is and always was wrong. Leaving aside all other historical considerations, it is worth asking if Holmes had a point, anyway. Yes, his famous judgement actually set pretty narrow terms on which free speech might be abridged in very specific circumstances. But should there really be legitimate grounds to limit speech as too dangerous?

The answer is no, there shouldn't be – once we are clear what free speech means. This point was spelled out in chapter 1. Explicit threats against specific targets are not free speech. Neither is giving a direct order to others to commit a crime or do somebody harm. Nor, we might concede, is it freedom of expression falsely to shout you-know-what, you-know-where, or to plant pretend bombs intended to terrorise people.

But that's why Holmes never had a case. He used a theatrical example that had nothing to do with free speech in order to attack something that definitely did – the freedom of political campaigners to criticise conscription. Whether or not there is a 'right' falsely to shout fire in a theatre, if free speech means anything there must be a right to protest against the government's war policies.

Justice Holmes's famous dictum was not about free speech at all. From today's perspective it sounds more like an issue of health and safety policy (one might only wonder that theatres and other public places don't include 'No falsely shouting fire' in their voluminous lists of posted safety instructions). On the other hand, firebrand speeches made by anti-war agitators, revolutionaries and even KKK racists most certainly are free-speech issues. They involve ideas, beliefs, passions and hatreds in an argument about what sort of society we want. There should never be any constraint on that sort of debate, however heated. We always need more speech rather than less to clarify the arguments and let people choose their idea of the truth.

Underneath all the legalese, the fire-in-a-theatre argument has often been an expression of elitist disdain for the masses. It rests upon the assumption that many people are ignorant and suggestible enough for a word out of place to start a riot, just as being told a theatre was on fire might start a stampede for the exits.

The wish to throw a bucket of ice water on 'inflammatory' speech often reflects the prejudice that the public are mostly highly flammable blockheads, so that public opinion might be a pogrom waiting to happen at the drop of a hateful word. That is the base view of humanity that those who lazily repeat the fire-in-a-theatre line to justify restricting speech are really signing up to today.

The list of types of expression that reverse-Voltaires want to see restricted on fire-in-the-theatre grounds seems to grow longer all the time. It now includes not only Islamist preaching or Islamophobic rhetoric, but also offensive jokes, football chants, sexist/gun-glorifying gangsta rap, homophobic dancehall reggae and much more. With any of these apparently considered capable of inflaming mob violence, it seems a wonder that the streets are not constantly running with blood. If listening to the 'wrong' sort of music can now be considered an incitement to riot, then surely any sort of political or cultural expression is at risk of being thrown onto the censors' bonfire.

But what is to be done about incitement? Any attempt to restrict or punish speech as incitement in a civilised society should surely be forced at the very least to pass the test set by the 1969 Brandenburg case cited above: to show that the speech was both intended to, and likely to, incite 'imminent lawless action'. Instead the tendency in the West today is to try to broaden the definition of incitement to include any 'inflammatory' words or opinions that are deemed too far beyond the pale. Broadening the legal definition of incitement risks criminalising arguments and opinions.

The verb 'to incite' can mean simply to urge somebody towards your desired goal. You are using words to try to persuade others to think and act in a certain way. There is often an immediate assumption that inciting others must mean incitement to commit a crime. But the origins of the term incitement are about urging somebody forward in a particular direction, prompting them to act as you suggest. In that sense countless types of speech could be branded as incitement – whether it's a politician inciting the electorate to vote for her, a corporation inciting consumers to buy their products, or a comedian inciting an audience to laugh at his jokes. As Justice Holmes of fire-in-a-theatre fame himself put it, in one of his other less-remembered Supreme Court opinions, 'Every idea is an incitement.'[9]

Of course it is also possible to try to incite somebody to commit a crime, whether that means to riot against the police or launch a racist attack, and for centuries that sort of incitement was itself a crime in Britain, the common law offence of incitement – persuading somebody else to do something that was already a crime. But we are still only talking about words, and context should be all-important in judging guilt. To express a general inflammatory attitude – for example, that the country would be better off if it could rid itself of ginger-headed people – is one thing; to urge a specific action in a particular context – 'let's get that ginger bastard over there!' – to a mob scared witless of being attacked by ginger thugs is another matter. The latter might sound like a criminal offence, the former merely an offensive opinion, and there should not be a law against it.

To what extent should a speaker be held responsible for the actions of others? A key legal consideration must be whether, in the context of the inflammatory remarks, the listener has an opportunity to reflect before acting. The 'incitees' themselves still have to choose to act on those words, and commit the offence being incited. They are not pre-programmed automatons having their buttons pushed, or actors following a script. They have to decide for themselves whether to do as they are invited or incited to do. Furthermore, since the Second World War, we have been generally reluctant to accept the excuse that somebody was 'only following orders'.

To claim that a speaker can be held directly responsible for the actions of others risks making the idea of personal responsibility meaningless. It infantilises the listeners, suggesting that they are childlike simpletons who will simply do as they are told. When I hear accusations of incitement being thrown around these days, it sometimes brings to mind the image of an exasperated mother demanding of her embarrassed son: 'Oh, little Johnny told you to do it, did he? And if Johnny "told you" to jump off a tall building, would you do that, too?' No doubt some might be more impressionable than others. The tendency of the fire-in-a-theatre advocates, however, seems always to generalise and judge the public to be one big susceptible infantile blob.

Broadening definitions of the crime of incitement risks blurring the distinction between words and deeds, speech and action. It means blaming those who imagine an outcome for the fact that others might choose to act out their fantasies. King Henry II of England did not commit murder when he (allegedly) demanded: 'Will no one rid me of this turbulent priest?' That crime was committed by the four knights who took their king's words as a licence to assassinate Archbishop Thomas Becket in Canterbury Cathedral. Today, Henry might find himself charged with 'encouraging or assisting' an offence (since 2008 the statutory replacement of common law incitement), or at least he would if it weren't for the small matter of the British monarch still being immune from prosecution. The collapsing of aggressive words into violent deeds is bad news for freedom of thought and speech in a free society.

The UK's more recent laws creating and extending the crime of incitement to racial or religious or homophobic hatred make clear the dangerous implications of this mission creep. We may find racial or religious hatred offensive. They should no more be a criminal offence than any other opinion or emotion. Yet the offence of incitement to hatred makes it a crime to say something which might persuade others not to commit a crime but simply to think in a way deemed unacceptable in polite society.

As Professor John Fitzpatrick of the Kent Law School made clear back in 1997, when the New Labour government embarked on its mission to develop further the law relating to racial hatred, UK law in this area was already deeply problematic. These measures made it 'a crime to incite somebody to do something which is perfectly lawful – to hate other people on account of their race. You are entitled, in a free society, to hate who you like, whether they be black, Arsenal fans or Jack Straw [the Labour minister pushing through the legal changes].' The exceptional law that made incitement to racial hatred a crime was based on 'three very dangerous assumptions – people are not capable of withstanding certain ideas, are not able to think or believe something without acting violently upon it, and are simply not entitled to have one type of belief ... It is a thought crime.'[10]

* * *

And what about in times of war, the precise and extraordinary circumstances in which Justice Holmes imposed his rules on restricting freedom of speech? It is not hard to see how it might have been in the interests of the UK or US state to restrict freedom of speech in the midst of the national crises occasioned by the First and Second World Wars. (Although, as Orwell pointed out, wartime government censorship was rarely necessary in Britain, due to the mood of self-censorship and conformism within the mainstream media world.)[11] From the point of view of defending the principles of a free society, however, some of us might think it important to advocate the right to dissent and argue for alternatives even – or especially – when democracy is on the line. The list of some of the offences for which Americans were jailed under Montana's First World War Sedition Act – for example, refusing to kiss the flag, or calling wartime measures such as Meatless Tuesdays and Wheatless Wednesdays 'a joke' – should remind us of the dangers of letting the censors run riot under the cover of wartime.[12]

Today we are a long way from those earth-shattering world wars of the twentieth century. Yet we are witnessing the resurgence of wartime arguments about the need to control 'dangerous' speech, in relation to the conflict between Western societies and Islamic terrorism. In comparison with the powerful enemies of the past such as Nazi Germany or the Soviet Union, these nihilistic Islamists – whilst posing a mortal threat to individuals – are effectively throwing snowballs at the West's castle walls. Nevertheless the conflict with them has been used to justify new measures against 'extremist' speech – whether of the Islamophobe or Islamophile variety – from the streets of Britain to UK and US university campuses.

The dangerous use of incitement laws to curb the expression of unpalatable opinions was laid bare in December 2014, when a 35-year-old Muslim mother of six was jailed in the UK for incitement to terrorism in Syria. Runa Khan from Luton was sentenced to five years and three months in prison, having previously admit-

ted disseminating terrorist material. That sounds like a deadly serious offence that decent people would want to see punished.

But what did she actually do? In the words of the BBC report,
Khan was imprisoned 'for promoting terrorism on Facebook'. She
had reposted an article aimed at Islamist mothers entitled 'Raising
Mujahid children', encouraged another poster (who turned out to
be an undercover police officer) to pursue his stated aim to go and
fight in Syria, and posted that, while doing up her eight-year-old
son's jacket, she imagined a future when she would be 'tying the
shahada [martyrdom] bandanna round his forehead and hand him
his rifle and send him out to play the big boys game'. She urged
Islamist women to encourage their older sons and brothers and
husbands to go to Syria and join the jihad – holy war. The court
also heard that police found a photograph of her two-year-old son
with a rifle – a toy rifle, that is.

Distasteful stuff, no doubt. But was it really deserving of a five-
year-plus prison sentence? Khan was described as an erratic,
unstable individual with a 'chaotic' life, five of whose children had
to live with their grandmother. Her online ranting seems to fit that
profile. In an interview with BBC TV's *Newsnight* programme, she
said: 'I was posting up my belief' on Facebook. However objectionable we might find her opinions, wasn't she entitled to express
them?

In sentencing Khan, the judge said she was an 'avowed fundamental Islamist, holding radical and extreme beliefs'. That is clearly
true. But since when was holding beliefs an imprisonable offence?
She was jailed for expressing those views online – the judge
pronounced that her postings were designed to 'further your own
deeply entrenched violent ideology and persuade others to violent
action, including suicide, martyrdom and other violence'. Even if
that was proven, this strange woman trying to persuade others to
fight for Islamist forces in Syria is surely not the same thing as
ordering acts of terrorism. Unless we believe in her powers to
brainwash her Facebook friends, it would still be up to them to

decide to take the path of martyrdom. If she had dressed her young children in suicide vests and sent them out to die in a bomb attack, that would be terrorism. But going online to argue that Muslim mothers should try to raise their sons to grow up as jihadis is something else entirely, more like perverse parenting advice than a military command. Words are not physical weapons and viewpoints are not violence, however 'radical and extreme' they might appear to most of us. The opinions expressed by the likes of Runa Khan need to be openly challenged. Trying to bury them instead in prison, on the ground that they are too dangerous to be let loose on Facebook, can only lend their radical message more credence.[13]

The attempt to extend the fire-in-a-theatre fears of the First World War to the conflict with cliques of radical Islamists today reveals the lack of faith in freedom at the heart of our societies. Are our leaders now so afraid of our own shadows, thoughts and words that they must try to restrict speech further, because they do not trust their ability to win an argument with such intellectually feeble opponents? To use the shouting-fire-in-a-theatre dictum to condemn or try to ban Islamist or anti-Islamist speech or cartoons suggests that the theatre of Western civilisation must be a crumbling edifice, if it can seriously be threatened with panic and destruction by a few shrill words from the wings.

If we are serious about defending freedom, it is precisely in these times of conflict that we need to stand up for 'freedom for the thought that we hate' – and then exercise our right to take up intellectual arms against it. The solution is as ever more speech and argument rather than less. Even in an era of war and terror, it is a matter of life and death for liberty that we reject the fire-in-a-theatre device for tricking us out of our rights and insist on fighting the free-speech wars against all-comers. The demand that we sacrifice free speech in the name of freedom is a theatrical twist that deserves to be booed off the stage of history.

8

'... but words will *always* hurt me'

The prosecution alleges that some speech, particularly 'hate speech', is just too hurtful and offensive to be allowed to go free.

In the aftermath of the murderous attack on the Paris offices of the satirical weekly *Charlie Hebdo* in January 2015, prominent people who had previously shown no interest in the subject suddenly seemed keen to insist that Muslims or other religionists 'have no right not to be offended'. Even the UK's Conservative prime minister David Cameron, whose coalition government was busy trying to tame the scandalmongering tabloid press at home, spoke up for the scurrilous magazine *Charlie*'s 'right to offend' in response to criticism from the Pope.

Wind the clock back just a few days from there, however, and a truer picture of the state of public debate about offensive or hateful speech was provided by the case not of *Charlie Hebdo*, but of a real-life cartoon character called Katie Hopkins. Hopkins is a British reality TV wannabe-turned-rent-a-gob social commentator, a 'professional troll' who has made a career out of offending people and winding up the media. In the space of a week at the very end of 2014 Hopkins twice made news by being reported to the police – not for committing any offence, but for saying offensive yet irrelevant things.

First, on a TV show she made about obesity, Hopkins was shown being reported to the Metropolitan Police for the 'hate crime' of being 'personally offensive' to a fat rights campaigner she had told to lose weight. Then she was repeatedly reported to Scottish police for alleged racism on Twitter, after chastising the 'little sweaty jocks' for 'sending us Ebola bombs in the form of sweaty Glaswegians'. An online petition calling for Hopkins to be arrested for her 'vile racist' tweets garnered thousands of signatures. What is more, the Scottish police made clear that they were taking this nonsense seriously, issuing a straight-faced statement that: 'Police Scotland will thoroughly investigate any reports of offensive or criminal behaviour online and anyone found to be responsible will be robustly dealt with.' Note the official use of the phrase 'offensive or criminal behaviour online' to conflate naughty words with crimes. Hopkins's acerbic opinions were being investigated as criminal offences.[1] Weeks later Hopkins was once more reported to the police for allegedly inciting racial hatred on Twitter – this time by a Labour MP, Simon Danczuk, who she had accused of 'not helping with community cohesion' and being 'inflammatory' after he posed with a Pakistani flag in his ethnically-mixed Rochdale constituency. Less than three months after the outpouring of sympathy for *Charlie Hebdo*, the UK's intolerant anti-offensiveness industry was back to business as usual.

And things soon went further still. On 17 April 2015, Hopkins used a column in the *Sun* to express her unpleasant views about the African migrants trying to reach Europe by boat from Libya, several hundred of whom had just drowned in the attempt. Hopkins called such migrants 'cockroaches' and 'feral humans', said she cared not if they died, and suggested Europe should send gunboats to drive them back rather than rescue boats to save them from drowning. It seemed as if Katie Hopkins the spite-fuelled cartoon character was becoming a caricature of herself. More remarkable than her worthless words of wine bar wisdom, however, was the response to them. Hopkins's column about migrants appeared to spark more furious outrage in Britain than the actual drownings that prompted it. Where the horrible deaths of hundreds of migrants had been met by a quietly sighing wave of public sadness, the few hundred nasty words she wrote about them caused a tsunami of public and political outrage. The online petition set up to demand that the *Sun* sack Hopkins quickly attracted more than a quarter of a million signatures – rather more than petitions calling on Europe to act to save the desperate Africans. Never mind addressing the problem of the UK and EU foreign and immigration policies that had helped to bring this tragedy about, what mattered most apparently was hounding a stupid writer out of the UK press. The notion that offensive speech can somehow be the worst offence of all has rarely seemed more perverse.

This is the intolerant attitude towards offensive speech that prevails in the West on every day when satirists are not being murdered for offending religion. Little wonder that, despite the initial outburst from Cameron and Co in defence of *Charlie Hebdo*'s 'right to offend', many others from the Pope to liberal novelists felt free to criticise the magazine for being too offensive and provocative. The instant display of empathy turned out to be like an emotional outburst by mourners at a funeral, who soon get a grip of themselves and return to the normal mode of moaning about the deceased.

The traditional playground chant that 'Sticks and stones may break my bones/But words will never hurt me' must now be one of the most unfashionable of old-fashioned wisdoms. These days it is treated with about the same level of popular respect as the Book of Leviticus in the Old Testament (the one that says God wants us to sacrifice animals and slaughter homosexuals).

The consensus now is that words hurt, by causing harm and offence. Indeed it is often argued that hurtful words cause emotional wounds and psychological scars that are worse and more lasting than the external marks of physical abuse. As the British celebrity intellectual Stephen Fry says, 'Sticks and stones may break my bones, but words will *always* hurt me.'[2]

The old rhyme, like many things children might say, is not strictly true. In the real grown-up world words can certainly hurt in their way, and not only the abusive ones; there are few things more painful than an unwanted 'Goodbye'.

But unlike Leviticus, the past wisdom of the playground still has something important to teach us. There is indeed a difference between sticks and stones and words, between speech and deeds, between offensive language and physical violence. The protection of the law must be upheld for those who are assaulted or oppressed (although paper 'rights' won't stop punches or bullets in the first place). But there can be (as was said by many with varying degrees of sincerity after *Charlie Hebdo*) no right not to be offended. Or to put it another way, anyone is entitled to take offence at anything said by anybody else. But taking offence does not give them any right to take away somebody else's freedom of speech.

Instead of free speech, however, the demand from radical campaigners these days is more often for freedom from offensive words. More than twenty years ago the American academic Stanley Fish published his provocative essay in defence of speech codes, 'There's No Such Thing as Free Speech – and it's a good thing too', arguing that since 'there is no class of utterances separable from the world of conduct' and all language is a potential incitement to action, then neither the First Amendment nor anything else should try to treat words differently from deeds.[3]

Twenty years later, few would endorse Fish's dismissal of free speech in principle. Yet in practice his conflation of harmful speech and action has been widely accepted, leading to the demand that hateful words should be policed as rigorously as harmful deeds.

Measures imposed to deal with the scourge of offensive words range from formal laws against 'hate speech' in the UK and Europe to the informal but pervasive conformism of the You-Can't-Say-That culture across the Anglo-American world.

We are not talking here primarily about the use of abusive language, but the expression of offensive opinions. Barely a day now seems to pass without another news story about somebody claiming to have been offended or harmed by what somebody else has said, and demanding that something must be done about it. Jokes are a constant target of the offence-takers. Postings found to be offensive on social media are likely not only to be ripped apart by an online lynch mob, but also reported to the police. And British police commanders, who seem more comfortable policing the tweets than the streets, have made it clear that they want to crack down not just on criminal offences online, but offensive words and opinions also.

From the point of view of the reverse-Voltaires, the beauty of this line of attack is that offensiveness is in the eye of the offended beholder. Whether or not you consider any speech offensive is an entirely subjective judgement, based on your feelings. Nobody else can disagree and tell you that you are not offended. For you to say 'You have offended me' thus becomes an apparently unanswerable argument for censorship. Determined to prevent and punish the expression of anything with which they disagree, the new censors have homed in on offensive speech as an easy target against which to assert their moral superiority.

The crusade against offensive speech now extends from the low comedy of social media 'banter' to high-powered political debates. As Richard King, author of *On Offence*, observes, going on the offensive has been part of political struggles since ancient times, as 'the word offend derives from offendere, a Latin word meaning "to strike against"'. Offensive arguments that strike against your opponents have long been the normal ammunition of a political fight. Things are different in politics today, however: '[I]n the twenty-first century, it isn't only offence, but also the *taking* of offence that is weaponised – that is, used to strike against opponents.'[4]

Taking offence at the other side's argument has itself become an easy knee-jerk intervention, without the awkward necessity of having to come up with an argument of your own. To claim that you feel offended by something your opponent says has become a short-cut to winning – or at least, ending – a political debate, regardless of the relative merits of debaters' points.

Back in the Seventies, feminists and other radicals first insisted that 'The personal is political'. Now it often seems as if politics is just personal, so that taking personal offence becomes the acceptable face of political censorship. Taking offence has become such an automatic political weapon that it is used by the conservative right as well as the 'politically correct' left. Thus in 2014, the UK Independence Party reported a green blogger to the Brighton police for posting 'offensive' remarks about them – and the language police of Sussex Constabulary duly went round and told him to desist.[5]

This habit of offence-taking hypersensitivity has become so normalised it might be hard to remember what a change it represents from the past. The sticks-and-stones rhyme captured the attitude that most adults once wanted to impart to their children: that in growing up in a free society you had to learn to cope with the rough and tumble of other people's words and opinions without shedding too many tears.

Once upon a time, the taking and giving of offence was seen as an inevitable part of a full life. Back in 1838, the Scottish historian and philosopher Thomas Carlyle published a short biography of the novelist Sir Walter Scott. Discussing how to present the life of a great man without making him appear too much like a plaster saint, Carlyle captured an important truth about life in a free and dynamic society when he wrote that: 'No man lives without jostling or being jostled; in all ways he has to elbow himself through the world, giving and receiving offence. His life is like a battle, insofar as it is an entity at all.'[6]

Elbowing through the world, giving and receiving offence, treating life like a battle? Today the cry would surely go up (probably via Twitter) to lock that man away, or at the very least take away his smartphone privileges.

The historic shift in attitude is illustrated by the attempt to rewrite one of the classical cases for free speech, J. S. Mill's *On Liberty* (1859), into a modern-day demand for restricting hate speech. Mill's essay was a ground-breaking argument for freedom. He argued that an individual should be sovereign over himself, and could not be compelled to do or say anything he did not want to even if it was deemed to be for his own good. The single exception to this rule, Mill allowed, was if he was harming somebody else: 'The only purpose for which power can be rightfully exercised over any member of a civilized community, against his will, is to prevent harm to others.'[7]

This subsequently became known as the harm principle. For Mill, it was almost an aside in his uncompromising defence of liberty. Yet today you could be forgiven for thinking that *On Liberty* was actually called *On Harm*, since the 'harm principle' is the only aspect of that work you are likely to hear reference to. What is more, Mill's carefully limited grounds for restraint have been expanded beyond recognition, so that 'harm' is now equated with being offended or upset by somebody else's speech. Mill's argument for free speech has been turned into its opposite. Some might call that taking liberties.

The attempt to de-normalise any speech which somebody finds offensive is having a stultifying effect on public debate, encouraging an atmosphere of tame conformism and mute self-censorship. The biggest victim is not the one who is taking offence; it is the rest of us, robbed of the opportunity for open-minded discussion and free debate that offers our best hope of getting at the truth and deciding a way forward on controversial issues.

How have we come to this state of affairs? It surely cannot simply be that more people are using more offensive forms of speech these days. What has changed is the way we respond to other people's speech, and the widespread propensity for taking offence at the drop of a disrespectful word.

Some critics see a central problem as the new outlets for outrage provided by the internet. The American writer Sara Stewart accurately characterises 'our age of ceaseless, monotonous outrage. Another day, another lone target for collective shaming ... I kept picturing a stoning. Contrary to that old biblical admonition, these are high times for rock-throwing.' For her the new villain of this story appears to be social media: 'Twitter, far from fostering debate and broadening minds, has turned us into a hive of scolds. Angry mobs wait on the sidelines to strike and then bask in the glow of their moral superiority.'[8]

Holding Twitter responsible for the 'age of ceaseless outrage' seems a little like blaming the stones for a stoning. The internet and social media have certainly facilitated the 'monotonous' outbreaks of mass rhetorical rock-throwing, and have granted some more faint-hearted rock-throwers the gift of anonymity. But they cannot really explain what has changed to make so many people keen to take advantage of the opportunity to cast the first, second and final stones. We should perhaps bear in mind that other old admonition, to beware shooting the messenger.

Something more substantial must have changed in society and the way that people relate to one another, to explain this epidemic of thin-skinned syndrome sweeping the Anglo-American world. It is significant in this respect that the most explosive incidents tend to be sparked by speech deemed offensive, not just to an individual, but to an entire self-defined group, be they Muslims or members of the transgender community.

The advance of the culture of offence-taking can be plotted in inverse proportion to the retreat into the politics of identity.

In recent decades Western societies have lost any powerful sense of an overarching belief system holding people together. Churches, political parties and other traditionally unifying institutions have fallen into public disrepute. The big ideologies of both left and right, which dominated Western thought for two centuries, appear exhausted and irrelevant to most people's lives. It has become commonplace for commentators to describe our societies today as atomised, individuated, a 'lonely crowd'. The angst-ridden question 'Who are we now?' forms the background to political debates such as the tortuous attempts to define the modern meaning of 'Britishness', and the endless Culture Wars in the USA.

Faced with a crisis of social cohesion and the lack of a moral consensus today, many still desperately want something to cling to that is bigger than their own selves. In search of that something, they have retreated from the failed society-wide Political (large P) projects of the recent past, into more segmented cultural and political (small p) identities. Alongside other consequences that are beyond the scope of this argument, the withdrawal into identity politics has had a serious impact on free speech and open debate.

A self-defined identity – whether it be as a black woman, gay man or Muslim – is seen as fixed; it is what you are, not something you are striving to be. As such it is a closed-off state, not open to question or challenge by anybody else. Moreover, since an identity is subjective – it is who you say you are – the members of an identity group assume the right to define the truth about themselves. They insist on a moral monopoly over their story. If you are not black, female or gay, you can have no say on issues which affect them.

Any outside attempt to challenge an identity group's worldview is likely to be condemned out of hand as offensive to the feelings of those involved, and met with a double dismissal: not only You-Can't-Say-THAT, but also YOU-Can't-Say-That. In an inversion of the old aristocratic rule that discussing politics was the preserve of the right class of person, the suggestion now is that only the right identity groups have the right to express opinions about certain issues.

The consequences of this for freedom of speech in society have been dire. It has created a sort of privatised form of blasphemy, where it is widely accepted that intruding on the personal space of an identity group – by, for example, questioning the institution of gay marriage, or gay adoption as Dolce & Gabbana did – puts you beyond the pale. Informal censorship and self-censorship are the inevitable results of what Frank Furedi, author of *On Tolerance*, defines as 'the criminalisation of criticism'.[9]

What passes for debate today often looks more like an arms race to see who can appear most offended. Identity politics is the sphere of competitive victimhood. Identity groups draw their moral authority from claims for redress for grievances and offences against them, past and present. The insistence that you are constantly vulnerable and victimised reinforces the tendency to take offence at any opinion outside your identity's narrow world-view. Since identity is defined subjectively, it matters not what the intention of the offending speaker or writer might have been. If the identity group says it is offensive, then it automatically must be so, and demands for a withdrawal, apology and possibly compensation will follow.

Taking offence is the perfect weapon for attacking free speech because it is defined subjectively. The Oxford English Dictionary, as Stefan Collini points out in *That's Offensive!*, includes this definition: 'The act of offending, wounding the feelings of, or displeasing another; usually viewed as it affects the person offended'. The emphasis on the subjective reaction and the realm of feelings ultimately means, as Collini says, that 'each individual is the only possible judge of whether or not they have been offended'.[10]

If you say that you're offended, who can disagree? Nobody is allowed to say that you have not been offended (they can of course insist apologetically that no offence was intended, but what does that matter when your feelings decide the truth?). Once the priority of subjective feelings of offence is accepted, it becomes difficult to resist the demands for apologies and withdrawal that will soon follow. This is different from an allegation of physical assault, where objective criteria can be applied – it is not solely up to you to decide whether you have been punched or not. A personal insistence that you have been offended, however, provides a seemingly unanswerable case for demanding redress in any situation.

This subjective interpretation of events has even been written into UK law. Following the recommendations of the 1999 Macpherson Report, into the London murder of a young black man called Stephen Lawrence, criminal law has been rewritten to define a 'racist incident' as 'any incident which is perceived to be racist by the victim or any other person'. If anybody says it's racist, then officially it is. New laws against 'hate speech' in the UK and the EU have ensured that this sweeping subjective definition applies to offensive words as well as actions.

There is nothing wrong with genuinely taking offence, of course, any more than with giving it by expressing an honest opinion. But what we have here is politicised instrumental offence-taking in the age of the reverse-Voltaires. Identity activists go out looking for some speech to be offended by, and when they find it (which they always will) they demand that the speaker cease and desist. The insistence that speech must be policed to protect the hurt feelings of a few who claim to find it offensive has far wider consequences. It is presented, and increasingly accepted, as an unanswerable case against unfettered free speech. As such it encroaches on the rights of us all, limiting our ability to generate much heat or light in public debates.

We might say that there is 'no right not to be offended'. But in fact many prominent offence-takers would not want any such right to be upheld anyway, if it meant they never had to hear another offensive word. Taking offence is as much a part of their lives as taking a breath. All that they ask is the right to demand redress for speech they deem offensive. They want the 'right' not to be offended only in order to protest that it has been violated.

Taking offence and outrage has become a legitimate source of self-righteousness. The -ism at work here most powerfully is not sexism or racism, but narcissism. In Greek legend, Narcissus fell in love with his own beautiful image, reflected in water. Today's reverse-Voltaires enjoy nothing more than looking at their own image twisted in outrage in the mainstream and social media. It was no surprise when a 2013 study by Tufts University in the US found that more viewers, of both left- and right-wing persuasions, were now obtaining their news from 'outrage-based' media shows. These offence-seeking outlets, the researchers concluded, 'offer flattering, reassuring environments that make audience members feel good'. Feeling superior by being outraged and offended is a fashionable look in our peculiar political times.[11]

This fashion for victim politics, in which activists search for something to find offensive to their fixed identity and demand redress, has grown over recent decades, as the old political movements and worldviews have declined in influence. In his 1993 study *Kindly Inquisitors: the New Attacks on Free Thought*, the American writer Jonathan Rauch (a gay critic of hate-speech laws and ardent supporter of gay marriage) noted how this trend had taken hold in the US during the supposedly conservative Reagan years. It was in the 1980s, says Rauch, that it first became common 'for activists and intellectuals to conspicuously take offence. Here, there, everywhere, they were offended. People began demanding public apologies when they were offended. Organised groups – gay activists, for example – began patrolling the presses and airwaves for offensive statements and promptly demanding apologies and retractions when they found cause for complaint.'[12] In the twenty-odd years since Rauch wrote this, conscious, conspicuous, offence-seeking has become accepted and institutionalised, with stultifying effects for free speech. As Rauch himself noted in a new afterword to the 2014 reprint of *Kindly Inquisitors*, 'What I called in 1993 "the new attacks on free thought" are no longer as new. Two decades on, the regulation of speech deemed hateful or assaultive or harassing has spread internationally and dug in domestically.'

One powerful indication of those trends is the way that laws against speech branded hateful or harmful have been introduced in the UK and the European Union. These 'hate-speech' laws truly mark the criminalisation of criticism.

The distinguishing feature of hate-speech laws is that they have managed both to restrict freedom of expression, and to further swell the tendency to take offence. Well done everybody.

In the UK, the New Labour government introduced hate-speech laws via the Racial and Religious Hatred Act of 2006, amended two years later to include hatred on the grounds of sexual orientation. The EU mandated Europe-wide hate-speech laws in 2008. These laws are officially justified with high-minded talk about encouraging tolerance and equality. But at the time when the EU endorsed its hate-speech laws, one European commissioner gave the game away about the Euro-officials' somewhat lower-minded motives; not so much instilling tolerance as appeasing the intolerant. These laws, the EU commissioner revealed, were intended to 'preserve social peace and public order' by protecting the 'increasing sensitivities' of 'certain individuals' who 'have reacted violently to criticism of their religion'.[13]

Far from bringing social peace and public order to Europe, however, the hate-speech laws appear to have helped to inflame the tensions around 'offensive' forms of expression that erupted in the Paris massacre. It is not too hard to see why. These laws officially sanction the notion that offensive speech is a crime, and that being offended is a cause for censorious action. Hate-speech laws give the green light to anybody with a grudge who wants to outlaw or suppress opinions they find upsetting.

As one conservative American commentator put it after *Charlie Hebdo*, these laws are 'part of the problem': 'Rather than promoting social harmony as EU bureaucrats had hoped, Euro religious hate-speech laws – like Pakistan's blasphemy laws – seem to fan sentiments of offence. Most dangerously, they give validity to expectations that speech disrespectful of Islamic symbols, practices and beliefs ought to be punished.' A few years before the murder of the cartoonists, Nina Shea notes, the French state itself had, at the urging of President Jacques Chirac, sought to 'avenge the prophet' by enabling the prosecution of *Charlie Hebdo* for anti-Islamic hate speech. In 2015, the gunmen decided to cut out the middleman and 'take it upon themselves to carry this [punishment] out.'[14]

Hate-speech laws set a dangerous precedent by writing into the statute book an entirely subjectively defined offence. Few can agree on what the term 'hate speech' really means (apparently it is popular with that equally loosely defined phenomenon, the 'troll'). They only agree that they all hate any speech that criticises their culture and identity. Little wonder that Europe's hate-speech laws have created a confusing mess of claims and counterclaims among competing groups claiming to be victims (often of one another).

In the UK, thousands of people are prosecuted each year under other laws which seek to police offensive speech in even more sweeping terms. Section 5 of the Public Order Act criminalised any words deemed 'threatening, abusive or insulting' until the government agreed to remove 'insulting' from the legislation in 2013. This concession was celebrated as a victory by civil liberties lobbyists, but as the police and prosecutors pointed out, the retention of 'abusive' made the law still vague enough to be used against anybody they might want to silence.

The consequence of all these laws is that people who have done nothing are being convicted and branded as criminals. Done nothing, that is, except to express an opinion deemed insulting or offensive to somebody else's religion or identity group. Almost 250 years ago, American Founding Father Thomas Jefferson defined the classic liberal attitude to keeping the law out of religious disputes and insults, declaring that 'it does me no injury for my neighbor to say there are 20 gods or no God. It neither picks my pocket nor breaks my leg.'[15] In the civilised capitals of twenty-first-century Europe, however, it is not necessary to pick a pocket or break a leg in order to be criminalised for criticising somebody else's beliefs.

The protection which Jefferson and his peers provided for free speech under the First Amendment means that there are no hate-speech laws in America. Not yet, anyway. But opinion polls show growing support for such measures. A Yougov poll from October 2014 found Americans almost evenly split between those who would support a hate-speech law (36 per cent) and those who would oppose it (38 per cent), with the remaining 26 per cent undecided; 51 per cent of Democrat voters favoured outlawing hate speech.[16] US campuses have already effectively banned any speech which identity groups find offensive. There are those who demand that America goes much further and faster down the slippery slope.

One influential British academic working in the USA has made heavy waves with a book arguing that America should adopt hate-speech laws. Jeremy Waldron's *The Harm in Hate Speech* tries to establish an objective basis for criminalising subjectively offensive speech. Waldron argues that such speech does more than hurt the feelings of an individual; it is intended to compromise the collective dignity of an entire identity group. Such 'group defamation', he says, poses a threat to 'public order' and so should be banned.

Waldron suggests that there is a precedent for this in England's old public libel offences – blasphemous libel, seditious libel and obscene libel – which were originally exported to the Crown's American colonies. Unlike civil libel offences against an individual's reputation, these forms of speech were criminal offences against God, the king and his government, and public decency. Waldron wants to adopt this model and prosecute hate speech for the good of society as a whole. Though presented as a forceful defence of tolerance, his argument exposes the illiberal intolerance at the heart of anti-hate-speech laws. Those ancient offences of public libel were political tools which the English Crown used for centuries in an effort to suppress free speech and any dissent from its orthodox views. Such ancient notions of legal restraint or repression of ideas which offend against the majority view should have no place in a free modern society where, as the civil liberties campaigner Josie Appleton responds to Waldron's proposal, ideas must prove their worth in open public debate, and '[t]here should not be a crime of bringing certain values into disrepute, or lowering certain ideas in public esteem'.[17] Far from protecting public order or social peace, laws against hate speech that prevent the honest airing of controversial views are more likely merely to suppress conflicts and intensify hidden hostilities; as the British comedian Rowan Atkinson said in opposing the UK's hate-speech legislation, they can impose 'a veneer of tolerance concealing a snakepit of unaired and unchallenged views'.[18]

And it gets worse. The proliferation of 'phobias' in public discussion is one symptom of the way that criticism and questioning are being delegitimised. It is apparently no longer enough simply to say that somebody's views are offensive. The person in question must be certified as suffering from a phobia – they are homophobic, Islamophobic, transphobic, etcphobic. These shorthand labels betray a deeper prejudice. They suggest that those who hold the opinions that offend are not merely wrong-headed, but are experiencing a form of mental illness. The spread of such '-phobic' name-calling effectively turns political or cultural dissent from the mainstream into a pathology. As such, it puts an immediate end to the debate. After all, who wants to waste time having an argument with the psychiatrically disturbed? Those suffering from these phobias are not to be conversed with or treated like normal people. Instead for the good of society they should be placed in a straitjacket and a padded cell, figuratively if not literally.

The rise of the concept of 'inter-sectionality' is another symptom of how the obsession with taking offence is making matters worse for free speech. The once-obscure academic jargon of inter-sectionality aimed to understand how different forms of inequality – on the basis of, say, race, gender, sexuality or class – interact in society. It has now become the language in which niche identity groups compete to claim which is the most oppressed. This marks a further retreat into fragmented identity politics, so that different groups assert their 'right not to be offended' not only against society, but against one another.

These sorts of identity wars waged between relatively small numbers of activists have commanded a remarkable amount of media attention of late. One notable focus has been on the issue of alleged 'transphobia' – fear and hatred of transsexuals – among prominent feminists in the UK. Feminist journalist and lobbyist Caroline Criado-Perez, feminist writer and lesbian and gay rights campaigner Julie Bindel and polemical writer Julie Burchill have all faced condemnation from other feminists, speaking bans and censorship for what one women's group called 'totally inappropriate and offensive' views on 'trans people'.[19] When Burchill defended another woman journalist from attacks by trans activists in typically forthright fashion – her article in the *Observer* newspaper likened such criticism to 'the Black and White minstrels telling Usain Bolt how to run' – she didn't just face the fury of the online feminist collective. In an extraordinarily supine display the *Observer* editors agreed with them, apologised for daring to publish the article and took it down from their website.[20]

These cases raise the question: why do transgender activists so often seem to be in the media front line of the battles over free speech and offensiveness? Obviously they are entitled to feel offended by other people's words and to respond as they see fit. But there must be something else going on here, to explain why a relative handful of trans activists have become such a *cause célèbre* for all those who want to restrict offensive speech today.

Perhaps the clue is that to be transgender is an entirely subjective, self-defined identity. As the leading LGBT lobby GLAAD defines 'gender identity' in its media reference guide, 'For transgender people, their own internal gender identity does not match the sex they were assigned at birth.'[21] Transgender people thus insist on their right to define their own gender identity, regardless of their biology. Trans activists take great offence at those – including the 'phobic' feminists mentioned above – who refuse to use the term 'cis' to describe those who were born female, aka 'non-trans' women. When the bearded, frock-wearing transgender singer Conchita Wurst won the 2014 Eurovision Song Contest, there was much tearing of hair and gnashing of teeth over the way that some in the offensive, transphobic media kept referring to the biologically male star as a 'he'.

The entirely subjective character of the transgender identity makes these few activists the perfect human shields behind which the reverse-Voltaires can pursue their crusade against free speech. They can decide they are women, in a triumph of personal will over physical reality. Then they insist that they have a moral monopoly over their truth, their story – and that everybody else must accept it unquestioningly. It is not necessary to insult them intentionally to cause offence. They will take exception to a factual description which fails to obey their rules. Thus to call these biological men 'he' is enough to make you an offensive, phobic bigot.

By changing the words we are allowed to use, the trans activists insist that they are altering reality. Hence they are determined to stop any 'not-trans people' saying or thinking anything about them that they don't like. It is this censorious subjectivity, this belief in a form of personalised blasphemy, that makes the transgender lobby such poster boys, or perhaps poster 'women without vaginas', for the new creed of intolerance in the name of tolerance. It is why this handful of trans activists is in the front line of the war against 'offensive' free speech. The power of veto over what others can legitimately say about them might even help to explain the appeal of adopting a trans identity to some. Just don't call them the tranny state. Or the trannyban.

* * *

What could be wrong with minorities and identity groups demanding freedom from offence? Anybody is entitled to be offended. But not to use that feeling as a weapon to curtail the rights of the rest of us.

What is really being said by these campaigns is that people can be the victims of words, in need of protection from speech. That they are objects to which things are done, rather than subjects who can shake things up and make change happen. So their interests are apparently best served by having less freedom rather than more.

This presents a striking contrast with the not-too-distant past. In times when women, black people, gays and other oppressed groups in the West faced far more abuse, discrimination and violence than today, they fought for greater freedom of expression to give them a voice. It was accepted that a precondition for fighting for equality and liberty was being able to speak, read and debate as you saw fit, regardless of how much it offended the other side. Their aim in speaking out was not to gain recognition as a closed, separate group with its own identity, but to win their freedom as equal citizens of a free society.

At the time of the First World War, Sylvia Pankhurst and the militant wing of the British Women's Suffrage movement joined forces with the Free Speech Defence Committee to demonstrate for their right to speak out against war and inequality, often being attacked in the street for their trouble. Around the same time in America, the immigrant workers of the IWW were engaged in running battles with the police in their Free Speech Fights for the right to speak in public.

In the late 1960s and 1970s, the explosion of the lesbian and gay rights movement had at its core the demand for freedom of expression. Gay men in Greenwich Village, New York started their own newspaper because even the radical *Village Voice* would not print the word 'gay'. The cry went up to sing if you're glad to be gay. Or, to put it more in the language of the moment, as expressed in a flyer announcing the formation of the Gay Liberation Front after the Stonewall riots in 1969: 'Do You Think Homosexuals Are Revolting? You Bet Your Sweet Ass We Are!'[22] If you seek some speech that was truly 'offensive' to the accepted ethics of the day, look no further than that.

For the most accomplished argument for free speech from those fighting against oppression, we might go back further to the black American anti-slavery campaigner – and former slave – Frederick Douglass. In 1860, faced with violent repression of debate by pro-slavery forces, Douglass wrote his famous pamphlet entitled 'A Plea for Free Speech in Boston', in which he argued:

> To suppress free speech is a double wrong. It violates the rights of the hearer as well as those of the speaker. It is just as criminal to rob a man of his right to speak and hear as it would be to rob him of his money … And until the right is accorded to the humblest as freely as to the most exalted citizen, the government of Boston is but an empty name, and its freedom a mockery. A man's right to speak does not depend upon where he was born or upon his color. The simple quality of manhood is the solid basis of the right – and there let it rest forever.[23]

If only. The former slave's appeal for free speech might sound like a foreign language to many claiming to stand for equality today.

All of these opinions were deemed highly offensive in their time, and the oppressed had to fight tooth and nail against the authorities for their right to express them. Are identity groups really so assaulted by hateful and offensive speech today that they must demand the authorities protect them from words by restricting the free speech of others? Though much has changed, to suppress free speech remains, in Douglass's words, 'a double wrong'. There is no way to emancipation through demanding bans and self-censorship.

The debate about curbing offensive and hateful speech might seem very modern, yet it too is not entirely new. More than 150 years ago John Stuart Mill dismissed suggestions that the free expression of opinions should be limited to those whose 'manner be temperate, and do not pass the bounds of fair discussion': 'Much might be said on the impossibility of fixing where these supposed bounds are to be placed; for if the test be offence to those whose opinion is attacked, I think experience testifies that this offence is given whenever the attack is telling and powerful.'

In other words, the more forceful the opposition's arguments, the more offence they caused. For Mill, complaints about 'offensive' speech were often really a response to opponents 'whom they find difficult to answer'. Mill himself was no fan of 'intemperate' debating methods. He believed in 'the real morality of public discussion', preferring calmness, honesty and candour to 'malignancy, bigotry or intolerance of feeling'. But these were questions for public judgement, he insisted: 'It is however obvious that law and authority have no business with restraining' any 'offensive attacks' by either side. We might wish that was so 'obvious' to the would-be prosecutors of offensive speech today.[24]

One last thought. The right to be offensive does not impose an obligation to be offensive. And defending the uncompromised right to be offensive need not mean endorsing the way the right is exercised by others.

The attempt to outlaw and delegitimise anything deemed offensive has sparked a phoney sort of backlash. Comedians, cartoonists, commentators and others have sometimes gone out of their way to cause offence, apparently as an end in itself, to make a name for themselves. (At least in the short term, before the online mob descends armed with petitions and forces them to apologise in tears.) Others have put these offence activists on a pedestal, as if being offensive to Islam or anybody else was an inherently progressive thing.

In fact there is generally little to celebrate in self-conscious and often self-serving acts of offensiveness. As William Hazlitt wrote,

'An honest man speaks the truth, though it may give offence, a vain man, in order that it may.'[25] We do not have to endorse those vain men – but we should defend their freedom to speak their version of the truth. And we should recognise that their token offensive gestures are a minor side effect of the far bigger problem of the culture of conformism and the war on 'offensive' free speech. Otherwise it may soon be a case of: 'When they came for the comedians and cartoonists, I did nothing because I was not a cartoonist or a comedian ...'

9

'Mind your Ps, Qs, Ns and Ys'

The prosecution alleges that some words are simply too evil to be tolerated, whatever the circumstances.

If a black man calls himself 'nigga', is it still racist? On a Sunday evening in April 2013 I happened to find myself trussed up in a dinner suit at the English Professional Footballers' Association awards dinner in a swanky London hotel ballroom, where they name the players' player of the year. The black American comedian Reginald D. Hunter, star of BBC panel shows, was the scheduled comedy turn, appearing between the pudding and the prize-giving. Hunter confessed that he knew nothing about 'soccer', and so just did his ironic 'nigga' routine about race and language. Our non-A-list party, tucked away on table 83, might not have found the act particularly hilarious, but we certainly did not think there was anything outrageous about it, especially coming from the comedian whose recent UK tours had gloried in such titles as 'Trophy Nigga' and 'Pride and Prejudice … and Niggas'. The only thing to send any shockwaves of outrage around our table was the discovery that the hotel bar wanted £8.45 for a small bottle of beer.

Despite having been a journalist for some years, I did not realise that we were in the middle of a major news story that evening. It just seemed like a good night of drinking and football blather with fellow United fans down from Manchester. Afterwards we all posed for red-eyed photos with Reginald D. and any passing United legends.

It was only on the following Monday morning that we awoke to discover that our grand night out had turned into a major controversy, with a 'race storm' breaking over the heads of Hunter and the Professional Footballers' Association. The PFA chairman was all over the media expressing his outrage at Reginald D.'s use of the n-word, and issuing unconditional apologies to 'everyone who was offended – and everyone who wasn't' (as one of the Great Unoffended I thought, thanks, but …). Self-righteous pundits, tweeters and phone-in hosts were quick to join the multi-media wave of condemnation. Before long, the PFA was demanding its money back from Hunter, and warning that it might have to drop the comic turn from future ceremonies. As top sports columnist Martin Samuel observed in the *Daily Mail*, 'That's right, comedy is the problem, rather than the febrile atmosphere in which football exists.'[1] None of this outrage, as I say, bore any relation to the reaction on the night. (Looking at the boozy photo of me posing with Hunter that was published online, one friend commented that I looked 'as outraged as a newt'.)

How could a black man's ironic use of 'nigga' in a comedy routine possibly be branded as racially offensive after the event? Only because, as a statement from the ruling English Football Association's official anti-racism lobby, Kick It Out, made clear, the British sports elite now 'condemns racial slurs, the use of the n-word, irrespective of context'.[2] The words which should seriously grate with any thinking person here are 'irrespective of context'.

That statement might sound high-minded, but in truth it is imbecility of the lowest order. Of course context matters. How can the use of the term 'nigga' in a black comedian's routine, or by one black man to another, be deemed the same as if being shouted by a racist? As students living in the multi-ethnic tower blocks of Moss Side and Hulme, Manchester, during the long, hot summer of 1981, we watched Greater Manchester Police beating their riot batons on the side of their vans while chanting: 'Nigger, nigger, nigger – Out, out, out!' They were not being ironic, and you did not need a degree in semantics to tell the difference.

One of the top groups of professional complainants about issues of racial language in the UK is called the Society for Black Lawyers. Would they accept that the use of the b-word in their own title is as objectionable as if it was used in a pub with 'bastard' attached? Far from being irrelevant, the context in which words are used, the deliberate meaning behind them, is what matters most in deciding whether or not language is discriminatory.

However, according to the gospel of Zero Tolerance, as preached by Kick It Out, the FA, the PFA and many other public bodies in the Anglo-American world, there are words which it is now a mortal sin to utter, regardless of what was meant by them. This sounds like a modern form of mystical mumbo-jumbo, echoing the Old Testament law that anybody would be damned and probably stoned to death if they dared to speak the name of God (Yahweh, if you're interested in tweeting Him). Or perhaps like Harry Potter's chums being afraid to mention the name of Voldemort, for fear that it might conjure up the dark lord before they got to the series finale.

Zero Tolerance means what it says. It is a blunt cudgel for hammering anybody who lets slip the wrong word. Sitting in the black-tie audience as Hunter did his act on that Sunday evening was Paul Elliott, the black former Chelsea defender who, by becoming a media spokesperson for Zero Tolerance, had got himself appointed to various high-powered football committees and as a trustee of Kick It Out. A couple of weeks after being appointed a Commander of the British Empire by the Queen, for 'services to equality and diversity in football', Elliott was forced to resign all of his posts after it was revealed that he called another black former player 'nigger' in angry private text messages about a failed business venture. The 'saddened' FA chief announced that 'the use of discriminatory language is unacceptable regardless of its context and in effect has made Paul's position untenable'.[3] Thus were the zealous crusaders for Zero Tolerance brought down by their own intolerance of a word 'regardless of its context'. It would have taken a heart of stone not to laugh. And yet, as Reginald D. Hunter was soon to discover, this is no laughing matter.

The concept of words being condemned 'regardless of context' has taken hold of the upper echelons of UK and US politics and culture as well as sport in recent years. It is the voice of institutionalised idiocy, turning everything from common sense to natural justice on its head. Yet experts and officials now apparently feel confident reeling off this mindless mantra in the media. After that PFA dinner, for example, one liberal newspaper's football columnist commented more in sorrow than in anger on Hunter's ironic 'nigga' routine that 'a racial slur is a racial slur'. What, even if the accused is obviously not a racist, and if he is not slurring anybody, either?[4]

Apparently, it is now even possible to be guilty of a racial slur whilst trying to draw attention to racism. In January 2015, the Oscar-nominated British actor Benedict Cumberbatch's appearance on a US TV talkshow reportedly sparked a 'race storm' in America. His crime was to have used the old-fashioned word 'coloured' while discussing the problem of racial inequality in the UK creative arts. 'As far as coloured actors go,' Cumberbatch told the TV host, 'it gets really difficult in the UK.' Few seemed to care that he had been trying to draw attention to racial inequality. All the anti-racism lobbyists heard was the c-word, and some reacted as if he had appeared on US TV in full black-and-white-minstrel regalia. Cumberbatch was obliged to issue a grovelling apology for having 'caused offence' by 'being an idiot', before praying that: 'I can only hope this incident will highlight the need for correct usage of terminology that is accurate and inoffensive.'[5] But who is to say what terminology is inoffensive these days? The incident certainly highlighted the way that language has become a minefield even for those trying to fight on the side of the angels.

Something important has changed. In recent years we have witnessed a stream of controversies and 'scandals' involving some celebrity or public figure being banned, investigated, suspended or censured for using language deemed too offensive or outrageous. It is not only the frequency of these media controversies that stands out. Something new is happening. It has become a war on words.

In the past, the free-speech wars tended to focus on ideas or arguments considered too subversive or dangerous to be allowed public expression. Those battles are still being fought, of course, albeit with new enemies and fresh weapons. But some more recent controversies have gone way beyond that. The backlash against Cumberbatch and other public figures focuses not on ideas and opinions, but on words. These people have been dragged over the coals for using words that nobody is apparently allowed to use in any circumstances, whatever they meant by them, and regardless of whether they are spoken in public or private – or even inside somebody's own head.

Once upon a time when it came to judging language, we sensibly believed that context and meaning mattered. The same words could mean something different, and be judged very differently, depending on whether they were used in an argument or a joke, in public or in private, as an outburst ('I'll kill you for that!') or as a real threat.

Now it seems that words themselves can be seen as inherently evil, regardless of context. This looks more like a modern version of the Middle Ages, when people believed there were 'words of power', the magic words that, whether uttered as a prayer, a spell or a curse, could themselves alter real lives and situations. Even the conjurer's cliché 'Abracadabra' was apparently once believed in as an ancient Hebrew phrase meaning 'I will create with words'. That other conjurer's staple, 'Hocus-Pocus', was originally a Protestant jibe aimed at the Latin words – beginning '*Hoc est ...*' – supposed to turn bread and wine into the body and blood of Christ in the Catholic Mass. As Sigmund Freud said a century ago, 'Words and magic were in the beginning one and the same thing.'[6]

But then Freud was talking about a time when our ancestors knew no better, the universe was incomprehensible, and everybody was grasping for some meaning in a world of mystery. The real 'magic' of language was easily expanded into a magical interpretation and explanation of events we did not understand. There is no excuse for living under such illusions in the present. To believe in the power of evil words today is about as reasonable as it would be to put pigs, bears and marble statues on trial for murder, which the ancients also did to try to make sense of their world; or perhaps to hang a monkey as a French spy, which legend has it the locals in Hartlepool, northern England, did only 200 years ago.

We know that the concept of 'Words of Power' has been recently revived in the fantasy arenas of movie-making and online gaming, where wizards and witches abound and a mystical utterance can save or savage the imaginary world. But that seems a poor excuse for importing it into real life, and behaving as if a word really does have the innate power to shape events regardless of what was meant by it.

Take even a word as extreme as 'Paki'. For years this was the British racist's insult of choice directed at immigrants from Pakistan, Bangladesh or even India, forever coupled in the bone-headed imagination with the blood sport of 'Paki-bashing'. It is not a word that ever seems likely to be acceptable in polite society. But is using the P-word, regardless of context, to be regarded as the same thing as assaulting Asians?

In 2009, a private video diary came to light (it had been filmed three years earlier), in which a young Prince Harry refers to one of his army colleagues as 'our little Paki friend'. For this the prince was accused of endorsing Seventies-style 'Paki-bashing' racism. Nobody should be surprised that posh boys and princes still have prejudices about the 'little people', especially their former colonial subjects; and yes, this is the same Harry who famously turned up at a fancy dress party in a hilarious Nazi uniform. Yet we should surely also be able to see that to use such a potentially offensive epithet among mates or comrades can be very different from shouting it aggressively at somebody in the street. When people in a city such as Glasgow talk casually about popping down to their local 'Paki shop' it might seem parochial and insensitive; but are they really spouting racism? Such considerations of context and intent no longer matter to the language-and-thought-policing authorities; the P-word is automatically deemed a verbal pogrom, to be not just frowned upon but effectively outlawed.

The importance of context in judging words should have become more obvious in recent years, as people from minority groups have sought to 'reclaim' the sort of language previously used against them. Young black people took to calling one another nigger/nigga, some of the lesbian and gay community appropriated 'queer', and you might even hear the British-born children of Asian immigrants talking about themselves with pride as 'Pakis'. All of which should have made it more obvious than ever that context is what matters in judging words, and that it is madness to equate such banter (another hated b-word in some circles) with bigotry. Was the American comedian Chris Rock guilty of peddling racial slurs in his famous routine about the differences between two groups – 'I love black people – but I hate niggaz'?

Yet as the pillorying of another black American comedian for using the n-word on a London stage shows, things have gone in the other direction. The language police have grown even less tolerant of the 'wrong' words regardless of who uses them where, when or why. And to think that we Brits used to say that it was Americans who 'don't do irony'.

*   *   *

We are faced with a lengthening and increasingly complicated list of words that can only be referred to by their first letter, stretching if not quite from a to z then at least from b to y. Some might have hoped that the problem labelled 'Political Correctness gone mad' had passed its peak back in 1999, when David Howard, a white aide to the black Washington DC mayor Anthony A. Williams, was forced out of his post for describing a budget as 'niggardly' (an oldish adjective meaning 'mean', which has nothing to do with the similar-sounding racial insult). The public backlash against this ridiculous incident led Williams to reappoint Howard, though not in his original post. Julian Bond, the chairman of the NAACP (a venerable black civil rights organisation which has always, we might note, had the word 'Colored' in its name), spoke for many in complaining that: 'You hate to think you have to censor your language to meet other people's lack of understanding.' Bond added that 'the mayor has been niggardly in his judgment on the issue', and suggested the administration should buy dictionaries for all its staff members.[7]

Fifteen years later, however, the demonisation of words seems less like an aberration than an accepted norm of Anglo-American society. It was always a mistake to attribute this problem to one of 'PC gone mad', since that pinned the blame on a few zealots and underestimated the wider influence and strengthening hold of these trends. Now we can see it is far more a case of the censorious standards of 'PC' gone mainstream, gaining widespread acceptance if not exactly enthusiastic support.

A sign of the times. Things have reached the point where a single word that nobody is sure they heard on a TV tape that was never broadcast can be turned into a national issue of political controversy.

In May 2014, another revealing n-word storm engulfed Jeremy Clarkson, former outspoken presenter of the BBC's worldwide hit motoring show *Top Gear*. Motormouth Clarkson found himself caught in a media car crash, after the *Daily Mirror* newspaper got hold of some never-broadcast *Top Gear* footage from a few years previously. In the film, Clarkson is seen reciting the old playground rhyme 'Eeny, meeny, miny, moe …' to help him choose between two sports cars, and twice mumbles through the part where his (and my) generation of English schoolchildren might have said 'catch a nigger by his toe'. Some 'experts' claimed to be sure that he actually used the n-word; most people just heard a mumble.

A furore followed, with Clarkson first denying he had ever used that word and then, under orders from BBC bosses, issuing a grovelling video apology for offending anybody in the first place, before completing another awkward U-turn and insisting that, while he often used the f-word and the c-word, he would never use the n-word. However, he revealed he had 'been told by the BBC that if I make one more offensive remark, anywhere, at any time, I will be sacked. And even the angel Gabriel would struggle to survive with that hanging over his head.'[8]

Some of us were left idly wondering why the petrolhead controversialist could not have managed to come up with a more suitably Clarksonesque version of the rhyme – say, catch a vegan by his toe? Or a cyclist? Others, however, reacted as if he had been swinging a black baby around by the toe while hollering the racist rhyme at full volume on prime-time TV.

In all the overblown controversy over a murky snippet of never-seen video from the BBC archives, the most worrying words were not Clarkson's inaudible mumblings. They were the clear and unambiguous statement made by Harriet Harman MP, deputy leader of the Labour Party and a minister in the previous government. In a post on Twitter (where else would a politician say Something Important these days?), Harman declared that: 'Anybody who uses the n-word in public or private in whatever context has no place in the British Broadcasting Corporation.'[9] The idea of politicians telling the public service broadcaster who to hire and fire would normally cause outrage in BBC circles, but not apparently where a rogue n-word is suspected of intruding.

Harman's intervention captured the intolerant essence of those calling for Clarkson's (admittedly swollen) head. For today's free-speech police, there is no difference between saying something in public or private or apparently saying it in your own head. Most importantly, they insist that somebody like Clarkson should be censored or sacked for using an offensive word 'in whatever context' – which, in his case, apparently includes possibly thinking it while trying to avoid saying it.

This illiberal idiocy drives an SUV through the principles of liberty and justice. The specific context in which anybody uses language matters. We properly judge people not merely by the words they use, but by what they mean. By which standard, mumbling an outdated nursery rhyme – and then trying to ensure that nobody sees the film of your mumble – is in no way comparable to using the n-word as a racist epithet.

Yet common sense seems to play no part in our public life today. British law now decrees that if anybody at all interprets any word or deed as racist then it is a hate crime, regardless of the intention of the 'offender'. Some joked during this ruckus that the c-word the British liberal elite seem to find most offensive is 'Clarkson'. The c-word they seem keenest to see removed from the language, however, is 'context'.

Thus words must be outlawed, the speaker punished 'whatever the context' in which they are allegedly used, and the cry goes up for a popular TV presenter to be banned from our screens based on the suggestion that he might have thought about using a word. As Jeremy Clarkson wryly observed after the Eeny Meeny scandal, 'I've always thought I'd be sacked for something I said. Not for something that actually, I didn't say.' In the end he was sacked in March 2015 for something that he did, after what the BBC called a 'fracas' with a producer. But the glee with which Clarkson's downfall was greeted in the upper echelons of the BBC and elsewhere in the liberal UK media was due to his record of breaking their speech codes and using the wrong words. A *Guardian* editorial even compared the etiquette-busting bruiser to an inhuman monster, declaring that 'ogres are fine, but only in fairy tales'. More relevantly it should surely be 'only in fairy tales' that evil words are deemed to have magic powers.[10]

As Britain's 'voice of the nation', the BBC has often been turned into the battleground for the official war on words – including unspeakable but unbroadcast ones. Five years before Clarksongate, when I first wrote about the new 'war on words', the BBC had just sacked Carol Thatcher from her role as a reporter on an anodyne early evening magazine show. The daughter of the former UK prime minister was reported to have referred to a mixed-race French tennis player as a 'Frog golliwog' over drinks in the hospitality green room after a programme. She claimed she had meant nothing by it. As I noted then:

> There may well be questions to be asked about why such a useless individual as Thatcher, who is stupid enough to use such language in front of the left-wing comic Jo Brand, was employed by the BBC as a high-profile 'journalist' in the first place. But as for whether such a woman uses a word she probably learnt as a child from her old Enid Blyton books, over a glass or several of wine in the back of the BBC TV centre, who really gives a golly's arse?[11]

Those in authority saw things differently. The BBC One controller Jay Hunt insisted that things allegedly said in the green room – off camera and away from the public eye – did not count as private. Indeed she went further, insisting that even if Thatcher had used such a word in the privacy of her own home, it still should not count as 'private' speech. 'I don't think it's fine that she [Thatcher] says this at home,' declared BBC boss Hunt.[12] And if you are not allowed to say something in your own bedroom, presumably you should not be thinking it in your head either.

As Catherine Bennett wrote at the time of 'Gollygate', 'perhaps the requirement to say nothing at home you would not say at work can't always be reconciled with freedom of expression', but then 'that liberty is increasingly trumped by the competing right not to be offended. Even in spirit.' Despite her 'offensive choice of words' at an off-camera party, argued Bennett, Thatcher 'had a reasonable expectation of privacy. And if we can't speak freely in private, we're finished.'[13]

This is where we end up once context and circumstances don't matter, so that words themselves can be seen as evil regardless. The logical outcome is that wicked words of power have to be policed even in private speech.

Like the riot cops forcing back the picket lines of striking workers twenty-five years ago, the cultural thought police have been busy pushing back important lines in the free-speech wars. They have blurred the traditional distinction between what people say in public and in private. And they have crossed the divide between words and deeds. The conventional notion that speech was 'only words', and that actions spoke louder, is as outdated as the n-word. It can now seem as if offensive words are treated as potentially more harmful than weapons.

The creeping intrusion into private words, the fudging of the lines between personal thoughts and public statements, has led to a string of controversies in the UK, US and Australia after the content of various public figures' phone calls, emails and text messages were made public. No doubt there will be many more such 'secret racism/sexism/homophobia' scandals to come, as more minds are turned inside out to see what is in there that shouldn't be. We need not endorse any of the unsavoury things that celebrities or sportsmen think or say in private in order to insist that they not be stuck in the public stocks for it.

Another sign of how far and fast things have changed. In 1999, when the senior UK judge Sir William Macpherson of Cluny published his official report into the murder of black London teenager Stephen Lawrence, almost all of its far-reaching proposals were accepted and written into law. These included the tectonic change in the legal definition of a racist incident, which henceforth would include any incident which 'the victim or any other person' considered racist. The one proposal which even Tony Blair's New Labour balked at implementing, however, was Macpherson's suggestion that it should be a crime to use racist language in the privacy of your own home. Fifteen years later, that proposal is being practically implemented by stealth rather than statute.

This word-hunting invasion of privacy should be a concern to us all. Not because we want to defend the 'right' to be a racist at home, but because we recognise the importance of the private sphere. Everybody needs a space where they can rant, rave and gather their thoughts free from the public gaze. The right to a private sphere where we can consider what to say to the world is the vital flipside of the right to free speech in public life. As the writer André Aciman puts it, 'If we can't say what we think under our roof, then we have no roof.'[14]

What explains the ferocity of the contemporary war on words? The modern-day belief in 'words of power' appears to be underpinned by an equally firm belief that most of us are what we might call 'people of weakness'. The elitist assumption is that people are so stupid, vulnerable and pathetic that they can be mortally offended or murderously incited merely by hearing, or even thinking they hear, a naughty word.

In this context (excuse use of c-word) it becomes clear why the popular public arenas of sport and television have been made the front lines in the war on words. These are among the few outlets where our political and cultural elites still feel able to connect with the masses. So they want to use the power of TV and sport to teach us all a lesson in the need to mind our ps and qs and ns and ys.

In the UK, football has been thrust into the frontline of the new war on words. The FA, the English Football Association, has for some time insisted that the use of 'discriminatory language' at matches will be punished 'regardless of the context' in which the offensive words are used. This led to the ludicrous spectacle in 2013 of Tottenham Hotspur fans being arrested for a racially aggravated public-order offence, because they called *themselves* the 'Yid Army' as a badge of pride. (The club's historical connection with the north London Jewish community led to its fans being branded 'Yids' by opposing supporters, so they adopted the name as a sign of defiance.) It also sparked the unfunny controversy over Reginald D. Hunter's ironic routine at the footballers' awards dinner.

This is where the phoney moral crusade against racism in Britain has come to. In the past, the campaigns against racism we revolting students took up were about big issues of power in society – opposing police brutality in black communities such as Brixton or Moss Side, or defending Asian immigrants being burnt out of their homes in east London. Now official anti-racism is apparently a petty attempt to police the language of celebrities, footballers and fans, as if words really could discriminate.

You need not be a fan of either *Top Gear* or Tottenham Hotspur (I am neither) to see the bigger dangers in this trivialisation of racism. The war on words risks creating a wider chilling effect on freedom of expression, making people too worried about linguistic etiquette to say what they really think and too anxious about possibly causing offence to speak clearly. In effect, like Clarkson and his nursery rhyme, we all start mumbling over the controversial parts of the argument. That does nobody any favours. What we need is clarity and the open clash of opinions, not unintelligible mumbles, awkward silences and empty apologies.

This does not mean upholding a right to hurl racist language around (although it is better if bigots come clean with their prejudices so that they can be challenged in public). What it does mean, however, is fighting for freedom of expression with no buts, as an inalienable and indivisible liberty for all. Contrary to what the authorities assume, most people are not stupid. All the media polls at the time of the Eeny Meeny ruckus showed that the vast majority of viewers were against Clarkson being sacked by the BBC – not because they like the n-word, but because unlike our cultural guardians they understand both the concept of innocent until proven guilty and the importance of context.

Those who want to police the words we use more firmly will insist, as the free-speech fraudsters always do in their silent war, that 'this is not a free-speech issue'. Instead it is about protecting the rights of others by refusing to endorse the use of racist or offensive language. But of course this is a free-speech issue. It is about the need for people to say what they think – rather than what they think they ought to say. That is our only chance of resolving arguments and tensions and getting closer to what we believe to be the truth.

Defending free speech these days can certainly mean standing up for some less than savoury characters, but to try to suppress words is simply to impose a polite etiquette, a snobs' speech code to make 'them' talk like 'us'. Imposing an etiquette or enforcing a speech code is not the same thing as having an argument, let alone winning one. It means telling people what they should say rather than engaging with what they think. In the interests of open debate and clarity of opinion, I have always felt that on balance people's prejudices are better out than in.

The alternative – of accusing people of racism for something they did not mean to say, and leaving others unwilling to speak because they are unsure of which words they should or shouldn't use – can only reinforce divisions and disaffection. That is quite a result for a policy which claims to be challenging prejudice and promoting tolerance. Meanwhile those who have been left behind by fast-changing fashions in acceptable language – see Gareth from the UK version of *The Office*, complaining that his old dad 'still says "darkies" instead of "coloureds"' – can find themselves denied a legitimate voice in public.

Those who think that banning words deemed offensive regardless of context is the way to change attitudes have it upside down. Words such as 'nigger' have faded from public use as more enlightened attitudes have taken hold across British and Western society. This is an important difference. The crusaders against evil words of power appear to believe that a volcano of hatred and violence lurks just beneath the surface of the Anglo-American world, only just held in check by their speech codes. Some of us believe that, on the contrary, if anything is likely to stir resentment amongst these largely tolerant peoples, it is constantly being ordered from above to watch their language.

At a deeper level the war on words reflects what many, particularly in authority, think about other people today. The thin-skin syndrome that makes people hypersensitive to anything offensive rests upon the divisive mood of mistrust in our atomised society and the sense that everybody is potentially a victim of somebody else's words. Things even reached the point in recent years where the far-right British National Party, self-styled champions of free speech, got the police to investigate a comedian on the basis that her words were inciting hatred of them as an ethnic grouping.

It would be better if we trusted others – and ourselves – to say what we really think and then respond accordingly. That might mean ignoring their nonsense, or telling them where to stick it – or having a proper argument where appropriate. What it should not mean, however, is calling in the language police. Instead we are entering a cultural age where people can be sacked, censured or censored for saying the wrong word, regardless of where they said it or what they meant by it. The inevitable consequence will be a freezing effect, making many people more cautious and further restricting conversation over a chilled glass of wine, never mind heated debate.

The chilling consequences for free speech of the war on words were strikingly illustrated in September 2014, at a meeting held at Smith College, a liberal arts college for women in Massachusetts. Entitled 'Challenging the Ideological Echo Chamber: Free Speech, Civil Discourse and the Liberal Arts', the panel was 'an apparent attempt to address the intolerance of diverse opinions that prevails on many campuses'.[15] Instead it became a powerful illustration of the new intolerance-in-the-name-of-tolerance, enforced by a movement of illiberal liberals.

Among the speakers was Smith alumna Wendy Kaminer – author, lawyer, campaigner and one of America's most forthright free-speech advocates. Answering a question about teaching materials that contain 'hate speech', Kaminer criticised the argument for censoring a classic book such as Mark Twain's *The Adventures of Huckleberry Finn*. A student on the panel protested that the book 'has the n-word'.

Well, Wendy Kaminer responded, 'let's talk about n-words. Let's talk about the growing lexicon of words that can only be known by their initials. When I say "n-word", what word do you all hear in your head? You hear the word ...' At that point, as a press report written by Harvey Silverglate, chairman of the pro-free speech on campus lobby FIRE put it, 'Ms Kaminer crossed the Rubicon of political correctness and uttered the forbidden word, observing that having uttered it, "nothing horrible happened" ... There's an important difference, she pointed out, between hurling an epithet and uttering a forbidden word during an academic discussion of our attitudes toward language and law'.[16]

That important difference, however, was apparently lost on the undergraduates, alumnae and academics who launched a backlash against Kaminer, accusing her of 'racist remarks' and even of launching 'an explicit act of racist violence'. Smith president Kathleen McCartney, who had chaired the panel, subsequently apologised to students and faculty who were 'hurt' and made to feel 'unsafe' by Kaminer uttering the wicked word in her defence of free speech (the horror, the horror).

When a recording and transcript of the controversial discussion were usefully posted online, it was preceded by the inevitable sweeping 'Trigger Warning' advising sensitive students not to go there: 'Trigger/Content Warnings: Racism/racial slurs, ableist slurs, anti-Semitic language, anti-Muslim/Islamophobic language, anti-immigrant language, sexist/misogynistic slurs, references to race-based violence.' Who would ever have guessed this warning about an apparent carnival of reaction was actually describing an academic discussion about free speech and education?

Things became even more surreal when Kaminer explained which words these Trigger Warnings had been used to replace in the transcript published in the campus newspaper.

Kathleen McCartney had joked, 'We're just wild and crazy, aren't we?' In the transcript, 'crazy' was replaced by the notation: '[ableist slur].' One of my fellow panellists mentioned that the State Department had for a time banned the words 'jihad,' 'Islamist' and 'caliphate' – which the transcript flagged as 'anti-Muslim/Islamophobic language.'[17]

It seems that the war on words does not only proscribe certain types of speech 'regardless of the context', and insist on what one academic who defended Kaminer called the tyranny of 'sanitary euphemisms' such as the n-word. It also dictates that there can be no legitimate debate about this assault on freedom of expression, unless it adopts those same sanitary euphemisms and gets itself tied up in Trigger Warnings. Such are the dire consequences for free speech of accepting the medieval notion that 'words of power' are too dangerous for mental weaklings such as us to be trusted to handle alone.

10

'Liars and Holocaust deniers do not deserve to be heard'

The prosecution alleges that censorship is sometimes necessary because there can be no right to spread lies or subvert incontrovertible truths – whether about the history of the Nazi Holocaust, the science of climate change, or much else.

What do you call somebody who still tries to defend old-fashioned capitalist economics and dissents from the mainstream media consensus about the dangers of rising inequality within the UK and US? A free marketeer, maybe? A Tory, Republican or some other brand of right-winger? Perhaps even a 'neo-liberal', if unlike me you have a notion what that pejorative name might mean.

But no, those labels all seem so last-century. According to the liberal Nobel Prize Winner for economics Professor Paul Krugman, the best way to dismiss these critics today is to accuse them of the heinous crime of 'inequality denial'.[1] That surely settles that. Nobody needs to argue the toss with lying deniers, after all.

Once upon a time we had political, historical and scientific debates. Those with alternative views were seen as intellectual opponents to be argued with and defeated. Today anybody questioning the dominant views on emotive subjects risks being accused of 'denial'. And those branded as 'deniers', accused of deliberately corrupting incontrovertible truths, have to be shut up or even locked up, not debated with.

The allegation of 'denial' has become a powerful device to demand that a discussion be closed down and an argument silenced. It began with the allegation of Holocaust denial, used to demonise and criminalise those few cranks and neo-fascists in the West who would question the truth of the Nazi genocide against the Jews. Now the allegation of denial is promiscuously deployed on all sorts of issues. Those whose views fall outside the mainstream of orthodox opinion have been variously accused of genocide denial, climate-change denial, Aids denial, racism denial, rape denial, inequality denial and even 'denial denial'. (In a twist of irony apparently lost on its accusers, the Vatican has even been accused of 'Inquisition denial'.)

The ease with which the denial label can be applied to dissidents on one issue after another suggests that it has little to do with the specific debates on these questions. Crusaders now yell 'Denier!' just as their predecessors yelled 'Witch!' – as a spell to discredit any opponent and short-circuit any argument. The vehemence of these accusations signifies less their strength of feeling on a particular issue than their general antagonism towards the free-for-all of open discussion.

Those waging war on denial will insist that this has 'nothing to do with free speech'. They are simply trying to protect the truth from liars, and in the process to protect the victims from harm.

But denial is a free-speech issue. Indeed opposing bans on those who would deny the Holocaust is an acid test for supporting free speech with no 'buts'. It is a stand-out case for defending the principle of 'freedom for the thought that we hate'. Challenging the wider use of the denial card to close down other debates is also becoming of undeniable importance, if we want to live in an open-minded society.

* * *

To call somebody a 'denier' is to allege that they have crossed a moral line. Their views are not just wrong, but have no right to be heard. That's why accusations of denial are among the favourite weapons *du jour* of the reverse-Voltaires, who do not wish to debate their opponents' views but to deny their right to express them. In this, the allegation of 'denial' has become the respectable face of intellectual intolerance today. That stands it in a long and inglorious historical tradition.

Like free speech, tolerance is a fairly modern idea. For centuries, Church and state in European societies combined to persecute those heretics who dared to deny some aspect of the orthodox beliefs of the age. Intolerance was the order of the day and free-thinking was an abomination to those who lived by religious orthodoxy.

The sixteenth-century friar–philosopher–astrologer Giordano Bruno was imprisoned and tried by the Roman Inquisition for denying the truth of core Catholic doctrines (among other things he insisted that Jesus had not been born to a virgin, was not God, and was not present in the bread and wine taken at Mass). Imprisoned through a trial lasting seven years, Bruno refused to recant his 'heretical' beliefs. The Pope pronounced him guilty of heresy and the cardinals of the Inquisition issued a death sentence. Bruno was burned at the stake in Rome's Campo de Fiori in February 1600, with his tongue tied down to suppress his 'wicked words', and all his books were banned.

In 1633, the Renaissance scientist and philosopher Galileo Galilei was tried by the Roman Inquisition and judged to be 'vehemently suspect of heresy' for holding the Copernican view which denied that God's Earth was the centre of the Universe and said instead that it moved round the Sun. Galileo's offending book was banned and he was forced publicly to renounce his heretical beliefs, under threat of torture and death, before being sentenced to house arrest for the rest of his life.

Nor did the Roman Catholic Church have a monopoly on heretic-hunting. When the radical thinker and scientist Michael

Servetus was pursued by the Catholic Inquisition for his denial of the doctrines of the Trinity and original sin, he fled to Protestant Geneva – only to find that the Calvinist authorities there were no more tolerant of heretics. They burnt him at the stake in 1553. A century later in 1656 the Jewish elders of Amsterdam found the young philosopher Baruch Spinoza (whose relatives had been persecuted by the Catholic Inquisition in Portugal) guilty of 'abominable heresies' after he publicly argued against the existence of a providential God, the immortality of the soul, and the idea of God-given laws governing man. Spinoza the denier was expelled from the synagogue and the Jewish community, with a blood-curdling send-off: 'Cursed be he by day, and cursed be he by night … The Lord will blot out his name from under Heaven.' Fortunately Spinoza survived to write his own name into history as the great Dutchman of the Enlightenment.

Despite the break with Rome and the establishment of the Protestant Church of England, the kingdom of the Tudor and Stuart monarchs was no safe haven for heretics and dissenters. Bartholomew Legate, an unorthodox preacher who denied the Holy Trinity and the authority of both powerful churches, was found guilty of blasphemous heresy. He refused to retract his opinions, and was burnt at the stake at Smithfield in March 1612 – the last such martyr to be burnt for his religious beliefs in London. The following month at Lichfield in Staffordshire his co-defendant Edward Lightman attained the distinction of becoming the last person to be burned for heresy in England.

In strictly Presbyterian Scotland, however, they carried a noose if not a torch for heretics somewhat longer. As late as 1697 Thomas Aikenhead, a twenty-year-old Edinburgh student, was condemned to death because he had 'rejected the mystery of the Trinity as unworthy of refutation; and scoffed at the incarnation of Christ'. Despite displaying remorse and penitence for what sounds like the seventeenth-century version of a drunken student prank, Aikenhead became the last person in Britain to be hanged for blasphemy, just ten years before the Act of Union between England and Scotland ushered in our modern nation state.

What all of these heretics had in common was that, in putting forward new opinions and challenging the old, they were questioning the unquestionable. Their arguments inevitably involved the denial of important aspects of the dominant religious orthodoxy. As one account has it, 'heretics were seen as religiously subversive, socially dangerous and even morally debased'.[2] Little wonder that some were sufficiently fearful of being branded a heretic that they hid their denial of the Church's teachings. Nicolaus Copernicus, the Polish astronomer whose belief that the Earth was not the centre of the Universe inspired Galileo and others, made sure that his book was not published until after his death in 1543. The Enlightenment scientist Sir Isaac Newton also protected his position by keeping his heretical denial of the devil's existence private.

The world, of course, has moved on a lot since those dark days, and not only in the sense that Copernicus meant. No Church exercises anything like unquestioned authority in the secular Western societies of the twenty-first century. Without a dominant orthodoxy, there can surely be no heretics condemned and punished in the West for denying the core truths of the age.

And yet … In the absence of an unquestioned moral code supposedly handed down by God, the moral guardians of the modern age have had to find new ways to draw a line between Good and Evil (or as they might be more likely to call it today, between Appropriate and Inappropriate words or behaviours). They have seized upon rare examples of unambiguous wickedness – child sexual abuse, say, or slavery – as secular evils against which all decent men and women must unite. These become the new taboos and none are allowed to question the orthodox teaching on such issues. The greatest new taboo of all is questioning the facts of the Nazis' genocidal massacre of six million Jews – what is now known as Holocaust denial.

Those who question the history of the Holocaust are treated as the secular equivalent of heretics today, pariahs to be cast out of civilised society and, in many European countries, cast into jail. It might seem a bit much to compare these fools, frauds and fanatics to the heroic heretics of the past, but it is worth recalling the point made in chapter 3: that the term heresy derives from the ancient Greek for 'to choose', in particular to choose to dissent from the dominant orthodoxy of the day. As Arthur Versluis observes in *The New Inquisitions*, 'A "heretic", then, is one who chooses, one who therefore exemplifies freedom of individual thought.' Thus what the Inquisition and the heretic-hunters of the twenty-first century do indeed have in common is that 'the "crime" in question is fundamentally a "crime" of thought'.[3] The fact that hate-mongering Holocaust deniers don't deserve to be mentioned in the same breath as Galileo or Spinoza cannot alter the fact that they too are being pursued for thought crimes.

The Nazi Holocaust of the 1940s stands unchallenged as the greatest crime against humanity in history. But when did Holocaust denial become the biggest thought crime in Western society?

Holocaust denial is currently a crime in almost twenty countries, most of which are European Union members, led by France and Germany. The UK parliament has so far rejected attempts to make Holocaust denial a specific crime – though the plethora of UK laws against hate speech and offensive language makes it easy enough for the British authorities to outlaw Holocaust deniers in practice, as with the ban they imposed in 2014 on the anti-Semitic French comedian Dieudonné M'bala M'bala.

These measures outlawing Holocaust denial were not imposed in the aftermath of the Second World War. Nobody seemed particularly concerned with 'denial' in the decades following the actual horrors of the death camps. Indeed the Holocaust itself was hardly discussed in the West in those years, since the Nazis' crimes stood as an embarrassing reminder of the racism and anti-Semitism that had been a staple of Western politics before the Second World War. In fact most European countries did not introduce laws against Holocaust denial until the 1990s, half a century after the liberation of the camps. This suggests their motivation had more to do with contemporary political problems than with historical events.

When the Berlin Wall came down in 1989 and the Soviet bloc followed soon afterwards, the post-Cold War era dawned on a world of uncertainties. Western politicians of both the traditional right and left found the ground shifting unnervingly beneath their feet. In these insecure times, striking 'Never Again' poses against dead Nazis and a handful of Holocaust deniers gave European politicians a rare opportunity to take a firm stand on the side of the forces of Good against a clear-cut Evil. Having been robbed of the Soviet bogeyman and the ideological cement of anti-Communism that had held their worldview together, many in the supposedly triumphant Western elites seemed unsure of what they were meant to stand for now. At a time when they did not know who they were, posthumous Holocaust-hunting at least allowed them to establish that they were Not Nazis.

That post-Cold War outburst of uncertainty and political posturing helped to explain why many EU states suddenly passed laws against Holocaust denial in the 1990s, using as a pretext the activities of a few 'revisionist' historians such as David Irving (whose major work, *Hitler's War*, had been published back in 1977). In Britain, Tony Blair's New Labour government attempted the same thing by introducing a Holocaust Memorial Day from 2001. More than fifty years after the Holocaust, European politicians plucked it out of its past setting and turned it into an ahistorical moral absolute, a universal symbol of evil to be exploited for political purposes in the here and now.

In many circumstances the Holocaust became less an historic atrocity to be taught, discussed and understood in its political context and more a matter of religious orthodoxy, a moral parable about human evil to be learnt by rote. This put the accepted version of what happened and why beyond question, something that secular authorities were no more prepared to have debated than the Pope might be willing to haggle over the truth of transubstantiation. The notion of banning (either explicitly or implicitly) those who dissent from this truth, the Holocaust deniers, followed logically from its elevation into pseudo-theology.

In recent decades the Holocaust has been turned into a moral absolute everywhere from classroom to courtroom. Once that was done, the next step was to convert it into an all-purpose brand that could be adapted to suit any agenda or campaign. Want to get a leg up onto the moral high ground in any debate? Just conjure up some comparison with the Holocaust, however far-fetched. So it is that pro-life crusaders will talk about the 'Abortion Holocaust', and that the US animal rights crusaders at PETA could seriously launch a campaign damning farmed meat as the 'Holocaust on your plate'. From the 1990s, those campaigning for Western military intervention around the world, for example in the conflicts in the former Yugoslavia, were also quick to compare these civil wars to the Nazi Holocaust.

Just as Holocaust denial has been made a taboo and a crime, so those accused of the secular blasphemy of denial on other issues now faced demands that they be silenced and censored. By 2006 one leading self-righteous British writer felt able to declare that 'almost everywhere, climate change denial now looks as stupid and as unacceptable as Holocaust denial'.[4] A more rational era might decide that it was 'stupid and unacceptable' to compare attempting to cover up the slaughter of six million Jews in death camps to the criticism of some numbers on a climatology graph. Today, however, such debased comparisons are widely accepted as good intellectual coin. And if questioning the official line on climate change is now as 'unacceptable as Holocaust denial', then there is surely no place for such sceptical opinions in the media, scientific circles or public debate.

Crusaders against the new variants of denial don't only wish to silence their opponents. In the true tradition of heresy-hunting, they also want to inflict punishment on those who deny the true faith. A writer on the US-based environmental magazine *Grist* sparked controversy and set the tone for the voice of the modern inquisitor in 2006, when he compared climate-change deniers to Nazi war criminals and argued: 'We should have war crimes trials for these bastards ... some sort of climate Nuremberg.'[5] Within two years that view had spread from the green fringe to near the top of the scientific establishment. Addressing the US Congress in 2008 James Hansen, top climatologist for the space agency NASA, reportedly called 'for the chief executives of large fossil fuel companies to be put on trial for high crimes against humanity and nature', accusing them of 'actively spreading doubt about global warming in the same way that tobacco corporations blurred the links between smoking and cancer'. In 2012 Hansen added that 'politicians who pretend that global warming is not man-made' should also be charged with 'crimes against humanity'. By 2014 radical UK-based media campaigners were arguing that Hansen's suggested 'Nuremberg-style trials' of climate-change deniers must include media executives as well as fossil fuel bosses and politicians. All were 'responsible for crimes against humanity and planet that almost defy belief. They must be held to account for their crimes.' Their major crime being 'actively spreading doubt' about the orthodoxy on man-made global warming.[6]

Three centuries ago, the Edinburgh authorities had insisted on hanging young Thomas Aikenhead not just for scoffing at their religion, but as a warning to any others who might be tempted to express such heretical ideas. Today's inquisitors similarly insist that banning or suppressing the secular blasphemy of denial is justified because it can protect other people from being infected with sinful notions about the Holocaust, Aids, the weather or whatever. The magic word 'denial' becomes the moral justification for restricting what others can say, whilst convincing yourself that such censorship has 'nothing to do with free speech'.

How did 'denial' achieve this status of something akin to secular blasphemy? A traditional dictionary definition would say that denial involves asserting something 'to be untrue or untenable'. That is what the unorthodox thinkers of the past were doing – denying the truth of an accepted opinion of their age, and offering an alternative interpretation.

But the allegation of 'denial' today is used to mean something different. It relates to a more modern definition, which states that denial can also mean a 'refusal to acknowledge an unacceptable truth or emotion, or to admit it into consciousness'. In our therapy-soaked psychobabbling culture, the definition that holds sway is this one relating to mental health; denial now allegedly involves a defensive suppression of knowledge that is too painful or traumatic to cope with. In short, deniers are pathological liars.

To accuse somebody of 'denial' no longer means merely that they are questioning or criticising some conventional wisdom. It implies instead that they are refusing to acknowledge what everybody knows is the undoubted truth – as with Holocaust denial. The crusaders who cry 'Denier!' are not just accusing their opponents of disagreeing, but of dishonestly refusing to face the undisputed facts. Those who are 'in denial' are thus low liars or sufferers from some mental aberration, who are not worth listening to and can safely be silenced if not straitjacketed.

Not only can they be silenced – it seems that they must be, in case their mental health problems are catching and could put others at risk. Some moral crusaders depict Holocaust denial as more than a thought crime, as both the justification of a past genocide and the prelude to another one. Gregory Stanton, the American professor of genocide studies and founder of Genocide Watch, describes denial not only as the last of eight stages of genocide, but also as one of the 'surest indicators of further genocidal massacres'.[7] So the deniers are more than misguided, they are complicit in mass murder.

A similar sleight of mind has become a common feature of the case for silencing climate-change deniers, with the alarmists arguing that the spread of 'denial' about man-made global warming is actually making the coming environmental apocalypse more urgent. In their view it follows that something must be done to silence the deniers, or we are all doomed. A narrow-minded argument for restricting freedom of speech is magically – sorry, scientifically – recast as a noble attempt to rescue the planet.

One other mover up the denialist chart is the increasingly common accusation of 'rape denial', which has been used to condemn or ban anybody from students and journalists to public figures such as Julian Assange of Wikileaks and left-wing MP George Galloway. At first sight it seems a curious charge. Who, after all, could deny the existence of rape? It turns out, however, that 'rape denier' can now mean anybody who questions any aspect of the feminist orthodoxy on rape – by, for example, suggesting that not all crimes categorised as rape are the same, or that a convicted rapist should be able to return to everyday life after serving his sentence. It is not only that the label 'denier' is being stretched ever wider and applied to more issues. It is also being used to close down more avenues of discussion and delegitimise more public debates.

There is nothing good to be said in defence of those who wish to deny the truth of the Holocaust, and attempt to write death camps and gas ovens out of our history. If there is one thing more stupid than that, however, it is surely imposing bans designed to turn Holocaust denial into a thought crime.

Some of us who entirely accept the historical truths of the Nazi Holocaust and the deaths of six million Jews nevertheless oppose bans and laws against Holocaust denial on two key grounds, one principled and one more practical. First, because we believe in freedom of speech as a fundamental political principle that has virtue in and of itself, regardless of the content of what might be said. And second because, in practice, trying to deal with a political issue such as Holocaust denial through bans can only make the problem worse, by encouraging cynicism and giving credence to conspiracy theories.

Whether some like it or not, treating Holocaust denial as a crime *is* a straightforward free-speech issue. It is a measure of how far the historic principle of freedom of speech has fallen out of fashion that so many should now believe that the way to deal with obnoxious opinion is through the law rather than argument. Thus a UK government and European Commission expert on anti-Semitism argues that Jews will be 'best protected in open and tolerant democracies that actively prosecute all forms of racial and religious hatred'.[8] Such one-eyed experts apparently see no contradiction in intolerantly banning speech and prosecuting 'all forms' of objectionable ideas, in the name of 'tolerance' and 'democracy'.

Freedom of speech is the eau de vie of a civilised society, without which many other liberties that we care about would not be possible. It is also an indivisible freedom. To have any real meaning, free speech must also extend to those that the mainstream deems irresponsible or unpalatable – be that the noble Greek philosopher Socrates, the brilliant Italian astronomer Galileo, or the anti-Semitic French 'funny man' Dieudonné.

Opposing the criminalisation of Holocaust denial is more than the right thing to do. It is an acid test for those who believe in the principle of free speech. After all, extreme ideas are the ones that most often need defending against bans. That should not imply any sort of support or sympathy for the historical falsehoods of the Holocaust deniers. It is instead in the spirit of the indivisible principle of free speech.

Once that principle becomes negotiable, there is no telling where it will end. Trying to make a 'special case' of Holocaust denial will not work. History demonstrates that, every time curbs are introduced on one type of speech, they serve as a cue for demands to censor something else. It is no surprise that the criminalisation of Holocaust denial has led to demands to repress other 'deniers' who diverge from conventional wisdom.

So much for the principle. The practical arguments against bans on Holocaust deniers are just as important today. The best way to confront bad ideas and distortions is always through debate and exposure – through more speech rather than less. To seek to repress them instead can only inhibit the search for clarity and truth. Attempting a bureaucratic solution to profound political and social problems through bans and proscriptions always makes matters worse. In the case of Holocaust denial, the practical consequences can be dangerously far-reaching.

In recent decades, the authorities across Europe and America have sought to erect a ring-fence around the question of the Holocaust, often treating it as a religious relic that cannot be touched, re-examined or in any way disrespected without calling down wrath from above. The Holocaust has been widely used as an all-purpose instrument of moral instruction, to drum into people – especially young people – the threat of Evil. Under New Labour, the Holocaust became the first historical event to enjoy compulsory status in the UK national schools' curriculum. It has often featured, not only as a history lesson, but also as a moral sermon on how children should behave today. One important theme of the Holocaust Memorial Day Trust's educational materials for UK schools, for example, has been how low-level playground bullying can be the first step on the return march to the death camps. As the Trust's national co-ordinator explained in 2009, 'It's about stopping little acts of hatred in everyday life. In schools, bullying is often on the basis of what you look like or where you come from. We're not at the point of Nazi Germany, but let's look at our actions and make sure that doesn't happen. It's not just about learning about history. It's about learning from history.'[9]

The danger of this approach is to obscure the unique historical significance of the Holocaust by talking about it in the same breath as 'little acts' of playground unpleasantness.

When people are denied the chance seriously to discuss or question an official orthodoxy in critical fashion, it is likely to prompt other unwanted questions. Such as 'What have they got to hide?' In trying to protect the truth about the Holocaust from the perfidies of the deniers through administrative and even authoritarian measures, government and judges only risk giving credence to their execrable conspiracy theories. Those who live by the ban can perish by it, also.

Nobody has been more forthright in challenging Holocaust denial than the American historian Deborah Lipstadt, Professor of Modern Jewish and Holocaust Studies and author of *Denying the Holocaust*. That book led to Lipstadt being unsuccessfully sued for libel by the British 'revisionist' historian David Irving, a case which cost her six years and a small fortune to contest before a London court finally found in her favour and declared Irving to be a racist and a Holocaust denier in 2000.

Yet when an Austrian court later jailed Irving for three years for the crime of Holocaust denial, Lipstadt warned against the dangers of trying to gag deniers. The way to defeat them was as she had done, through open public debate and exposure and establishing the facts, rather than with laws and bans. 'Ironically,' she said of her public demolition of Irving's historical distortions, 'none of this would have happened had the UK had laws outlawing Holocaust denial. I shudder at the thought that politicians might be given the power to legislate history. They can hardly fix the potholes in our streets. How can we expect them to decide what is the proper version of history?'[10]

After her libel trial win, Lipstadt also made clear that, whilst Holocaust denial was a lie, it should not be illegitimate to question the known details of the Nazis' historic crime – after all, she said, 'this is not theology'. That must be news to the many zealous crusaders who seek to restrict free speech by treating denial as the new form of secular blasphemy.

Promiscuous allegations of 'denial' and the blood sport of heretic-hunting have now spread from the Holocaust to other important issues. The fact that even some leading scientists are seemingly prepared to treat their critics as 'deniers' to be silenced, rather than sceptics to be answered, confirms the dangers of this newly respectable form of intolerance.

Take the issue of climate change. We are often assured these days that the science of man-made climate change is settled, the debate is finished, the question is closed. No further indulgence of 'climate-change deniers' is therefore necessary or acceptable. Indeed if, in the words of one writer, challenging the mainstream consensus on climate change is equivalent to 'shouting fire in a theatre' (see chapter 7), then there can surely be no free speech for sceptics.

Now, I claim no insight into the science of climatology, but you need not be a scientist to grasp the important role that open-ended debate and the encouragement of scepticism has played in the advance of science through history. And you need only be a democrat to insist that it is not up to scientists to dictate what can and cannot legitimately be discussed in a free society.

The crusade to silence climate-change deniers has inevitably encouraged an attitude of intolerance in scientific circles. In 2011, the UK government's then chief scientific adviser, Sir John Beddington, openly demanded that the science community take an attitude of 'gross intolerance' towards 'pseudo-scientists', comparing their attitude to racism and 'anti-homosexuality'.[11] It was not difficult to see the implications of his words for sidelining and silencing 'climate-change deniers'. Those implications were spelt out in 2014, when a report from a committee of UK members of parliament called on the BBC and other media to stop giving time and space to climate-change sceptics. The committee chairman, Labour MP Andrew Miller, likened 'climate-change deniers' to the Monster Raving Loony Party and suggested that at the very least their appearances on news programmes should be accompanied by a 'health warning' about their dangerous views. Or perhaps a Trigger Warning to protect us from harm.[12]

Think about this. If the censorious attitudes of these scientists and politicians had prevailed over the past centuries, it seems unlikely that a scientific outlook would ever have broken through in Western societies. It was only by overcoming the intolerance of the past, such as that which the Inquisition showed to Bruno and Galileo, that science was able to advance and flourish in the more tolerant age of Enlightenment. Do scientists seriously wish for a new attitude of intolerance to banish ideas with which they disagree, to burn the books if not the authors? That can be the only consequence of comparing 'pseudoscience' to racism.

How then should we deal with those who question accepted wisdom and try to separate the truth from the lies? It's not a new problem. Almost 200 years ago John Stuart Mill complained about a 'flowering of quackery and ephemeral literature' and promotion of mock science through the new 'arts' of the media. Yet Mill did not advocate 'gross intolerance' towards all this quackery and nonsense.

Instead he argued for the tolerance of all ideas, even those we believe to be lies, as the best way to establish the truth for all to see. Mill's warnings about the dangers of allowing those who are sure they are right to silence alternative views should ring in the ears of the heretic-hunting protectors of Scientific Truth today: 'To refuse a hearing to an opinion, because they are sure that it is false, is to assume that their certainty is the same thing as absolute certainty. All silencing of discussion is an assumption of infallibility.'[13] And mystical notions of infallibility should surely be left to popes rather than men and women of science.

Mill was clear on the distinction between opinions and facts. Even so, he insisted on the right to publish what were considered falsehoods. For Mill, alongside his firm adherence to the principle of free speech, the practical virtue of allowing heretics and the holders of 'false opinion' to question received wisdom is that it forces the mainstream to defend and prove its viewpoint. He summed up beautifully two different bases for assuming your argument is true – a good one, based on tolerance and refutation of criticism, and a bad one based on intolerance of any scepticism or questioning: 'There is the greatest difference,' wrote Mill in *On Liberty*, 'between presuming an opinion to be true, because, with every opportunity for contesting it, it has not been refuted, and assuming its truth for the purpose of not permitting its refutation.'[14]

It was in this spirit that, back in the 1660s, the Royal Society was founded in London with the motto *Nullius in verba*, which translates as 'On the word of no one', or as we might say today 'Take nobody's word for it'. Everything was open to question and demands for proof, nothing was set in stone (except that motto), scepticism was the very stuff of scientific inquiry. By contrast today's champions of 'gross intolerance' in science seem to live not just in a different century from the founders of the Royal Society or the likes of Mill, but on another planet. Their attitude is to treat those who disagree with them as lying deniers, to be dealt with by moral condemnation and censorship rather than argument and evidence.

So it was that in 2013, leading UK scientists and lobbyists demanded that shops should stop selling an alternative health magazine, *What Doctors Don't Tell You*, because it published pseudoscientific and misleading information about health issues. One prominent science writer, Simon Singh, who prides himself on being pro-free speech and had campaigned for the reform of Britain's restrictive libel laws, nevertheless supported the calls to suppress *WDDTY*, insisting that 'it's not a free-speech issue – it's about public health and responsibility'. But as the doctor and author Michael Fitzpatrick responded, 'this is very much a free-speech issue. No matter how stupid or irresponsible *WDDTY*'s articles are, it is an important matter of principle that we uphold its right to publish and distribute them. We in turn insist on our right to challenge and to expose what we consider are its stupid and irresponsible articles. Let the public decide.'[15]

The responsibility not only of scientists, but also of historians and journalists, remains to question everything. The new intolerance that would condemn its opponents as 'deniers' to be outlawed rather than exposed is undeniably a fashionably dangerous and dangerously fashionable excuse for attacking free speech, and denying the public the chance to judge the truth for themselves.

A footnote. In April 2015, loud protests broke out in Australia after Bjorn Lomborg, Danish author of global bestseller *The Skeptical Environmentalist*, was appointed to run a government-funded think-tank at the University of Western Australia. Dr Lomborg said that his new Australian Consensus Centre would study 'where Australia's A$5 billion in aid, and the world's $US140 billion, spent every year can be spent – better. It's about the 2.5 billion people who are desperately poor and need access to clean water and sanitation.'[16] This did not assuage the protests from Greens, the liberal media, academics and student activists, who demanded that Lomborg be kicked out of UWA for his record of 'downgrading' the importance of global warming and generally being a 'climate contrarian'.

Note the new language. Lomborg, you see, cannot be branded a 'climate-change denier'. He agrees that climate change is a real problem and needs to be addressed. Yet he dissents from the mainstream view by insisting that climate change is not the biggest problem facing humanity, and that it should be tackled by encouraging development – especially among the poorer nations on earth – rather than through the Greens' preferred policies of cutting back and imposing a form of eco-austerity. That is apparently now enough to put his views beyond the pale and spark calls for him to be denied a platform in Australian academia.

The UWA Student Guild's demand for Lomberg to be sent packing spelled it out. 'While Dr Lomborg doesn't refute climate change itself', the student protestors conceded, he does have a 'controversial track record [as a] climate contrarian'. He is controversial! He says things 'contrary' to the eco-orthodoxy of the day! Cut off his funding, if not actually his head! The new spirit of intellectual intolerance has reached the point where controversy is to be barred from universities, and a writer can be demonised simply for expressing different views.

As often in the age of the reverse-Voltaires, the demand to censor one type of speech leads inexorably to attempts to deny others the right to freedom of expression. So the snowballing campaign against 'climate-change deniers' accelerates down the slippery slope, threatening to sweep away the new category of 'climate contrarians' too. Who's next?[17]

11

'Free speech is just a licence for the mass media to brainwash the public'

The prosecution alleges that 'ordinary people' cannot cope with the power of the media and corporate advertising, so it needs to be restrained.

Steve Coogan, Brit comedian turned Hollywood actor, delivered his most melodramatic line not on starry stage or silver screen but at the dull September 2012 conference of the misnamed Liberal Democrats, then part of the UK coalition government. Addressing a meeting in his role as celebrity voiceover artist of the Hacked Off lobby for state-backed regulation of the press (a part in which he generally understudies Hugh Grant), Coogan gave his political groupies the punchline they were gagging for. 'Press freedom,' announced the former funny man, 'is a lie peddled by proprietors and editors who only care about profit!' He was not joking.[1]

Meanwhile in London, the Metropolitan Police were putting the press-bashing political mood into practice. After the scandal of phone-hacking at the *News of the World* exploded in the summer of 2011, the Met launched three major investigations into the UK tabloid press. Involving 200 officers and an apparently unlimited multi-million-pound budget, these operations amount to the biggest criminal investigation in British police history. To put that in some perspective: the scandal was sparked by revelations that the Sunday tabloid the *News of the World* had listened to voicemail messages sent to an abducted and murdered schoolgirl, Milly Dowler, in 2002. Ten years after she disappeared, there were many more police officers investigating who had hacked Milly's phone messages than had ever searched for the missing teenager or her murderer.

Police arrested more than sixty journalists who worked for the Rupert Murdoch-owned *Sun* and *News of the World* (which had closed in July 2011), many in dawn raids on their family homes. Dozens of these journalists were then left in limbo on police bail for years, their lives and careers on hold while they waited to discover if they would face trial and, in some cases after a jury failed to convict, retrial.

It proved to be the most extraordinary state crackdown on a supposedly free press in a modern Western society. Police treated tabloid journalists more like members of a terror cell; as Trevor Kavanagh of the *Sun* summed it up in April 2015, after another dock full of journalists had been found not guilty by an Old Bailey jury: 'Police ransacked homes, held terrified children in their nighties, ripped up floorboards and confiscated bags of private papers, love letters and computers still not returned. Not one scrap of this "evidence" was ever used in court.'[2]

To pursue Operation Elveden, the huge investigation into journalists allegedly paying public employees for information, state prosecutors dusted off a thirteenth-century common law which made 'misconduct in public office' a crime. Then they gave it a modern twist by adding on the previously unheard-of offence of 'conspiracy to commit misconduct in public office', which allowed them to prosecute journalists who are not public employees at all. It looked as if the authorities were effectively making up a law as they went along, specifically to nail tabloid reporters. What is more, this nonsensical new offence aimed to criminalise the normal practice of reporters searching for inside information and trying to expose stories that the secrecy-obsessed authorities want hidden. As I wrote after four *Sun* journalists were eventually acquitted in March 2015: 'Never mind all the lectures about how journalists are "not above the law"; we must insist, as the jury's verdicts did on Friday, that they are not "beneath the law" either, to be singled out in a legal witch-hunt.'[3]

Yet the 'I-blame-the-meejah' climate hanging over British politics and culture meant that there were few political protests or civil-liberties complaints over journalists being treated more like suspected jihadists. As one of the arrested (and eventually cleared) *Sun* journalists told me, 'If this was happening in Zimbabwe, China or North Korea, there would be a shit-storm of opposition here – protests outside the embassies, the NUJ [National Union of Journalists] would be on its high horse, all that. But if it's British redtop journalists working for Rupert Murdoch? "Naa, fuck 'em."'[4] When the big trials of these tabloid journalists finally started in 2014, jurors showed they did not necessarily share the political elite's fear and loathing of popular journalism – what one top prosecutor called, in open court with open contempt, the 'gutter press' – by refusing to convict reporters who were 'guilty' only of being journalists. By April 2015, 34 journalists had been arrested under Operation Elveden with only one conviction.

Arguments about regulating free speech now take place in a febrile atmosphere where the popular press and the mass media are depicted as society's supervillains. There is no real free speech for powerless 'ordinary' people, the prosecution alleges, who are at the mercy of the megaphone media. This is perhaps one of the most insidious – and increasingly influential – arguments for reining in free speech: that freedom of expression and of the press is effectively 'a lie', because that freedom is only really available to the rich and powerful, via the mass media and the power of corporate advertising. The demand to restrict media freedom can then be presented as progressive, providing an apparently anti-capitalist excuse for censorship and control.

The blame-the-media mood has been used to justify the push for new regulations on publishing and broadcasting in the UK. There have been moves to tighten controls on what advertisers can say and where. And the British political class has united to try to impose the first system of state-backed press regulation in more than 300 years, via the Royal Charter which the political party leaders agreed with Grant and Coogan's Hacked Off lobby at a late-night meeting in March 2013. Even in the US, growing hostility in high places towards the tabloid press and Fox News alongside complaints about advertisers allegedly holding sway over consumers and voters has sparked calls for the First Amendment to be interpreted less leniently in regard to 'lower-value' types of speech, such as advertising, and even for the state to subsidise more 'serious and substantive' media coverage of political affairs.

None of this, we are assured, has anything to do with attacking freedom of speech. It is simply about curbing the ability of the mass media to spread lies and manipulate public opinion, whether in advertising or election campaigns. That might sound all well and good and might be thought attractive to an old Marxist like me. The trouble is there are two ugly illiberal prejudices underpinning the liberal media-bashing.

It involves a low view of the importance of the freedom of the press. That liberty has been fought for and defended over five centuries as the practical expression of free speech, by people who were prepared to suffer and even to die for their cause. If only these heroes could have had access to the wisdom of Steve Coogan/Alan Partridge, they could have saved themselves a lot of trouble. After all, what fool would go to the Tower of London or the gallows in support of 'a lie'? The entire discussion of press regulation in the UK today is premised on the myth that the press is somehow 'too free' to run wild and make trouble. It would be far more true to say that the press is not nearly free or open enough.

The blame-the-media mood is also based on a low view of the public. Attacks on the influence of the mass media are often coded assaults on the intelligence of the masses. The assumption is that people are so gullible and greedy they can easily be manipulated by the media into doing the 'wrong' thing, whether at the supermarket check-out or the ballot box.

The cry 'I blame the meejah!' has become a constant feature of Western cultural debates. There is scarcely a social problem from global warming to Islamophobia that is not casually attributed to the malign influence of the allegedly unethical mass media – often by those looking down from the allegedly ethical upper echelons of the liberal media. After the England football team's ignominious exit from the 2010 World Cup in South Africa, the *Guardian*'s senior columnist, Polly Toynbee, even demanded: 'Was it Rupert Murdoch wot lost England the World Cup?'[5] Ours, it appears, is an age when shooting the messenger can compete with football to be considered Britain's national sport.

But should it matter what anybody says about the mass media and corporate advertising? What do campaigns to ban fast food advertisements, or to make tobacco companies sell cigarettes only in plain packages, or in various other ways to counter and control media influence and bias, have to do with freedom of expression? More than some would have us believe.

This might seem like safe ground for the 'it's-not-a-free-speech-issue' crowd. Restricting media advertising or banning tabloids from campuses appears more of a blow against narrow corporate interests than a broadside against the democratic rights of the rest of us. But that is just another face of the free-speech fraud.

These things *are* free-speech issues. Not only because they infringe on the right of corporations and newspapers to say what they want (if free speech is supposed to be for all, then why not for Philip Morris and Ronald McDonald, too, just as it should be for their critics?). But also, more importantly, because it infringes on the other side of free speech – the right of the public to hear and see whatever we want, judge for ourselves, and make our own choices.

The progressive-sounding attack on media influence is almost always underpinned by reactionary notions about the masses who are deemed too pathetic or childlike to cope with or resist whatever the mass media tells them. So people must be 'protected' from dangerous ideas and images, inconvenient facts, and ultimately from themselves.

Most attacks on the power of the mass media, corporate PR and advertisers' puff in Anglo-American culture are really a coded way of dumping on the supposedly feeble-minded public. The ostensible targets are such powerful hate-figures as media moguls and corporate fat-cats. The underlying target, however, is the mass of 'sheeple' who supposedly do the bidding of these super-rich Svengalis. To accuse the media of 'dumbing down' is really to say that they are pandering to the base tastes of the mass of dummies.

This is a hidden front in the silent war on free speech. It is presented as a well-intentioned attempt to rein in corporate power, prevent media manipulation and censor damaging words and images that could cause crime, cancer or obesity. Yet at root these are swingeing attacks on free speech. They deny the right of freedom of expression to those of whose messages they disapprove. And they would deny the public the right to hear and judge for themselves. In a free society of morally autonomous adults, the right to make your own choices – even the right to make the 'wrong' choices – should be resolutely defended in the consumer marketplace as well as the 'marketplace of ideas' covering politics or religion.

As with so many battles in the free-speech wars today, the underlying lack of faith in free speech reflects and reinforces a lack of belief in humanity. It says we cannot be trusted to resist the siren calls of the media and the advertisers. Which raises the question – who is really showing contempt for the public as mugs and muppets in this discussion?

* * *

Of course the media can exert a powerful influence in shaping perceptions of events. But to go further and try to blame the media for what happens in the real world makes little sense. The clue is in the name: media. Whether we are talking about traditional print newspapers or up-to-the-microsecond online outlets, they are still only a collective 'medium' for transmitting information and images between people. The media reflects real life and helps to shape perceptions of it. But it cannot create reality at will. As Karl Marx wrote in one of his first German newspaper columns back in the 1840s, the press is ultimately about as responsible for changes in the world on which it reports 'as the astronomer's telescope is for the unceasing motion of the universe. Evil astronomy!'[6]

The only way in which the blame-the-media case makes sense is if one accepts the fairy tale assumption that the public really does what it is told by the media mirror on the wall.

Take the unending rows about politics and the media. In the UK, losing Labour Party leaders have long suggested that the tabloid press was responsible for deciding the outcome of British elections – a patronising notion which denigrates the intelligence of the electorate and conveniently lets the politicians off the hook. In the US, too, it has become common for high-minded liberals to blame political setbacks on the supposed brainwashing of the gullible masses by the mass media. 'People getting their fundamental interests wrong is what American political life is all about,' notes Thomas Frank in *What's the Matter With Kansas?*, his 2005 US bestseller (published in the UK as *What's the Matter with America?*), which sought to explain how the much-derided George W. Bush had managed to defeat the Democrats in two presidential elections. Had they not been duped by the media, he suggests, how could they possibly vote Republican? A liberal columnist such as Arianna Huffington can seriously suggest that in recent elections Americans voting Republican are using their 'lizard brains', which 'are not susceptible to rationality' but are instead manipulated by fearmongering politicians and the media. Exactly how a 'lizard brain' could make voters behave like sheep or lemmings might be beyond the grasp of us non-neurologists, but we get her message about the mass of voters.[7] These arguments about the media manipulating elections are conveniently set aside when the 'correct' candidates win.

Complaints about manipulative media advertising often contain similar 'hidden messages' about brainless consumers. Campaigners might be keen to stress that they are gunning for the corporate giants of Big Tobacco, Big Alcohol or Big Food. Yet the ultimate target in their sights is the Big Public, viewed as only one jingly advert for fast food or cheap booze away from being reduced to a blob of obese alcoholics. The anti-advertising crusaders always urge us to 'think of the children!', but their campaigns treat consumers as incapable infants.

A glance at the activities of Ofcom or the Advertising Standards Authority in the UK – two priggish quangos with the power to punish broadcasters or ban adverts – shows their apparently high-minded rulings dripping with low contempt for the public's right to choose. The ASA is supposed merely to ensure that advertising is 'legal, decent, honest and truthful'. Yet it goes beyond that brief, to ensure that the childlike public gets taught the 'right' lesson.

In a typical case from August 2014, the ASA banned a light-hearted advert for the British supermarket chain Morrisons, which depicted a mother preparing a burger-in-a-bun for her daughter, who then takes the salad out before she eats it. A scene familiar to parents who have ever tried to feed their children dull, healthy food. The humourless ASA, however, did not get the joke. Its ruling concluded that the advert 'condoned poor nutritional habits or an unhealthy lifestyle, especially in children, and that it disparaged good dietary practice'.[8] The fact that this little ad was entirely 'legal, decent, honest and truthful' was cast away like an unwanted lettuce leaf. All that mattered to the po-faced ASA was that if this thirty-second scene was allowed onto the nation's TV screens, irresponsible parents everywhere would automatically think it OK to stuff their already obese kids' faces with fatty food. The truly unhealthy thing on display was the authorities' patronising attitude to grown-ups in general and parents in particular.[9]

Smoking brings out the worst in them. The consumer-bashing zealots have gone way beyond offering straight information and advice on the proven health threats associated with smoking. They are pursuing a crusade aimed at eradicating any sign of (perfectly legal) tobacco products from the face of the Western world – banning advertising, hiding cigarettes from public display and stuffing them into plain packaging, and even trying to outlaw e-cigarettes, surely the best aids to stopping smoking ever invented.

All of this is based on the assumption that we can be seduced into addiction and an early death by bright colours and the merest mention of the c-word (cigarette). Contributions to the UK government consultation on proposals for plain packaging from anti-smoking campaigners even suggested that young women could be tempted by 'girly' pink and black packaging on fag packets, the silly things![10] The Australian authorities set the standard with a system where, as the writer Christopher Snowdon notes, '"plain" means "grotesque"'. Cigarette packs are plastered with morbid images of death and disease, like medieval warnings of mortality. As Snowdon says, 'These are people who think that it is better for children to see corpses than colours.' And the crusade against Big Tobacco has become a template for similar campaigns against Big Food and Big Booze: 'In Australia, public-health lobbyists are already pushing for the same law to be applied to hamburger packaging and beer bottles, and even campaigning for smokers to be required to carry licences as the "next logical step" after plain packaging.'[11] It is a wonder they don't want us to qualify for a licence before being allowed to watch television or read the news.

The Canadian-based Adbusters Media Foundation has sought to create a global network of environmental and anti-consumption activists, using the tools of the new media to counter corporate media influence and advertising. Adbusters' campaigns such as 'Buy Nothing Day' and 'TV Turnoff Week' might seem to carry an anti-capitalist message. Yet as so often, the mass media-bashing is underpinned by anti-consumer prejudices about the gullible masses. One of the founders explained their aims thus: 'We take the environmental ethic into the mental ethic, trying to clean up the toxic areas of our minds. You can't recycle and be a good environmental citizen, then watch four hours of television and get consumption messages pumped at you.' Or as the Adbusters' advert for 'Buy Nothing Day' (timed to coincide with the pre-Christmas shopping rush on 'Black Friday') put it, 'in a world where every inch of the capitalist system is bullying you into submission, can you resist? When advertisers hound you day and night, can you escape?' Only, it seems, with the enlightened guidance of those activists who are somehow immune to the siren calls of the advertisers that bully and hound the rest of us 'into submission'.[12]

In 2014 the unremarkable town of Rotherham in Yorkshire in the north of England became the scene of a remarkable double scandal which exposed the poisonous consequences of the media-bashing culture. A top-level report revealed that an estimated 1,400 young girls had been abused, exploited and raped by gangs over a period of twenty years. Most of the victims were white or mixed-race, and most of the alleged perpetrators were unnamed Muslim men of Pakistani extraction.

Almost as shocking was the second scandal the report revealed – a concerted official cover-up. *The Times* began publishing Andrew Norfolk's investigations into child sexual exploitation in Rotherham from June 2012. The immediate response of the local Labour council and the police, a government investigation later revealed, was to dismiss these reports as politically motivated lies, peddled by 'the Murdoch press', and to spend thousands of pounds of council tax payers' money in an abortive attempt to get the courts to suppress them.[13] It would be another two years before the full story of the Rotherham sexual abuse scandal was revealed by a top-level inquiry and splashed across all of the media.

Why did the local authorities try to close down media reporting and public debate of the child sex scandal? Not because the council and police in Rotherham had some sort of soft spot for sex criminals. It was because they were afraid of being accused of racism, and exacerbating community tensions, by allowing it to be said that Asian men were abusing white girls. They did not want to suppress the story because it was false. They wanted to suppress it because it was true.

As Professor Alexis Jay's report said: 'Several councillors interviewed believed that by opening up these issues they could be "giving oxygen" to racist perspectives that might in turn attract extremist political groups and threaten community cohesion.'[14] In other words they feared the reaction of local people if the media were permitted to report the truth and people were allowed free discussion of the facts. Or to put it more bluntly, they suspected that the Rotherham public were a malleable lynch-mob-in-waiting, a collection of puppets that could be inflamed into race riots by a spark from a Home Office report or a newspaper investigation.

As former Rotherham Labour MP Denis MacShane, who lost his seat and was jailed as a consequence of the parliamentary expenses scandal, admitted: 'There was a culture of not wanting to rock the multicultural boat.'[15] The authorities feared that there might be race riots in Rotherham if locals heard a bad word about child sexual exploitation from the press or right-wing politicians. So interfering in the right of the public to know the facts and judge for themselves became the first instinct of liberal-minded officials and politicians. Rather than have uncomfortable truths in the public domain, they tried to keep the free-speech genie in the bottle.

This was not done in the name of restricting free speech of course, but of protecting the innocent and maintaining community cohesion. Whatever they called it, the result of interfering with free speech and limiting debate was, as always, to make matters far worse. When the long-suppressed truth finally came out there were no race riots in Rotherham – people are not the mindless automatons that some appear to believe. But the scandal left deep divisions and scars that threatened to sink, never mind rock, the multicultural boat.

The Rotherham child abuse scandal revealed a wider truth about attitudes to freedom of speech today. We have reached the point where the instinct of those who think of themselves as enlightened is often to demand less free speech and to restrict the freedom of the press – key gains of the Enlightenment – all in the name of protecting 'ordinary people' from the evil media.

Listening to those who want more controls on the hated 'popular press' and the 'mass media', one might almost think it was better to be unpopular. It helps, I have long thought, to recall that the word 'popular' has its origins in the Latin *populus* – the people. Attacks on the 'popular press' and 'mass media' are often code words for the elite's fear and loathing of the populace, the masses who are supposedly stupid enough to be duped by media messages telling them how to vote (in reality TV shows and real elections), who to hate, and which celebrities to worship.

In our allegedly enlightened age, it is no longer considered decent (at least outside the more old-fashioned gentlemen's clubs) to talk about 'ordinary people' as if they were proletarian scum or tasteless chewing gum stuck to the bottom of one's riding boot. The fall of a UK government minister who insulted policemen in Downing Street as 'fucking plebs' in 2012 was instructive. Tory MP Andrew Mitchell lost his power and the subsequent 2014 libel case, not for using the f-word – nobody cares about that anymore – but the degrading p-word. Labour MP Emily Thornberry was promptly 'resigned' from her front-bench post in November 2014 without saying a word, after she tweeted a photograph of a white van outside a house festooned with England football flags, interpreted as a snapshot of the Labour Party's contempt for its traditional working-class voters.

If you cannot insult the populace directly, however, you can do it via attacks on the popular press that imply the moral inferiority of those who put the mass in the mass media. This is the respectable way to draw a line between the enlightened few and the herd who are prey to the dark arts of the media manipulators.

There is a long history here. Arguments about controlling the media's output have often been underwritten by attitudes to controlling the people's thoughts. Those who fear and loathe the mass of people and their passions tend to favour more control over what they are allowed to see, hear or read. Those who believe in an unfettered media are more likely to believe in people's capacity to consider everything and choose what is right for themselves.

When popular movements to change society are on the up, support for media freedom tends to rise with them – from the flourishing printing presses in England and America during their respective revolutionary eras of the seventeenth and eighteenth centuries, to the many political online blogs that sprang up during more recent popular protests around the world. But when faith in humanity is out of fashion, as across much of Western culture today, media-bashing comes more into vogue as a proxy for expressing contempt for the masses who have disappointed their betters.

The struggle over how free the media should be to educate, inform, entertain, outrage and entice the populace has raged for more than 500 years, since William Caxton introduced the first printing press into England in 1476. Through the sixteenth and into the seventeenth century, the English state imposed a system of Crown licensing to control what could legitimately be published and read. Nothing could be legally printed without the prior approval of the Star Chamber, a secret court of king's councillors and judges, and the official Stationer's Company. State licensing also spread to the American colonies in an attempt to control what could be printed there.

It was during the English Revolution of the 1640s that the popular demand for freedom of the printing press first exploded. Amid the power struggle between King Charles and parliament came 'the revolt of the pamphleteers', who published their unlicensed writings demanding religious and civil liberty and saw freedom of the press as a vital tool to hold government to account. John Lilburne of the radical Leveller movement called for a free press and an end to state licensing, demanding of parliament 'that you will open the press, whereby all treacherous and tyrannical designes may be the easier discovered, and so prevented ... which such only as intend a tyrannie are engaged to prohibit'.[16]

The first aim of many pioneers of the popular struggle for a free press was to win the freedom to express their heretical religious beliefs. Yet their argument was as much about Man as it was God. They believed that God had granted them the ability to separate truth from falsehood. There was no need for earthly authorities to control what was published, since Man was capable of reading all sides and judging what was right. The poet John Milton spelt it out in his call for an end to licensing in *Areopagitica* (1644):'God gave him reason, he gave him freedom to choose, for reason is but choosing.' To use God's gifts of reason and freedom of choice, mankind must have 'the liberty to know, to argue, and to utter freely according to conscience, above all liberties'.[17]

These seventeenth-century Puritans believed that those whom Lilburne called 'the meanest' in society could be trusted to think and say what their conscience suggested, without the need to protect them from dangerous ideas by policing what was published. Their faith in God went alongside a faith in humanity. (Though they drew the line at any notion of extending freedom of the press to 'Papists'.) Today, by contrast, our allegedly liberal elite often appears to have lost faith in our humanity – and hence in freedom of the media. The Puritans of the past can almost look like open-minded humanists compared with the misanthropic attitudes of some modern illiberal liberals.

It is in the modern age that the practice of attacking the mass media as a proxy for attacking the masses has really come into its own. By the approach of the twentieth century, the British working classes were becoming better organised and educated. Three UK parliamentary reform acts, the last in 1884, had extended the right to vote to more working men (women would be denied the vote until well into the twentieth century). The industrial trade union movement was gaining members and clout. And British workers were devouring the new industrially printed mass newspapers such as the *Daily Mail*, launched by Lord Northcliffe in 1896 to 'deal with what interests the mass of people' (and thus to maximise sales).

The rise of these uppity plebs who no longer appeared to know their place horrified many among the upper classes and their political supporters. Yet they could not respond like the lords of old. No longer able to give the lower orders a public flogging, the elites instead appointed the popular press as a whipping boy. Flaying the vulgarity of the new mass media became a proxy for beating the vulgar masses. Newspapers were denounced from on high as an evil of the modern age for debasing public culture by pandering to 'what interests the mass of people'.

The new proxy war on the mass media was often led by highminded intellectuals and literati who, lacking the political skills of those who wanted the masses' votes, failed to conceal that their loathing of the press was really aimed at the readers. For German philosopher Friedrich Nietzsche, the rabble 'vomit their bile, and call it a newspaper'.[18] English author D. H. Lawrence wanted schools closed and reading discouraged to protect workers from those 'tissues of leprosy', popular books and newspapers'.[19] The writer H. G. Wells hated newspapers because he considered their readers as fearsomely alien as the Martians in his novel *The War of the Worlds*. Professor John Carey, author of *The Intellectuals and the Masses*, is clear on the prejudice underpinning Wells's hatred of 'popular newspapers': 'Newspapers were dangerous, Wells believed, because the profit motive forced them to appeal to the most crude and vulgar passions, such as patriotism and war-fever. This made them prime organs of mass hatred. A popular newspaper was, in a quite literal sense, a "poison rag".[20]

The elites of the first half of the twentieth century decried the mass media as a cipher for expressing their disgust at the masses. Their real concern was not so much low media standards as the low culture of the lower classes who consumed it.

In more recent times, the elites' proxy war against the mass media in the UK and US – now including television and the internet as well as traditional newspapers – has been joined by the modern left, seeking scapegoats for their frequent failure to win over the mass of voters.

Hume's law of inverse proportion states that 'the less fulsome support Labour and the Left receive from voters, the more fierce their attacks on the mass media become; the less certain they are of the loyalty of working people, the more certain they become that the popular press is exerting malign influence'.[21] All political parties on both sides of the Atlantic have at times been guilty of peddling this it-was-the-media-wot-lost-it excuse, though Labour and the US Democrats have pushed it hardest of late. The Anglo-American left has projected its disappointment with the masses onto the mass media.

In the eighteenth century, English MPs wanted to restrict the reporting of parliament in order to prevent the people being 'misled by printers', and to protect them from newspapers 'for their good'. Today's politicians similarly seem to believe that gullible and apathetic voters are at the mercy of the modern mass media and should be protected for their own good.

When Margaret Thatcher's Conservatives were sweeping all before them in the 1980s, the Labour Party blamed the influence of the Tory press, displacing its own political crisis onto the mass media. Labour demanded statutory backing for stronger press regulation, in the apparent belief that paper rules could alter political realities. Meanwhile the Tory government was keen to blame its problems on the influence of BBC television and radio, accused of displaying an 'institutional left-wing bias'.

The political row about alleged media influence over the passive masses famously came to a head around the 1992 UK general election. Labour lost for the fourth successive election, despite Thatcher having been ousted and Britain being in an economic mess. 'It's the *Sun* wot won it!' boasted that paper's front-page headline. Labour leader Neil Kinnock had an anti-tabloid tantrum, blaming the press for his defeat and threatening to report it to the Press Complaints Commission, as if that regulatory body could award him the election. The *Sun* responded that Kinnock's claim that it had duped the electorate was 'an insult to the intelligence of the 14 million people who voted Conservative'.[22] In fact both the original headline and Kinnock's tantrum insulted the electorate, who were accused of dancing to the tune of the Pavlovian press.

Rather less was heard from Labour about the evils of the mass media later in the 1990s, when Tony Blair courted the support of the Murdoch press and New Labour romped to victory in three UK general elections. However, as his government's fortunes plummeted, Blair suddenly rediscovered the evil of mass media influence over politics. Shortly before being replaced as prime minister by Gordon Brown in 2007, Blair turned on the media 'feral beast' that 'hunts in a pack' with a 'seriously adverse' impact on 'the way public life is conducted'. He confessed New Labour had paid 'inordinate attention' to 'courting, persuading and assuaging the media'. Few could dispute that the convergence of the UK's political and media elites into a single oligarchy had become a serious issue. However Blair apparently noticed this was a problem only once he could no longer court, persuade or assuage the electorate to vote for him.[23]

In the 2010 general election the *Sun* deserted New Labour and Prime Minister Brown lost power. The result sparked a violent spasm of media-bashing as Labour supporters sought a scapegoat for their dismal failure. Having effectively gone into hiding after his defeat, Brown appeared in parliament to make one speech, accusing News International of having 'descended from the gutter to the sewer' as part of a 'criminal-media nexus'.[24] Did Brown raise these criminal allegations during his many meetings as prime minister with NI editors and executives? Miraculously it appears that the scales only fell from New Labour eyes once they fell from office. Does anybody seriously believe that Labour MPs would have pursued the phone-hacking scandal with the same ardour if the *Sun* had stayed loyal to Brown? Or is it a coincidence that Labour discovered its belief in limiting media ownership only after it had lost the support of the Murdoch press?

The attack might be on the mass media, but the underlying message is that stupid voters are to blame for being brainwashed. It was telling that when Rupert Murdoch appeared before the Leveson Inquiry into the press in April 2012, the front cover of the *New Statesman*, house journal of the Labour left, called him 'The puppet master'[25] and accused him of manipulating our democracy. The implication appeared clear enough; puppet masters, after all, can only really manipulate wooden-headed marionettes which they dangle on strings.

In American politics, meanwhile, a similar law of inverse proportion appears to operate. The more the Democrats lose the support of working people, the more wildly they will lash out at the media they blame for (lizard-)brainwashing the electorate. This came to a head at the end of 2014, when Obama's Democrats sought a scapegoat for their trouncing in the mid-term Congressional elections. Karen Carter Peterson, chair of the Louisiana Democratic Party, had a perfectly rational explanation for her party being all but wiped out in a state they once dominated. The 'fact of the matter', she said, was that 'the non-stop onslaught of negative and inflammatory Koch Brothers ads, added to the toxic media environment driven by Fox News and the right-wing echo chamber, have made it challenging for us to drive out our message to voters'.[26] It could not be that those voters actually got the message about what the Democrats had done in office and voted them out accordingly. No, it was all the fault of the 'toxic' right-wing media and 'inflammatory' adverts funded by the Kochs' political action committee, which somehow tricked no fewer than 56 per cent of the electorate into voting for Republican Bill Cassidy rather than three-term Democrat Senator Mary Landrieu.

The left cannot claim a monopoly on the blame-the-meejah PR line. At the same time as leading Democrats were blaming the conservative Fox News for their electoral problems, Republicans were up in arms about the liberal bias of the mainstream network news. The suspension of NBC news anchor Brian Williams in February 2015, over allegations that he had embellished the truth in reporting from wars and disasters, was seized upon as proof of the sort of mainstream media manipulation that the Republicans alleged had helped win the White House for President Obama. 'If they lie about things like this,' demanded defeated Republican vice-presidential candidate Sarah Palin, 'what and who else do they lie about?' It brought to mind an earlier age when Senator Jesse Helms, leader of the Republican right, had branded CBS news anchor Walter Cronkite as 'a participant in a vast ultra-liberal mechanism tirelessly dedicated to brainwashing the American public'.[27] At least nobody could accuse Senator Helms of delivering his attack in code.

It is undeniable that newspapers, television and now the web have a big influence in politics. It is also evident that, with the decline of political party membership and activism, the media sphere has become the big battleground in UK and US politics, with more and more political events fitting Daniel Boorstin's definition of a 'pseudo-event' – non-spontaneous events that are staged primarily in order to be reported in the media.[28] Understanding that process, however, is a long way from swallowing the notion that the mass media has exerted an authoritarian malign influence over politics or even that, as in the conspiratorial mind of one leading Labour MP, the Murdoch media has had 'a poisonous, secretive influence on public life' and 'orchestrated public life from the shadows'.[29] That remains an easy excuse with which politicians of all parties can seek to explain away their own loss of influence and authority among the public. The underlying sentiment expressed is too often a disdain for the masses, and a wish to regulate people's thoughts and actions by curbing the media that supposedly manipulates them like puppets.

When all of that is said and done, and we have separated the propaganda from the proof, it remains indisputable that the rich and powerful inevitably have more opportunity than others to exercise their right to free speech via the media. Even in Anglo-American societies where formal free speech prevails, having a voice that can be heard is not something most of us can take for granted.

The question is, what is to be done about it? And the answer should be that whatever response we choose, supporting efforts to get the state to curb the freedom of the media can only make matters worse. The only way any of us can have a proper opportunity to exercise freedom of speech is if that right is defended across society and not undermined further for anybody.

Free speech is an indivisible liberty. You cannot start tampering with it for one group – even if the group is press barons or PR executives – and expect it to remain intact for everybody else. Once the bulwark has been breached and the cultural support for the principle of freedom of the press and of speech is compromised, everything is called into question. And once free speech is openly called into question it ceases to be a right.

Free speech is not a zero-sum game, where you somehow have to decrease the rights of others in order to increase your own. It is not a negotiable commodity that can somehow be 'redistributed' away from the rich and powerful towards the rest. To infringe on the right to free speech of others can only risk undermining your own capacity to exercise it. Those who fought, suffered and sometimes died for freedom of speech and of the press through the history of the West demanded the extension of those rights to the lowest and 'the meanest' in society, not their removal from the upper echelons.

When the former slave Frederick Douglass made 'A Plea for Free Speech in Boston' in 1860, after a meeting to discuss the abolition of US slavery was attacked by 'a mob of gentlemen', he was adamant that the 'sacred' right to free speech in America would mean nothing unless it was extended to all: 'When a man is allowed to speak because he is rich and powerful, it aggravates the crime of denying the right to the poor and humble.' Yet Douglass's demand was for freedom of speech to be allowed across society, not removed from the powerful pro-slavery gentlemen: 'There can be no right of speech where any man, however lifted up, or however humble, however young, or however old, is overawed by force, and compelled to suppress his honest sentiments.'[30]

A key issue in the modern debate is our attitude to the state. State regulation and control has long been the enemy of freedom of speech and of the press. Granting the authorities more power to decide who deserves those freedoms, however progressive-sounding the pretext might be, can only open the door for the state to extend its deadening influence over public debate.

As the media has fallen deeper into disrepute in enlightened quarters, an argument has surfaced that says freedom of speech for individuals and freedom of the press should be considered separately: the first is a Good Thing, the second not necessarily. Putting forward her proposals for a tighter system of statutory regulation of the UK press, ethics professor Onora O'Neill told the Leveson Inquiry in 2012 that: 'An argument for free speech for the powerless will not make a case for free speech for powerful organisations' and that the media do not qualify for self-expression because they

are not 'selves'.[31] Such legalistic wordplay and dancing on the head
of a philosophical pin ignores the way that freedom of speech and
of the press have advanced hand-in-hand through the historic
struggle for liberty; there is a good reason why the US First
Amendment couples them together as rights to be equally
protected from the sort of state intrusion which Professor O'Neill
et al. support for the UK press. Despite their patronising claims to
speak for 'the powerless', the ethical elite's underlying concern in
encouraging the state to limit free speech for 'powerful organisations' is that the public lack the mental powers to resist media
brainwashing and so need protecting for their own good.

There is always a difference between formal legal equal rights and
real inequalities in society. As the old saw goes, it is equally illegal
for either the rich or the poor to sleep on park benches, but somehow only the poor get arrested for it. Similarly, since the abolition
of state licensing it has been equally possible for anybody to establish a national newspaper or (if they can get the regulators' permission) a television station. Yet somehow only the very rich seem to
do so.

The power which a few large entities can exercise over much of
the Anglo-American media is a longstanding problem. It is likely
to remain so at least until we are all billionaires or the billionaires
all become socialists. In the meantime, we can moan about media
empires and encourage the state to restrict their freedoms. Or we
can strive to remove all legal and cultural obstacles to freedom of
expression, in order to maximise the opportunities for broadening
the debate and creating an alternative media.

One historical trend that the discussion of Western media
empires tends to avoid is the consistent failure to create any popular alternative media. There have always been big barriers to
successful media 'start-ups', yet the internet has already given a
glimpse of opportunities to create a new media on an unprecedented scale. Thirty years ago those of us involved in the 'alterna-

tive' press in the UK were selling small radical newspapers and magazines on a few street corners. Today we can talk to the world through internet publications such as the web magazine of which I was founding editor, Spiked-online.com. Other online publications such as Huffpo, Salon and Guido Fawkes have shown the possibility of popular challenges to the mainstream. The problem is that, for all of its flashy formats, far too much of the 'new' media has adapted to the wider climate of dull conformism in its content. If all those who spend their time and energy bemoaning the 'toxic' influence of the mass media instead devoted their efforts to creating a serious alternative via the web, and developing some new ideas to spread through it, who knows where we might end up?

One area which we should definitely be concerned about is the ability of the rich and powerful to prevent critical voices being heard, through the libel laws. Despite recent liberalising reforms, the UK's notoriously censorious laws of defamation remain among the worst in the civilised world (as I believed and argued even before I lost a punitive libel case in 2000). The huge costs and penalties involved, and the way the rules are stacked against defendants, do not only punish those relative few who fight and lose a libel suit in London's Royal Courts of Justice. They also have a far wider 'chilling effect' on the exercise of free speech, making many reluctant to risk the wrath of the corporate lawyers by publishing anything too critical. The American system which, since 1964, has effectively made it impossible for a public figure to sue for libel, unless the publication was motivated by malice, is far friendlier to free speech and open debate of important issues. The US also now refuses to enforce judgements obtained by 'libel tourists' in London courts. Defenders of press freedom might do even better to revive and update the spirit of the great London newspaper essayist of the eighteenth century, 'Cato', who declared: 'I must own, that I would rather many libels should escape than the liberty of the press should be infringed.'[32]

It would be good to strive for a freer, more open and open-minded media via the web, that could provide outlets for more voices and different opinions. But it would not be good to imagine that situation can be brought about by greater state intervention and regulation of press freedom. Yet today one-eyed campaigners for UK media reform demand compulsory state-enforced 'diversity'.

One 'Manifesto for Media Reform', issued by prominent lobby groups for the 2015 UK general election, sums up the problem. Its ostensible aim is to make the media 'more accountable and more responsive to the public they serve'. Yet the only way these media activists can envisage that is through more state intervention and control, not just to limit concentration of media ownership but to regulate what the media does. Never mind that freedom nonsense, they demand that 'communications should be organised and regulated in the public interest'. The question such committee-speak always raises is: who is going to do the organising and regulating, and who will decide what we mean by 'the public interest'? And the answer is: not the public. The manifesto wants 'stronger powers' for the government's regulatory quango, Ofcom. It also demands that 'the nations of the UK through their elected assemblies should be granted greater powers over the regulation of the media'. This might sound nice and people-friendly, but is basically a coded way of calling for greater political control, something that defenders of freedom of speech and of the press have fought against for 500-odd years.

These radical reformers also appear to think that they could encourage greater diversity of media ownership by getting the state to fund alternative media from the public purse. Even if it were possible to obtain such funding in an age of austerity, there would be far too high a price to pay for it. Such officially sanctioned 'diversity' would inevitably involve applying for state funding by ticking enough boxes. The results of the process are evident across the UK's publicly-funded cultural sectors – more politically and culturally-correct conformism, imposed in the name of greater diversity. Nothing could seem more certain to crush the spirit of new voices in the media than having to dance to the tune of a new breed of state licensers.[33]

In America, meanwhile, some radical Democrats have even begun to see the First Amendment as a problem rather than a precious resource – because of the way it grants freedom of speech to pro-business voices of which they disapprove. Writing for the *New Republic*, stalwart journal of American liberalism for the past century, Professor Tim Wu of Columbia Law School warns that corporations have 'hijacked the First Amendment'. He cites cases such as the tobacco industry's 2012 'use of the First Amendment to have new, scarier health warnings on cigarette packaging thrown out on the grounds that the labels constituted compelled speech'. Judgements such as that one, says the liberal law professor, are 'what makes the First Amendment such a dangerous weapon' today.

No doubt it is true that top lawyers will use US free speech law to try to justify all manner of corporate messages and evade regulation. That is no reason to start condemning the First Amendment, the best legal safeguard of freedom in the Western world, as 'a dangerous weapon' against liberalism. Once the First Amendment's defence of free speech for all is called into question for some, nobody's rights will be safe. As the veteran liberal lawyer Floyd Abrams, who won fame representing the *New York Times* in the 1971 Pentagon Papers case and has more recently represented corporations in First Amendment cases, told the nonplussed Professor Wu, 'Speech is so important, we must refuse to limit it. It doesn't matter who is speaking.' That principle of defending 'freedom for the thought that we hate' should surely apply to corporate PR just as much as to Islamist preaching or KKK propaganda.[34]

Once media freedom is portrayed as the problem, the 'solution' tends to be more state intervention and regulation. Professor Cass

R. Sunstein, an influential legal scholar who was a member of the Obama administration, has long led calls for the US authorities to get tougher with the media in order to diversify freedom of speech. Sunstein has proposed that the US government should take 'affirmative action' to ensure that all points of view are heard on controversial issues, and that the Supreme Court should offer less First Amendment protection to 'lower-value' speech such as advertising, hate speech and violent pornography (of the heterosexual though not the homosexual variety).

Sunstein has also called for a New Deal for speech, involving government intervention to ensure an hour of public affairs programming every night, enforce a mandatory right to reply, and subsidise 'higher-quality' TV shows as well as a more 'serious' and 'substantive' press. This amounts to a manifesto for snobs and social engineers, proposing how the US state should use the mass media as an instrument for re-educating the masses in order to emulate their cultural betters. As one conservative reviewer of Sunstein's original book on these issues had it twenty years ago, he ultimately 'endorses the Orwellian view that in order to safeguard freedom of speech, what is needed is more regulation'.[35]

These schemes for state-sponsored diversity are really about trying to change the media to suit the agenda of social engineers. They are a recipe for conformity in the name of diversity, sanitising that which is not to the taste of those for whom 'popular' is a dirty word. They would also mean handing more power to interfere in press freedom to the state authorities. As ever, the question is: who do you trust to regulate public debate and decide what should be published, and by whom? Some of us would always rather leave it up to the public rather than the state to see everything and judge for themselves what is good for the 'public interest'.

* * *

In various ways, the arguments for greater restrictions on the power of the mass media all rest on the myth that the press and the media are too free to do as they like. This turns an important truth on its head. Especially in the UK, the media is nowhere near free or open enough even before any new rules and regulations are imposed.

There are already far too many formal rules and regulations, such as the execrable libel laws, impinging on freedom of the press. More dangerous still is the informal culture of conformism across much of the media that makes official censorship largely unnecessary. In his 1945 essay, 'The Freedom of the Press' George Orwell admitted that, for much of the Second World War, state censorship in Britain had not been 'particularly irksome'. Instead the media and cultural elites had generally censored themselves, particularly by rejecting criticism of Britain's ally, Stalin's Soviet Union: 'Unpopular ideas can be silenced, and inconvenient facts kept dark, without the need for any official ban ... [T]hings which on their own merits would get the big headlines [have been] kept right out of the British press, not because the Government intervened but because of a general tacit agreement that it "wouldn't do" to mention that particular fact.'[36] This 'tacit agreement' to suppress the truth not only covered the newspapers owned by rich press barons, but 'the same kind of veiled censorship also operates in books and periodicals, as well as in plays, films and radio. At any given moment there is an orthodoxy, a body of ideas which it is assumed that all right-thinking people will accept without question ... Anyone who challenges the prevailing orthodoxy finds himself silenced with surprising effectiveness. A genuinely unfashionable opinion is almost never given a fair hearing, either in the popular press or in the highbrow periodicals.'

Today's pervasive culture of You-Can't-Say-That has much the same effect on narrowing the minds of the media as the 'It wouldn't do' wartime consensus – and a new generation of the 'renegade liberals' whom Orwell identified as deserting the cause of freedom are enforcing the orthodoxy. We are often warned in the multi-media age that people are bombarded with too many adverts and images. A bigger problem in the one-note media age is that we are presented with far too few choices in the marketplace of ideas and news reports.

No doubt there are many problems with the press and the wider media. But history suggests there is always one thing worse than a free press, and that is its opposite. Nowhere in the world today is the problem with the media that it is 'too free'. When I have made that point in public debates, by the way, my opponents have several times demanded 'What about Rwanda?' Their argument is that the bloody 1994 massacres there happened after an extremist radio station demanded it – therefore, a less free Rwandan media might have averted genocide. The notion that Africans are simple folk who would take up machetes and massacre each other for no more complex reason than that the radio told them to reveals the sort of anti-popular prejudices that too often lie behind the apparently radical demands for more control of the media.

Putting up with the broadcast of what you might not like in the media and letting others choose what they see or read or consume or vote for is part of the price of defending freedom of expression for us all. As the young Karl Marx told the Prussian state censors almost 150 years ago, when they tried to suggest that only what they deemed a moral and decent press should be free: 'You cannot enjoy the advantages of a free press without putting up with its inconveniences. You cannot pluck the rose without its thorns! And what do you lose with a free press?'[37] Without defending freedom for the press and the media against state intrusion and sanitisation, however, we risk losing a big battle in the free-speech wars.

A short summation
for the defence

What, in the end, do we lose if we quietly give up on defending free speech as an indivisible liberty? Fighting for freedom of speech has played a crucial role in the advance of civilisation and liberty through history. But what will we really be giving up today if we allow new restrictions, formal and/or informal, to be placed around that freedom?

Nothing that is worth defending, say supporters of measures to curb offensive speech. Some might lose the 'right' to spout racist or homophobic bigotry, but who wants to fight for that? Meanwhile what we all gain, they will claim, is a safer, more civil society where people have to respect each other. After all, it's not as if the UK and US are about to be turned into Saudi Arabia, where bloggers can be flogged for offending the authorities, is it?

Nice try. The problem is we risk losing far more than that if we allow free speech to be but-ed into submission today. And the losers will be more than a few extremists.

What we are facing in Anglo-American society today is not old-fashioned censorship, but new forms of strait-laced conformism. There is a prohibitive atmosphere hanging over many public discussions, where the threat of being told that You-Can't-Say-That always seems to be just a rhetorical slip away. People might not be formally barred from expressing an opinion, but are often unsure of where the limits of acceptable speech lie.

There is no need to dream up horror fantasies of a dystopian future in which freedom is crushed under a jackboot. The real trends in our culture that have been discussed here already point the way towards a society in which the stymying of debate and the fettering of free speech risk robbing us of the chance of a better future.

One thing we are in danger of losing is the meaning of words. What language is anybody allowed to use to express themselves today? The rules and codes are always shifting and, generally, narrowing the acceptable terms of debate. The award-winning actor Benedict Cumberbatch can be hauled over the coals for letting slip the word 'coloured', even though he was trying to highlight racial discrimination. When the *Sun* accurately described the pilot who deliberately crashed a passenger plane into the Alps, killing 149, as a 'madman in the cockpit', it was widely lambasted for giving what one academic called 'a kick in the teeth for people who suffer from mental health issues'.[1]

In a world where there is such confusion about the meaning of language, and nobody can be sure what they are allowed to say anymore, the danger is that words lose their meaning. Instead of meaningful debates, we are left with empty exercises in tiptoeing around words that have become detached from reality. An obsession with using the correct language and code words, rather than saying what we believe to be right, is a recipe for self-censorship and apologies rather than clarity through argument.

We also risk losing sight of new ways to advance human knowledge. How can knowledge flourish in an atmosphere where there are questions that cannot be asked and arguments that cannot be had? For example, when debates about anything from the history of the Holocaust to the causes of climate change or the efficacy of rape laws can all be ended with a shout of 'Denier!' it is not only the proponents of alternative or crankish views who lose out. Some of the well-founded arguments of modernity – the undeniable case for racial or sexual equality, for example – risk losing their intellectual dynamism without being tested, and instead become arid prejudices that are never properly justified but only repeated by rote. That is unlikely to advance our knowledge, or to convince future generations to accept the traditions and values of our society. From science through history or politics, open discussion and the ability to question everything are the tools we need to keep sharp if we hope to test what is right and prove what we believe to be the truth.

We are in danger, too, of losing the lifeblood of important political and moral debates. In a world where You-Can't-Say-That, for fear of causing offence or inflaming opinions, many controversial issues will be taken off the table for debate and put into suspended animation. There can be no free and open debate about the pros and cons of immigration, for example, or the morals of Islam, in case these issues prove 'inflammatory' to some section of the allegedly wooden-headed public. There can be no proper discussion about the future of the family, or same-sex marriage, due to anxieties about attracting a charge of homophobia.

It is a sign of the times that in US court hearings about the legality of same-sex marriage in 2015, no top law firms proved willing to represent the traditionalists who oppose gay marriage on religious principle. In the past leading American lawyers have recognised that even such unpopular figures as British soldiers accused of the 1770 Boston massacres, or opponents of racial desegregation in schools, or Guantanamo Bay detainees accused of al-Qaeda links, were entitled to the best legal representation. Now opponents of gay marriage, who still reflect a sizeable minority of American public opinion, are not to be allowed proper representation.[2]

Without full and frank debate of controversial issues there can be no proper conclusions, simply declarations that 'the issue is settled' leaving unresolved tensions waiting to burst forth. We are left uncertain of what minorities or the majority in society really believe or deem acceptable. Young people in particular will be taught how to follow – or secretly reject – rules and etiquettes, but not how to make properly-informed moral judgements or arguments about what is good or bad.

We are also in danger of losing the ability to be different, to say something out of the ordinary and shake up the world. We live in an Anglo-American culture where the emphasis seems always to be on the need for safety, for avoiding offence and making others feel comfortable. If this continues the likely upshot will be an anodyne culture in which any opinion considered too strong or colourful or strange must be toned down, whether it is expressed in a satirical magazine, a football chant or a university seminar. If you want to imagine that grey future, picture not Orwell's image of a boot stamping on a human face, but the human mind and imagination drowning slowly in a bland blancmange of colourless conformity.

And we are in danger too of losing our sense of independent adulthood. Too many demands for restricting freedom of expression today reflect the assumption that adults need to be treated like vulnerable children, swaddled in protective blankets for their own safety and security. The phrase 'Not in front of the children' has traditionally been used to distinguish between what is considered fit to say or show to adults but not to our offspring. That line is becoming increasingly blurred.

These patronising attacks on freedom of expression infantilise adult life. They risk robbing people of the moral autonomy that is central to a system based on free speech – the freedom to listen, think, and judge for yourself. And they inevitably hand the authorities the power to act *in loco parentis*, to protect us from each other and ourselves.

Freedom of thought and speech is essentially about the liberty to make your own choices. That has long been a mark of mature adulthood, as opposed to the childish acquiescence in doing what you are told is good for you. Dependent children have to learn to talk. Autonomous adults have to learn again how to deliberate and argue for themselves. Unfree speech is for children, who should sometimes still be seen but not heard and protected from bad words. Free speech is for adults in a grown-up world of give and take who do not need to be spoilt, cosseted, coddled or swaddled for our own good.

So yes, we have a lot to lose by giving up the fight for freedom of expression. The one thing we do need to lose instead is the fear of free speech. As the subtitle of this book suggests, it is the fear of being offensive that risks 'killing free speech'.

Far too much public discussion today focuses on the dangers of allowing speech to run wild and free. If we let any Tom, Dick or Ali say what they like, we are warned, it runs the risk of encouraging extremism – inciting hatred of Muslims, or provoking Islamic terrorism, or in some other way letting loose the beast supposedly lurking within us all. (All of us, that is, apart from the enlightened few who issue these warnings.)

Fear of free speech is about far more than the unlikely prospect of being shot for your opinions or cartoons. That is the far end of a spectrum of fear that begins with the embarrassment of saying something different from what is expected, and the sense that one should apologise the moment anybody takes exception.

That fear is not entirely unfounded. Free speech is far from being the risk-free easy option. Words can hurt, talk can start trouble and even wars, there are words and opinions that some might reasonably think would be better unsaid, and freedom does inevitably mean that other people are free to talk and tweet out of their backsides as well as their frontal lobes.

Yet whatever discomforting symptoms it might bring on or risks it might entail, in the end free speech is always a price worth paying, and the alternative of restricting it out of fear is always worse.

But, some might say, what about *Charlie Hebdo*? Wasn't that massacre a consequence of the cartoonists 'going too far' with their insulting caricatures of Muhammad? Wasn't it 'natural', as the Pope suggested, that their provocations would be met with 'a punch', or worse? Wouldn't a little less freedom and a little more discretion have avoided the tragedy? The implication is that had the cartoonists been a bit more fearful of the consequences of free speech, they might still be here. Some others may draw that conclusion to be careful about what they say or draw in future.

But the *Charlie Hebdo* massacre was not provoked by too much press freedom. To suggest that it was is to give in to the murderers.

If that violence was invited by anything, it was actually the public displays of fear of free speech and the over-sensitivity about giving offence in the upper echelons of French and wider Western society. The authorities have legitimised and institutionalised the culture of You-Can't-Say-That. That official fear of free speech, as I argued at the start of the book, can only have handed the murderers political ammunition by endorsing the idea that the offensive cartoonists had gone too far.

To suggest now that the *Charlie Hebdo* victims provoked the attack and would have been better off using blunter pencils is little different from how the police and Labour council not only tried to blame those girls in Rotherham for their own abuse but also attempted to stop the press reporting it, for fear of how people might react. Freedom of speech is not the problem. Fear of it is.

No doubt the right to free speech has been used to pursue all manner of offensive ends down the centuries. But we should not accept that as an excuse for limiting it today. The value of free speech outweighs the possible harm, and defending 'freedom for the thought that we hate' is the only sure way to protect it for all. As the Polish-born leader of German revolutionaries Rosa Luxemburg nailed it a century ago: '*Freedom* is always and exclusively *freedom* for the one who thinks differently.'[3] Some of those who fought the historic battles for freedom of speech and of the press used it for low purposes, from John Wilkes, the English scandalmonger and pornographer in the eighteenth century, to Larry Flynt, the *Hustler* publisher in the twentieth, who pithily captured the essence of why it is important to defend the right to be offensive: 'If the First Amendment will protect a scumbag like me, it will protect all of you.'[4]

Defending the right to be offensive need not mean celebrating obnoxiousness or looking for the opportunity to exercise that right at somebody else's expense. It is about upholding the freedom to think what you like and say what you think. It is for others then to take offence or not (which they are fully entitled to do, so long as they don't imagine that gives them the 'right' to take away yours). Our sole responsibility should be to ensure that we have expressed the truth as we understand it, clarified the argument or cracked the joke to the best of our abilities, then allow others the same freedom to respond.

The fear of free speech for all is often ultimately based on fear and loathing of the masses, who might dare to use that freedom as they see fit rather than as they are told. Support for freedom of expression always blooms at moments in history when humanity is marching forward and filled with confidence in itself; it shrivels in more fearful and misanthropic times. That is why supporting unfettered free speech today is a declaration of faith in the future, an invitation to an open, no-holds-barred debate about the sort of societies in which we, and our children, might want to live. To accept instead that it should be restricted would be an admission that we fear the future too much to trust people to think and decide for themselves. We need more free speech and open debate if we are to stand a chance of resolving the conflicts in our society today and creating a less fearful tomorrow.

If anything, public debate today would benefit from some more seriously offensive – or offensively serious – arguments. It would be good to use the right to be offensive in a more meaningful fashion, and not just to draw naughty cartoons or make edgy jokes (although there is nothing wrong with either of those) but to pose some bigger questions about many of the accepted truths of our culture today, starting with questioning the notion that free speech is too offensive to be let loose.

Over the past century, many of the great debates about free speech and its limits in the Anglo-American world have focused on cases heard in the US Supreme Court. Perhaps then we might leave the final thought on the fear of free speech to Justice Louis Brandeis, from a 1927 Supreme Court case that considered the conviction in California of Anna Whitney, a member of the Communist Labor Party of America, for engaging in speech deemed to have threatened society. Justice Brandeis insisted that, before speech could be restrained, 'there must be reasonable ground to fear that serious evil will result if free speech is practiced' and reasonable ground to believe that the danger is 'imminent'. He dismissed the notion that mere fear of what might happen could be ground for suppressing speech, in words that echo down the decades: 'Fear of serious injury cannot alone justify suppression of free speech and assembly. Men feared witches and burnt women. It is the function of speech to free men from the bondage of irrational fears.'[5]

Despite that rousing declaration, Brandeis then went on to vote with the rest of the Supreme Court judges to uphold Whitney's conviction for speech crimes. Proof, if any more were needed post-*Charlie*, that whatever fine words we hear from the Western authorities, free speech is never a liberty that can be taken for granted.

Epilogue

The Trigger Warnings we need

Trigger Warnings have become symbols of the culture of You-Can't-Say-That. Those ominous letters 'TW' have spread across university campuses, the Atlantic and the web like banners of the forces driving back free speech. As the title of this book suggests, it is time we raised new banners to warn about the dangers posed by the silent war on free speech today.

Trigger Warnings point a gun at the head of free speech and demand it surrenders. They appear at the start of books, films, articles or news reports to warn that the following contains words or images which some might find harmful or disturbing, followed by a list of all the things we are supposed to be wary of – from A for Ableism or B for Bi-phobia, to X for Xenophobia or Z for Zionism.

The idea began as a questionable attempt to warn mental health sufferers that an online posting contained violent or sexual content that might 'trigger' an unhappy memory and cause a disturbed reaction. Now it seems as if encountering any sort of potentially challenging or offensive speech can be equated with a damaging mental health episode.

Trigger Warnings have become the modern equivalent of those 'Here Be Dragons' notices that used to be inscribed on uncharted areas of ancient maps. They are an invitation to self-censorship, to cover your eyes and ears pre-emptively – and in the process, to close your mind. And they point the way towards more official censorship by our increasingly offence-sensitive authorities. Trigger Warnings are the enemies of freedom of expression and open discussion.

We are living, as this book argues, in the age of the reverse-Voltaires, who would far rather close down debate than suffer others' freedom of speech, and whose core belief can be summarised as 'I know I will detest what you say, and I will fight to the end of free speech for my right to prevent you saying it.' The reverse-Voltaires love Trigger Warnings, which enable them to tell us what we should – and more importantly, should not – see, read or hear, for our own good of course.

Time we turned the situation around, and set up some alternative Trigger Warnings to alert us to attacks on free speech.

If we are to expose the free-speech fraud and defend our liberties today, we need a different kind of internal Trigger Warning. One that will alert us whenever we hear the sort of coded language and weasel words in which the free-speech wars are now being fought.

The phrases listed here are all invitations, if not orders, to shut up and withdraw from the rhetorical fray. The code words used are changing and mutating all the time, but the essential message is always the same: either You-Can't-Say-THAT, or YOU-Can't-Say-That – and quite possibly, both. The reaction of those who care about freedom should be to do the opposite, and insist on the right to think what we like and say what we think.

Yes, we do need to be more sensitive. We need to be more sensitive to what's really being said in these double-talk debates, the dangerous implications of the demand to restrict speech however it is excused. And then we need to crack the code and bring the free-speech frauds to book.

Here are just some of the coded arguments I have come across in the course of writing this short book that should trigger a fighting response for free speech.

'This is not a free-speech issue.'
This a pretty sure sign that, yes, it is.

The first shot fired in the silent war on free speech is often an assurance that the bans or proscriptions on speech being demanded really have nothing to do with attacking freedom of expression. Of course the fraudsters assure us that they all support free speech, but this is about something else – hate or harassment, national security or personal safety. The reverse-Voltaires are so impressed with the magic power of words (especially their own) that they appear to believe if they say something is so, we must all believe it to be true.

What they usually mean is 'This is not a me-speech issue'. It is not infringing on their free speech, so it's not a problem. But free speech is not the same as me-speech, never mind me-me-me speech. It is always primarily about defending freedom for the other fellow, for the one who thinks differently. Not everything is a free-speech issue – direct threats of violence don't count, for instance, and neither does swearing too loudly in a bar or the library. But anything that interferes with anybody's right to express an opinion, tell a joke, chant a song – or their right to criticise somebody else for doing so – *is* a free-speech issue, whether some might like to think so or not. Not just an 'issue' that needs to be discussed, either, but one that should be straightforwardly resolved in favour of free speech. The biggest free-speech issue of all should be any attempt to restrict it whilst claiming that you're not.

'Of course I believe in free speech, but …'
This is the one most often guaranteed to give the game away that no, in fact, you don't.

Ours is the age of the but-heads, when almost nobody opposes free speech 'in principle', but Principle is seemingly another country and they do things differently there. In Practice, back here on Earth, many have a 'but' to wave around in the face of free speech to explain why the freedom to express an opinion should go thus far, but no further, like 'free'-range livestock caged in a pen.

This might sound reasonable. But (to use the only language some people seem to understand) the problem is that, like all meaningful liberties, free speech has to be a universal and indivisible right. Once you apply a 'but', impose a condition or attach a string, it ceases to be a right. Instead it becomes a concession to be rationed by somebody in authority. (If the but-heads stopped at 'but I don't believe in the right to demand money with menaces', few would disagree; their multiplying buts, however, are aimed against 'offensive' ideas and opinions with which they simply disagree.)

Those ubiquitous 'buts' don't just qualify a commitment to free speech, they crush it. To claim to believe in free speech, but … is akin to insisting that you believe in an Almighty God, but you don't think He's all that. It might be better if the but-heads came clean and confessed that they don't really believe in free speech after all.

'We should defend free speech, but not hate speech.'
That might sound a no-brainer. After all, who could be in favour of hate speech? But the tougher questions are these: Which words exactly should qualify as hate speech? And who would you trust to decide which forms of speech should be sent to the chopping block?

There is no more agreement on the meaning of hate speech than on the definition of an internet troll. One person's heartfelt opinion or religious belief might be another's hate-filled rant. By the same token, nobody has the universal authority to float above the fray and make impartial decisions about which form of words to punish or prohibit. Everybody has an agenda and interests of their own. And control-freak governments and judges will always take requests to restrict one kind of speech as an invitation to restrict another.

The hard truth is that, to be free, freedom of speech and thought must include the right to hate who you choose – just as much as to love who you want. To defend free speech but not the freedom to spout 'hate speech' is a contradiction in terms. Don't you just hate it when your no-brainer turns out to be nonsense?

'Check your privilege before you speak to me.'

Perhaps those who use this excuse could check their self-righteousness before they say that. Free speech is a right for all, not a privilege to be restricted to a few – whether they be the lords of the manor or the activists of the transgender lobby.

This is one of the newer generation of coded assaults on free speech. It expresses the notion that only certain people should have the right to speak about certain issues, that the 'privileged' should not presume to talk about issues of oppression or inequality. It is about identity groups claiming a monopoly on the truth about themselves. So don't talk about racism unless you're black, but black men have no business sticking their noses into black women's affairs. Woe betide any man or 'person without a uterus' who wants to express an opinion on abortion, or a 'cisgender' individual of either sex who dares to disagree with the transgender lobby's self-definition. (Variations on the 'privilege' theme might include being accused of 'mansplaining' an issue to women, or 'straightsplaining' a question to gays. Some straight talking would surely be a welcome alternative.)

The demand to 'check your privilege' is posed as an anti-elitist attempt to give a voice to the voiceless. The irony is it expresses an inverse elitism, a wish among some to keep free speech for themselves. Once upon a time we were told that public discussion of important matters was the exclusive preserve of kings and cardinals, barons and bishops. Now we have a new version of that selective attitude to speech, updated for the age of identity politics. The effect is the same – to turn speech itself into a privilege, not a right, to be granted only to the 'right' class of people.

The demand to restrict speech on these issues stands in stark contrast to the attitude of past campaigners for black, women's or lesbian and gay rights, who understood that winning free speech for all was the necessary precondition for their liberation. The language may have changed, but the truth remains that making speech less free is no path to liberation for anybody.

'Rights come with responsibilities.'

No, they do not. Otherwise they cease to be liberties belonging to us by right, and transmogrify into concessions granted by governments and judges with conditions attached like chains.

It would be good to hope that everybody might use their right to free speech in a responsible fashion, and take responsibility for what they say or write. That does not mean, however, that they should be restricted to saying only what others approve of. The right to free speech has to mean that other people are not responsible to you or me for what they say or think. Nobody has to pass an ethics test or gain a licence in logical argument in order to qualify for freedom of expression. If we have a responsibility it is only to speak what we believe to be the truth – and leave others free to disagree.

'We have the right to feel safe and comfortable.'

If you're talking about the need to feel safe from violence and comfortable in decent housing, fine. But as a demand to be protected against other people's opinions – that 'right' is wrong.

The fashion for 'safe spaces' in universities is code for turning campuses into gated comfort zones, where nobody has to confront challenging ideas or opinions. That's the opposite of the open-minded debate and inquiry upon which university life depends. Safe-space policies and the demand to be 'comfortable' have spread from US campuses across the Anglo-American world. They are used to demand the exclusion of any speech students claim to find upsetting, whether that be alleged Islamist extremism or alleged Islamophobia. After the *Charlie Hebdo* massacre, a UK student official made clear that the satirical magazine would have been banned from his campus anyway for infringing 'safe-space' policies.

These measures risk turning campuses into soporific cocoons, where students and academics are protected from anything that might wake them up or ask them to think differently. They don't just infringe on the free-speech rights of a few, but rob the rest of the freedom to listen and judge for themselves – and possibly even to change their minds. To use 'feeling comfortable' as an excuse for restricting free speech puts the risk of a tummy upset above the principle of moral autonomy. It treats students – young adults – as a cross between helpless toddlers and stuck-in-their-ways pensioners. Free speech and open debate can certainly be uncomfortable, and you are entitled to shelter from it if you prefer. But that does not give you the right to stick your fingers in everybody else's ears so they can't listen either.

'We cannot tolerate intolerance.'

This is really a cute way of justifying censorship in the name of freedom from oppression. That ought to be an intolerable twisting of the truth.

An avowed refusal to tolerate intolerance has been used to ban speakers or adverts accused of anything from homophobia to Islamophobia. It brings to mind Big Brother's official language, Newspeak, from Orwell's *Nineteen Eighty-Four*, which is notorious for making words such as 'freedom' mean their opposite. The new use of 'tolerance' as a justification for censorship fits that bill.

True tolerance means precisely allowing the expression of ideas and opinions which you find objectionable, including those that are intolerant of other people's freedoms. It does not mean stamping on 'intolerant' views with a politically correct boot. But neither does it mean pussy-footing around the problem and allowing everybody to express their prejudices with impunity. True tolerance is about bringing it all out into the open, to allow the fullest and freest debate. It is about enabling a battle of opinions to the bitter end. By contrast, the fashion for intolerance in the name of tolerance means closing down that debate before it has even begun. The only tolerable response to bad speech is more speech, not just those two little words 'zero tolerance'.

'That's x-phobic!'

It seems madness to try to brand opinions you disagree with as mental health problems.

There is an apparent epidemic of phobias in Anglo-American society, and it is spreading. First the emphasis was on the problem of homophobia, then on the rise of Islamophobia, now there is talk of transphobia, Afrophobia, fatphobia, whatevaphobia. A phobia, lest we forget, is defined as 'an irrational fear of or aversion to something'. To call the expression of different ideas 'phobic' means to damn them not just as objectionable opinions, but as symptoms of a psychiatric disorder. It says that your own views on, say, Islam or homosexuality are so normal and unquestionable that any opposite opinion must be the product of a disturbed mind. And of course there is no point debating with the opinions of the 'phobics', since they are irrational and dangerous. Far better to muzzle and quarantine the carriers, as one would mad dogs suspected of hydrophobia.

If there is a 'phobia' on display here (though we should perhaps hesitate to use the word), it is surely the fear and loathing of other people's speech and non-conformist opinions. It might even look like a symptom of your own narcissistic personality disorder to imagine that anybody with the opposite strongly held views to you must be slightly mad. It is worth recalling that the authoritarian Stalinist regime in the old Soviet Union was keen on accusing its political critics of mental health problems and imprisoning them in psychiatric institutions. That seems a poor role model for anybody interested in challenging prejudice today.

'You're a Denier!'

To accuse your opponents of telling lies about an issue is no excuse for denying them their right to freedom of speech.

Along with all those multiplying phobias, there appears to be a dangerous epidemic of denial across Western societies. First the focus was on the problem of Holocaust denial. Now we are also warned that public debate has been infected by climate-change denial, racism denial, rape denial, inequality denial and many more variants up to and including 'denial denial'.

And as with allegations of 'phobia', the consequences of accusing somebody of denial are far-reaching. It means that they have crossed the line from expressing an honest opinion to acting out a psychiatric disorder. To call somebody a denier these days is not simply to accuse them of honestly disputing the orthodoxy of the day, like old-time heretics such as Socrates or Galileo. 'Denial' is now bandied about in the language of psychiatry, to mean that somebody is suppressing some unquestionable truth about the Holocaust or climate change – denying facts which everybody knows are true. As such, there is deemed to be no point in debating with them. Instead their views – and possibly their persons – should be locked away in a straitjacket to prevent them doing any harm.

Yet even if you think they are twisted liars, those branded deniers should still have the right to free speech for reasons of both principle and practice. In principle, free speech must be defended for all or it will be safe for none at all; and it is the extreme or unpalatable opinion that needs protecting most. Defend free speech for them and the mainstream will look after itself. In practice, the only way to be sure of the truth is to allow it to be tested from all directions. Of course we know that the Holocaust is an historical fact. But that does not mean its history is beyond debate; as Deborah Lipstadt, American author and scourge of Holocaust deniers, says, it is not theology. Far from affirming the truth, to try to silence critics and opponents instead by beating them with the allegation of 'denial' inevitably raises the question: what have you got to hide?

'You're an apologist!'

To accuse somebody of being a dishonest apologist for some evil is a sorry excuse for avoiding engaging with their arguments.

Apologists appear to be close relations of deniers. They too are not to be treated as the holders of honest, if arguably misguided, opinions. Instead they are accused of spreading disingenuous arguments as a cynical excuse for something or somebody beyond the pale. Question changes to UK law that might make it harder for men to defend themselves against accusations of sexual assault, and you risk being branded a 'rape apologist'. To criticise plans to confine cigarettes to plain packs is to invite the allegation that you are just an 'apologist for Big Tobacco'. And so it goes.

The implication is that, since these opinions fall outside the conformist consensus in the media and politics, they cannot be real. Nobody could seriously think that! Instead the alleged apologists are essentially accused of spreading black propaganda for the forces of darkness – and often accused of being paid to do so. In which case, why should anybody bother engaging with their arguments? Just shout them down or shut them up instead. The irony is that brandishing the accusation 'apologist!' becomes a handy excuse for those lacking persuasive arguments of their own.

Sorry, but nobody should have to apologise for their opinions – or be denied the right to express them by being branded with a scarlet letter 'A' for apologist, like the shunned Adulterers of Puritan times.

'The debate is over!'

Perhaps a more honest way of putting it might be: 'I am so Over having a debate with You!'

First we were told that the debate about man-made global warming was over. Now the same line turns up in regard to multiple other issues; President Barack Obama even suggested that the debate about his contentious 'Obamacare' programme was over. The US writer Joel Kotkin calls this spreading phenomenon 'Debate is Over Syndrome', and it appears to be contagious. When such a syndrome moves so easily from one issue to another, it is a sign that the specifics of those issues are less important than the broader underlying hostility to free speech and open-minded debate.

The assertion that the debate is over and, therefore, you should have no right to speak is rather like the modern, secular version of the religious Inquisitors of old declaring that 'I can persecute you because I am right and you are wrong'. It denies the legitimacy of any challenge to the orthodoxy of the day. But in a free and civilised society, no debate should ever really be declared over. Even in the field of science. Scepticism and questioning everything remain the stuff on which the scientific method is based. And how much more important that openness is when you move to the fiercely contested arena of political debate over the future direction of society.

If you don't want to engage in a debate, that's your business. Nobody is under any obligation to exercise their right to free speech. But don't presume to tell anybody else what they can or cannot say, and which debates are 'over'. Closed debates are not for open minds.

'Your words oppress me – that's microaggression.'
Those who want to restrict free speech today tend to imbue words with magic powers, like ancient curses. That can involve debasing both the language, and the meaning of a real-life problem such as oppression.

The notion that words can oppress makes a nonsense of the concept in the present and insults the struggles of the past. Oppression involves the denial of equal legal and social rights to a group. That is what women, black people, gays and colonial peoples fought against in the past, often suffering and even dying in the struggle for liberty. It does not mean somebody being a bit rude or making you feel uncomfortable with the way they talk.

When racist language was commonplace in UK and US society, it was a reflection of the real power and respectability of racism in our politics and culture. Now that racism is no longer respectable, and old-fashioned racist language is rarely heard, we are left with a ghost struggle against often-ordinary words which are accused of 'unwitting racism'. The concept of 'microaggression' takes things a step further, finding oppression in the most minor interactions of everyday life – such as somebody using the pronoun 'him' or, in one reported case, a US college professor being accused of racism for correcting his students' spelling and grammar.

Words can be weapons in a battle of ideas or a slanging match. But words are not literally weapons with which to do violent harm, or magic spells with the power to oppress. We need to give more power to speech, not less, and set it free to debate issues from the real meaning of oppression to the correct use of language.

'Stop your dog-whistle arguments!'
It is a dog of an argument that would suggest the public are a pack of dumb beasts.

A dog whistle gives off a high-pitched note that is undetectable to the human ear; only dogs with their sensitive hearing can detect and respond to it. The allegation of using a dog-whistle argument or dog-whistle politics means that you are deploying language whose hidden message will only be picked up and responded to by a particular 'breed' of listener – more often than not those considered susceptible to racism or other political prejudices. Just as a high-pitched whistle can make trained dogs come running or attack a designated target, so the claim is that a shrill scream can provoke the pack animals among the public to use their votes or violence as they are told by the whistler.

This seemingly liberal argument reveals what some who would restrict free speech really think about 'ordinary people'; that they are dumb animals to be turned into a rabid pack by a whistle from an inflammatory orator. As always, your view of free speech reflects and reinforces your opinion of humanity.

However shrill they might seem, speakers and writers are not animal-trainers, and the public is not a pack of dogs to come running at their whistle. It would be better to stop such people-baiting complaints and get on with winning the argument.

'By calling for a ban on your speech, we're exercising our free speech!'

Are we living in such a looking-glass world that the reverse-Voltaires can seriously claim their loud demands for censorship demonstrate free speech in action?

It is a hallmark of what I have called the silent war on free speech that few want to admit that they are against that liberty in principle. The reverse-Voltaires insist that their attempts to restrict what somebody else can say are not really an attack on his freedom of speech. This reaches its nadir in the argument that the ones demanding a speaker be 'No Platformed' into silence are true champions of free speech. They are exercising the inalienable right to express their opinion, which just happens to be that you should not be allowed to express yours.

Anybody does indeed have the right to use their freedom of speech in order to argue against it. Free speech is for fanatics and hysterics, too. And anybody has the right to deliver a forceful response to what somebody else has to say. Although it is normally considered good practice to hear what that might be first.

But nobody has the 'right' to deny freedom of expression to somebody else in the name of freedom, however objectionable their opinion might appear. To try to do so is an act both of censoriousness and of stupidity, since it denies us the chance to decide for ourselves and does nothing to refute the other's argument. Nor will the argument wash that 'it's not censorship because it's not the state doing it'. The informal, unofficial censorship exercised by the online mob of reverse-Voltaires is the most commonplace and pernicious threat in the age of the silent war.

However you try to dress it up, demanding No Platform for opinions you dislike is the reactionary action of cowards (who don't trust their own ability to win an argument) and prigs (who don't think others should be allowed to hear naughty words). You are free to call it the exercise of free speech if you choose. Just as long as we're free to tell you what you can do with your No Platform placards.

'There is no freedom to shout "Fire!" in a crowded theatre!'
Who exactly is demanding the 'right' to do that? But there must be a right to express an opinion, however inflammatory the authorities might think it.

The old ones are the worst. This one-line dismissal of the right to unfettered free speech has been around almost 100 years, yet if anything is trotted out more often than ever these days. It was first coined by Justice Oliver Wendell Holmes of the US Supreme Court in a 1919 case, to dismiss the free-speech defence of Socialists convicted of agitating against military conscription during the First World War.

The full story of the shouting-fire-in-a-theatre ruling is told in chapter 7. Suffice to say here that it was wrong then, is wrong now, and has not even really been part of American law since the 1960s. So why does this outdated theatrical line still make such frequent appearances in arguments about everything from Islamophobia to climate change or sexist comedians?

The allegation of shouting-fire-in-a-theatre has become an access-all-areas ticket to justify restricting any sort of speech which somebody deems inflammatory. It usually rests on the assumption that the public, like a panicking crowd who think there's a fire in a theatre, will stampede at the mention of a 'trigger' word. That assumption in turn rests on a view of people as a wooden-headed mob-in-waiting, who can be set ablaze by a spark from an inflammatory orator.

This view of the public is more than a rhetorical prejudice. It has been used to jail people in the UK for nothing more than the words they used on social media. They have been convicted of offences ranging from 'incitement to racial and religious hatred' to 'incitement to terrorism' merely for expressing opinions which the elites feared might inflame the great British public. As so often, the disdain with which the authorities view freedom of speech in the fringe political theatre reflects the contempt in which they hold the wider audience.

In fact it is acceptable to shout fire if the theatre is ablaze. In any case it is a health and safety issue that has nothing to do with anybody's free speech. There should, however, be a right to express an opinion – including, or especially, in times of crisis and war when the future of society is up for grabs. Inciting the commitment of a crime is a crime. However, today's attempts to broaden the definition of criminal incitement pose an unwarranted danger to free speech. To 'incite' can mean simply to urge others to act in some way. So all arguments are an 'incitement' of sorts. We should not allow anybody to pick and choose which opinions to allow to be expressed on the basis of a judge's misruling from another century. That is an attack on free speech for us all, no matter how you dress it up for a night at the theatre.

'Free speech is all well and good but you don't have the right to insult other people's beliefs.'

In fact if you don't have the right to be offensive to others' beliefs – and if others don't have the right to do the same to you – then free speech is not 'all well and good'. It would be worthless and dead.

The right to be offensive is not, as the Pope seems to think, about being able to curse somebody's mother with impunity. It does not mean making a virtue of personal insults. And it is not only about the freedom to publish provocative cartoons (although that right should be defended).

It is primarily about the right to offend other people's beliefs, by challenging their fundamental worldview and questioning what they deem the unquestionable. And it is not only, as some seemed to think after *Charlie Hebdo,* about the right to offend Islam. No belief-system should be immune from being interrogated and offended, be it fascism or radical feminism, flat-earthism or environmentalism.

The right to be offensive is not an optional bolt-on to free speech, to be 'butted' out of existence leaving the principle intact. What is 'free' about speech if we are only permitted to say that which others find agreeable? Without fighting for the heretical right to offend against society's consensus views and to question the unquestionable orthodoxies of the age, many of the great political, cultural, scientific or artistic breakthroughs that we now take for granted would have been hard to imagine.

The right to be offensive does not, of course, imply any obligation to offend others. Just because you can say it, does not mean you always should. And the fact that there is no law against it doesn't necessarily make it morally right. There is nothing big or clever about being offensive as an end in itself; but as a means to striving for the truth, whether through politics or comedy, it is often unavoidable and always indispensable. A wise writer said that: 'An honest man speaks the truth, though it may give offence; a vain man, in order that it may.' An important distinction, so long as we remember that, just as the rain falls on the just and the unjust, so the right to free speech must fall on those who speak out of vanity as well as honesty.

'Trigger Warning'
Trigger Warnings themselves speak volumes about what is wrong with contemporary attitudes to freedom of speech. They are the

battle standards of the army of reverse-Voltaires and but-heads who insist that You-Can't-Say-That, listen to this, or read the other. They encapsulate the attitude that potentially hurt feelings are more important than universal free speech, and that freedom of expression is not a right but a privilege that should come with conditions, chains and warnings not to step off the edge of the known world.

Let the spreading appearance of those letters 'TW' be a warning to those who appreciate free speech as the most important liberty of all. Trigger Warnings that hold a pistol to the head of free speech should have us all reaching for our metaphorical guns to fight for the right to think what we like, and say what we think.

Notes

Prologue: 'Je Suis Charlie' and the free-speech fraud

1. The audio recording of the attack on the Copenhagen meeting is available at https://audioboom.com/boos/2897267-audio-of-copenhagen-shooting#t=0m0s
2. *Daily Mail*, 15 January 2015.
3. *International Business Times*, 12 January 2015, www.ibtimes.com/charlie-hebdo-china-limited-press-freedom-will-prevent-similar-attacks-state-media-1780304
4. Professor Marc Lynch, cited *Washington Post*, 11 January 2015.
5. Tony Barber, *Financial Times*, 7 January 2015.
6. http://www.theguardian.com/politics/2011/jul/08/david-cameron-speech-phone-hacking
7. Quoted *Guardian*, 7 January 2015; *Guardian*, 7 February 2015.
8. *Guardian*, 9 February 2015.
9. Labourlist.org, 7 January 2015, labourlist.org/2015/01/harman-warns-against-chilling-effect-on-free-speech-after-charlie-hebdo-attack/
10. *Press Gazette*, 25 February 2015, www.pressgazette.co.uk/harriet-harman-labour-will-have-mandate-follow-through-leveson-if-it-wins-general-election
11. Will Self, 'The Charlie Hebdo attack and the awkward truths about our fetish for "free speech"', Vice.com, 9 January 2015.
12. *London Review of Books*, vol. 37, no. 3, 5 February 2015.

13. http://www.c-span.org/video/?323637-2/secretary-state-john-kerry-paris-terror-attack

14. www.mediate.com, 26 January 2015.

15. Catholicleague.org, 7 January 2015.

16. Becky Ackers, 'Sticks and stones aren't the only things that break bones', Lew Rockwell, 8 January 2015, www.lewrockwell.com/lrc-blog/sticks-and-stones-arent-the-only-things-that-break-bones/

17. www.kittystryker.com/2015/01/unpopular-opinion-satire-should-punch-up-charlie-hebdo-did-not/

18. npr.org, 6 February 2015, www.npr.org/blogs/ombudsman/2015/02/06/382170260/last-thoughts-npr-and-the-balance-between-ethics-and-the-nation

19. http://reason.com/blog/2015/01/08/charlie-hebdo-agnostics-im-against-murder

20. Cited *New York Daily News*, 11 January 2015, http://www.nydailynews.com/news/world/charlie-hebdo-cartoonist-scoffs-vomits-supporters-article-1.2072906

21. http://www.frontpagemag.com/2015/truthrevolt-org/andrew-klavan-attack-of-the-but-heads/

22. Cited *Guardian*, 7 February 2007.

23. Bruce Crumley, 'Firebombed French paper is no free speech martyr', *Time*, 2 November 2011, http://world.time.com/2011/11/02/firebombed-french-paper-a-victim-of-islamistsor-its-own-obnoxious-islamophobia/

24. *Private Eye*, no. 1386, February 2015.

25. Quoted mediaite.com, 15 January 2015.

26. *Living Marxism*, no. 63, January 1994.

27. K. Malik, *From Fatwa to Jihad: the Rushdie Affair and its Legacy*, Atlantic Books, London, 2010, p. 145.

28. Quoted in *Spiked*, 6 December 2007, http://www.spiked-online.com/newsite/article/4159#.VRajq-FsycE

29. Faithinourfamilies.com, 8 January 2015.

30. *The Times*, 17 March 2015.

Notes

1: A few things we forgot about free speech

1. Thomas Paine, *The Age of Reason*, 1794, from *Selected Writings*, The Franklin Library, 1979, p. 236.
2. Orwell, 'The Freedom of the Press', 1945, cited in Appendix I to George Orwell, *Animal Farm*, Secker & Warburg, 1987.
3. Quoted mediaite.com, 15 January 2015.
4. *Chaplinsky v. New Hampshire*, 1942, www.law.cornell.edu/supremecourt/text/315/568; *Street v. New York*, 1969, www.law.cornell.edu/supremecourt/text/394/576; *Gooding v. Wilson*, 1972, www.supreme.justia.com/cases/federal/us/405/518/case.html
5. *Gettysburg Times*, 24 June 1999.
6. Benedict de Spinoza, *A Theological-Political Treatise*, 1670, http://www.sacred-texts.com/phi/spinoza/treat/tpt28.htm
7. Cited in Louis Edward Ingelhart, *Press and Speech Freedoms in the World, From Antiquity Until 1998: a Chronology*, Greenwood Press, Connecticut, 1998, p. 61.
8. Speech published by the Colonial Williamsburg Foundation, www.history.org/almanack/life/politics/giveme.cfm
9. Alabama Department of Archives and History, www.archives.state.al.us/teacher/slavery/slave1.html
10. 'A Plea for Free Speech in Boston', 1860, classiclit.about.com/library/bl-etexts/fdouglass/bl-fdoug-freespeech.htm
11. Reprinted by Reporters Without Border, www.rsf.org/IMG/pdf/Charter08.pdf
12. http://www.imdb.com/title/tt0118715/quotes
13. David Feldman, *Civil Liberties and Human Rights in England and Wales*, Oxford University Press, 2002, p. 753.
14. ibid., p. 752.
15. ibid., p. 770.
16. Cited in Anthony Lewis, *Freedom for the Thought That We Hate: a Biography of the First Amendment*, Basic Books, New York, 2009, p. 107.
17. Mehdi Hassan, 'As a Muslim, I'm fed up with the hypocrisy of the free speech fundamentalists', *New Statesman*, 13 January 2015, http://www.newstatesman.com/mehdihasan/2015/01/muslim-i-m-fed-hypocrisy-free-speech-fundamentalists
18. J. S. Mill, *On Liberty*, 1859, Oxford World's Classics, 1998, p. 9.

2: The age of the reverse-Voltaires

1. www.frontpagemag.com/2015/truthrevolt-org/andrew-klavan-attack-of-the-but-heads/

2. *Sunday Mirror/Independent on Sunday* political poll, 13 June 2014.

3. Mark Johnson and Conor Gearty, 'Civil liberties and the challenge of terrorism', in Park, A., J. Curtice, K. Thomson, M. Phillips and M. Johnson (eds), *British Social Attitudes: the 23rd Report*, Sage, London, 2007, p. 168.

4. http://www.newseum.org/wp-content/uploads/2014/08/connect_blog_SOFA14-infographic.jpg

5. Evelyn Beatrice Hall, *The Friends of Voltaire*, 1907 (originally published in 1906 under the pseudonym S. G. Tallentyre).

6. Philip Johnston, *Feel Free to Say It*, Civitas, 2013, p. 7.

7. ibid., p. 3.

8. *Washington Post*, 1 July 2014.

9. Quoted in *Guardian*, 7 April 2012.

10. www.state.gov, 15 July 2011.

11. *Daily Mail*, 19 November 2014.

12. *Guardian*, 19 November 2014.

13. Nadine Strossen, *Defending Pornography: Free Speech, Sex and the Fight for Women's Rights*, NYU Press Paperback, 2000 edition, pp. 41–2.

14. John O'Sullivan, 'No Offense: The New Threats to Free Speech', *Wall Street Journal*, 31 October 2014, www.wsj.com/articles/no-offense-the-new-threats-to-free-speech-1414783663

15. Karl Marx, 'Censorship', *Rheinische Zeitung*, no. 135, 15 May 1842.

16. For a full list of the signatories see Hacked Off website, 18 March 2014, http://hackinginquiry.org/mediareleases/declarationmarch18/

17. *Mail on Sunday*, 19 June 2014.

18. Quoted in the *Observer*, 28 September 2014.

19. Lee Jasper, Operation Black Vote, 1 September 2014.

20. Cited in the *Independent*, 24 September 2014.

21. *New York Times*, 26 April 2014, http://www.nytimes.com/2014/04/27/sports/basketball/nba-clippers-owner-donald-sterling.html?_r=0

22. *Mirror*, 10 May 2014.

23. *Daily Mail*, 21 August 2014.

24. Cited in Catherine Bowen, *The Lion and the Throne*, Hamish Hamilton, 1957, p. 298.
25. Thomas Hobbes, *Leviathan*, Part One 1651, Wildside Press 2008 edition, p. 61.
26. Kathleen Parker, *Washington Post*, 29 April 2014.
27. Twitchy.com, 30 April 2014.
28. 'Policing private speech: the new inquisition', Spiked-online.com, 22 May 2014, http://www.spiked-online.com/freespeechnow/fsn_article/policing-private-speech-the-new-inquisition#.VRa86uFsycE
29. George Orwell, *Nineteen Eighty-Four* (1949), Penguin 1979 edition, p. 169.

3: A history of free-speech heretics

1. Lord Denning, former Master of the Rolls, cited magnacarta800th.com/schools/downloads-and-resources/magna-carta-quotations/
2. E. P. Cheyney (translator), *Translations and Reprints from the Original Sources of European History*, University of Pennsylvania Press, 1898, vol. IV, no. 3, pp. 3–5.
3. BBC Radio 4, 'Voices of the powerless – readings from original sources', 25 July 2002, www.bbc.co.uk/radio4/history/voices/voices_reading_revolt.shtml
4. family.twinn.co.uk/The-Trial-of-John-Twyn-for-High-Treason-16634.html
5. Cited in Tzvetan Todorov, *In Defence of the Enlightenment*, Atlantic Books, 2010, p. 70.
6. David A. Copeland, *The Idea of a Free Press: the Enlightenment and Its Unruly Legacy*, Northwestern University Press, 2006, p. 39.
7. Arlene W. Saxonhouse, *Free Speech and Democracy in Ancient Athens*, Cambridge University Press, New York, 2006, p. 30.
8. ibid., p. 105.
9. ibid., p. 212.
10. http://files.libertyfund.org/pll/quotes/51.html
11. Cited http://spartacus-educational.com/STUputneydebates.htm
12. John Locke, *A Letter Concerning Toleration*, 1689, Broadview Press, 2013.
13. Cited in George Rudé, *Wilkes and Liberty*, Lawrence and Wishart 1983 edition, p. 162.
14. Louis Kronenberger, *The Extraordinary Mr Wilkes*, New English Library, 1974, p. 33.

15. David A. Copeland, *The Idea of a Free Press: the Enlightenment and Its Unruly Legacy*, Northwestern University Press, 2006, p. 164.
16. ibid., p. 186.
17. Leonard Levy, cited in Walter Berns, *The First Amendment and the Future of American Democracy*, Gateway Editions, Illinois, 1985, pp. 84–5.
18. ibid., p. 117.
19. Karl Marx, 'On Freedom of the Press', first published 1842 in the *Rheinische Zeitung*, www.marxists.org/archive/marx/works/1842/free-press/
20. J. S. Mill, *On Liberty*, 1859, Oxford World's Classics, 1998, p. 21.
21. Michael Kent Curtis, *Free Speech, 'The People's Darling Privilege': Struggles for Freedom of Expression in American History*, Duke University Press, 2000, p. 117.
22. Philip S. Foner, *The Industrial Workers of the World 1905–17*, New World Paperbacks 1980 edition, p. 195.
23. ibid., p. 213.
24. *New York Times v. Sullivan*, https://supreme.justia.com/cases/federal/us/376/254/case.html
25. *Brandenburg v. Ohio*, https://supreme.justia.com/cases/federal/us/395/444/case.html
26. *Cohen v. California*, https://supreme.justia.com/cases/federal/us/403/15/case.html

4: The Internet Front: hunting for trolls down 'memory holes'

1. Quoted on technocrunch, 5 June 2013.
2. John Lindow, *Swedish Legends and Folktales*, University of California Press, Berkeley, 1978, p. 33.
3. Yougov survey, 10 October 2014.
4. Backbytes, computing.co.uk, 27 October 2014, www.computing.co.uk/ctg/news-analysis/2377787/backbytes-america-a-nation-of-online-trolls
5. CNN International Edition, 28 November 2014.
6. The Verge, 4 February 2015, www.theverge.com/2015/2/4/7982099/twitter-ceo-sent-memo-taking-personal-responsibility-for-the
7. Media Guardian, 22 March 2012.
8. *Guardian*, 20 May 2011.
9. *Mail on Sunday*, 18 October 2014.

10. *Mirror*, 19 October 2014.
11. *Independent Voices*, 20 October 2014.
12. *Watts v. United States*, https://supreme.justia.com/cases/federal/us/394/705/case.html
13. Quoted *Independent*, 5 October 2014.
14. *Washington Post*, 31 October 2014.
15. Cited Jeffrey Rosen, 'The right to be forgotten', *Stanford Law Review*, 13 February 2012.
16. BBC News online, 12 October 2014.
17. Orwell, *Nineteen Eighty-Four*, Penguin 1979 edition, p. 199.
18. ibid., p. 34.
19. Orwell, *Nineteen Eighty-Four*, ibid., p. 198.
20. Cited Techcitynews.com, 6 August 2014.

5: The University Front: students fight for 'freedom FROM speech'

1. Cited Mediaite.com, 31 October 2014.
2. See Tom Slater, 'When students believed in liberty', *Spiked*, 26 September 2014.
3. Cited on *Spiked*, 4 November 2014.
4. BBC News online, 25 October 2014.
5. Disraeli, Speech to the House of Commons, 11 March 1873.
6. BBC News online, 7 October 2014.
7. Isabel Hardman, *Spectator* blogs, 20 November 2014.
8. BBC News online, 28 November 2014.
9. *Guardian*, 31 March 2015.
10. *New Statesman*, 20 February 2015.
11. Greg Lukianoff, 'Freedom From Speech', Encounter Broadside no. 39, New York, 2014, pp. 30–33.
12. Ann Wroe, 'The Necessity of Atheism: 200 Years Young', in *Grasmere 2011: Selected Papers from the Wordsworth Summer Conference*, ed. Richard Gravil, Wordsworth Conference Foundation, 2011.
13. IowaStateDaily.com, 20 October 2014.
14. 'The trouble with teaching Rape Law', New Yorker.com, 15 December 2014.
15. Jenny Jarvie, 'Trigger Happy', *New Republic*, 3 March 2014.
16. *Columbia Daily Spectator*, 30 April 2015; legalinsurrection.com, 3 May 2015.

6: The Entertainment Front: football – kicking free speech with impunity; comedy – no laughing matter

1. talksport.com/football/he-role-model-and-should-know-better-fa-explains-ludicrous-ferdinand-judgement-141105122950
2. Mick Hume, 'Hillsborough: only half-remembered', *Spiked*, 15 April 2009.
3. *Sunday Times*, 19 May 1985.
4. *Daily Mail*, 13 July 2012.
5. *Guardian*, 9 August 2014.
6. ibid.
7. Stuart Waiton, *Snobs' Law: Criminalising Football Fans in an Age of Intolerance*, Take a Liberty, 2012.
8. STV News, 4 December 2014.
9. Kentonline.co.uk, 6 April 2014.
10. *Spiked*, 17 October 2008.
11. Adrian Hart, *That's Racist! – How the Regulation of Speech and Thought Divides Us All*, Societas, 2014, p. 109.
12. http://www.kickitout.org/news/lord-ouseley-comments-after-chelsea-fans-racist-behaviour-in-paris/#.VRbo-OFsycE
13. Quoted in *Newsweek*, 28 June 1993.
14. Mondoweiss, 26 July 2014; https://www.youtube.com/watch?v=Et38_Ufv-Jw
15. Quoted on Inquisitor.com, 6 August 2014.
16. *Daily Mail*, 28 February 2013.
17. Nancy McDermott, *Spiked*, 5 September 2014.
18. law2.umkc.edu/faculty/projects/ftrials/bruce/brucecourtdecisions.htm
19. CNN.com, 24 December 2003.
20. *Guardian*, 3 April 2014.
21. http://www.chortle.co.uk/correspondents/2014/10/08/21082/youve_helped_create_a_rapists_almanac; http://www.newstatesman.com/internet/2014/11/why-you-should-be-worried-about-dapper-laughs-he-s-making-sexism-mundane
22. vice.com, 10 June 2014.
23. http://www.huffingtonpost.com/2014/12/01/chris-rock-colleges-conservative_n_6250308.html
24. *Guardian*, 31 May 2015.
25. *Observer*, 28 September 2014.

26. The Wrap, 26 November 2013, http://www.thewrap.com/alec-baldwin-joan-rivers/

7: 'There is no right to shout "Fire!" in a crowded theatre'

1. http://www.econjobrumors.com/topic/i-am-not-charlie-hebdo-david-brooks/page/2; http://www.newsmax.com/Headline/bill-donohue-paris-attacks-muslim/2015/01/08/id/617451/
2. https://supreme.justia.com/cases/federal/us/249/47/; Walter Berns, *The First Amendment and the Future of American Democracy*, Gateway Editions, Illinois, 1985, pp. 150–5; Anthony Lewis, *Freedom for the Thought That We Hate*, Basic Books, New York, 2009, pp. 26–7.
3. BBC News online, 12 February 2009.
4. Adam Weinstein, 'Arrest climate-change deniers', gawker.com, 28 March 2014.
5. Reader's comment in the *Observer*, 8 November 2014, http://www.theguardian.com/commentisfree/2014/nov/08/dapper-laughs-vile-humour-misogyny-banter-itv
6. https://supreme.justia.com/cases/federal/us/250/616/; Berns, *First Amendment*, pp. 151–5; Lewis, *Freedom for the Thought*, pp. 28–37.
7. https://supreme.justia.com/cases/federal/us/279/644/case.html; Lewis, pp. 37–8.
8. https://supreme.justia.com/cases/federal/us/395/444/case.html; Lewis, p. 124, p. 159.
9. *Gitlow v. New York*, 1925.
10. *LM* magazine, issue 105, November 1997.
11. Orwell, 'The Freedom of the Press', 1945, cited in Appendix I to George Orwell, *Animal Farm*, Secker & Warburg, 1987.
12. Patrick Sauer, 'The year Montana rounded up citizens for shooting off their mouths', Smithsonian.com, 14 January 2015/www.smithsonianmag.com/history/year-montana-rounded-citizens-shooting-their-mouths-180953876/?no-ist
13. *Daily Mail*, 11 December 2014; BBC News online, 11 December 2014.

8: '... but words will *always* hurt me'

1. http://www.independent.co.uk/news/people/katie-hopkins-reported-to-police-for-hate-crimes-against-overweight-people-in-new-tv-show-9951155.html
2. Stephen Fry, *Moab is My Washpot: an Autobiography*, Hutchinson, 1997, p. 113.
3. Stanley Fish, 'There's no such thing as free speech, and it's a good thing too', in Paul Berman (ed.), *Debating PC: the Controversy over Political Correctness on College Campuses*, Dell Publishing, New York, 1992, pp. 244–5.
4. Richard King, *On Offence: the Politics of Indignation*, Scribe Publications, 2013, p. 42.
5. *Guardian*, 12 May 2014.
6. Thomas Carlyle, 'Sir Walter Scott', in *Carlyle's Works*, vols 15–16, New York International Book Company, 1869, p. 407.
7. J. S. Mill, *On Liberty*, 1859, Oxford World's Classics, 1998, p. 14.
8. Sara Stewart, 'Internet's outrage factory turns on Philip Seymour Hoffman', *New York Post*, 9 February 2014.
9. Frank Furedi, *On Tolerance: a Defence of Moral Independence*, Continuum Books, 2011, p. 153.
10. Cited in King, *On Offence*, p. 217.
11. Cited *New York Post*, 9 February 2014.
12. Jonathan Rauch, *Kindly Inquisitors: the New Attacks on Free Thought*, University of Chicago Press, 1993, p. 18.
13. Nina Shea, 'Hate-speech laws aren't the answer to Islamic extremism – they're part of the problem', *National Review*, 9 January 2015.
14. Ibid.
15. Thomas Jefferson, *Notes on the State of Virginia*, 1782.
16. Yougov, 'America divided on hate speech laws', 2 October 2014, https://today.yougov.com/news/2014/10/02/america-divided-hate-speech-laws/
17. Jeremy Waldron, *The Harm in Hate Speech*, Harvard University Press, 2012; Josie Appleton, 'There ain't no harm in hate speech', *Spiked Review of Books*, 26 October 2012.
18. Cited in *National Review*, 9 January 2015.
19. Varsity, 24 October 2014, http://www.varsity.co.uk/news/7663
20. http://www.theguardian.com/media/2013/jan/14/observer-withdraws-julie-burchill-column; Burchill's censored column is

available at http://blogs.telegraph.co.uk/news/tobyyoung/
100198116/here-is-julie-burchills-censored-observer-article/

21. http://www.glaad.org/reference/transgender
22. Cited in David Allyn, *Make Love, Not War: the Sexual Revolution, an Unfettered History*, Taylor and Francis, 2001, p. 157.
23. Frederick Douglass, 'A Plea for Free Speech in Boston', 1860, classiclit.about.com/library/bl-etexts/fdouglass/bl-fdoug-freespeech.htm
24. J. S. Mill, *On Liberty*, ibid., pp. 59–60.
25. Cited King, *On Offence*, p. 221.

9: 'Mind your Ps, Qs, Ns and Ys'

1. *Daily Mail*, 30 April 2013.
2. http://www.kickitout.org/news/the-pfa-comments-on-awards-ceremony-comedian/#.VRfYs-EZOcE
3. http://www.thefa.com/News/thefa/2013/feb/paul-elliott-statement-230213.aspx
4. *Independent*, 29 April 2013.
5. *Sun*, 27 January 2015.
6. Sigmund Freud, *A General Introduction to Psychoanalysis*, 1917, cited in Craig Conley, *Magic Words: a Dictionary*, Weiser Books, 2008, p. 12.
7. *LA Times*, 29 January 1999, http://articles.latimes.com/1999/jan/29/news/mn-2884
8. http://www.thesun.co.uk/sol/homepage/suncolumnists/jeremyclarkson/5605287/Jeremy-Clarkson-on-n-word-rhyme-scandal.html
9. https://twitter.com/harrietharman/status/462271405024108544
10. *Guardian*, 11 March 2015.
11. 'Now it's a war on words', *Spiked*, 11 February 2009.
12. Cited *Observer*, 8 February 2009.
13. Ibid.
14. www.goodreads.com/quotes/tag/freedom-of-speech?page=3
15. *Wall Street Journal*, 9 November 2014.
16. ibid.
17. *Washington Post*, 20 February 2015.

10: 'Liars and Holocaust deniers do not deserve to be heard'

1. *New York Times*, 1 June 2014.
2. Stephen Snobelen, 'Isaac Newton, heretic: the strategies of a Nicodemite', *British Journal for the History of Science*, 1999, vol. 32, p. 381.
3. Arthur Versluis, *The New Inquisitions; Heretic-Hunting and the Intellectual Origins of Modern Totalitarianism*, Oxford University Press, 2006, p. 7.
4. George Monbiot, *Guardian*, 21 September 2006.
5. http://www.epw.senate.gov/fact.cfm?party=rep&id=264568
6. *Guardian*, 23 June 2008; ABC News, 16 April 2012; Media Lens, 25 February 2014.
7. Gregory Stanton, *The Eight Stages of Genocide*, 1998, www.genocidewatch.org/genocide/8stagesofgenocide.html
8. Ivan Hare and James Weinstein (eds), *Extreme Speech and Democracy*, Oxford University Press, 2009, p. 543.
9. *TES*, 23 January 2009.
10. Deborah Lipstadt, 'Denial should be defeated by facts, not laws', *Spiked*, 16 July 2007.
11. *Research Fortnight*, 16 February 2011, http://www.researchresearch.com/index.php?option=com_news&template=rr_2col&view=article&articleId=1032320
12. 'Crackdown ordered on climate change sceptics', *The Times*, 2 April 2014.
13. J. S. Mill, *On Liberty*, 1859, Oxford World's Classics, 1998, p. 22.
14. ibid., p. 24.
15. Michael Fitzpatrick, 'Even quacks must have free speech', *Spiked*, 19 November 2013.
16. *The Australian*, 25 April 2015.
17. Brendan O'Neill, 'Are you now or have you ever been a climate contrarian?', Spiked, 27 April 2015.

11: 'Free speech is just a licence for the mass media to brainwash the public'

1. Quoted by Guido Fawkes, 25 September 2012.
2. *Sun*, 18 April 2015.
3. Mick Hume, 'The *Sun* 4: "Guilty" of being journalists', Spiked, 23 March 2015.

4. 'If this happened in China there'd be a shitstorm here', *Spiked*, 6 July 2013.

5. *Guardian*, 29 June 2010.

6. Karl Marx, 'On Freedom of the Press', *Rheinische Zeitung*, no. 139, 19 May 1842.

7. www.newsbusters.org/blogs/matt-hadro/2010/10/29/arianna-huffington-thinks-america-voting-gop-out-fear-using-lizard-brain#sthash.fJA8An1q.dpuf

8. ASA adjudication 6 August 2014, asa.org.uk/Rulings/Adjudications/2014/8/Wm-Morrison-Supermarkets-plc/SHP_ADJ_270040.aspx#.VRf7ZuEZOcE

9. *Spiked*, 14 August 2014.

10. Action on Smoking and Health, 'Response to government consultation on standardised packaging of tobacco products', submitted 13 July 2012.

11. 'Plain packs: a grotesque illustration of modern politics', *Spiked*, 8 April 2014.

12. Quoted in *E – the Environmental Magazine*, 30 April 1996, www.adbusters.org/campaigns/bnd

13. *The Times*, 5 February 2015.

14. 'Real or imagined: racism "fear" over Rotherham child abuse', BBC News online, 27 August 2014.

15. *Daily Telegraph*, 27 August 2014.

16. David Copeland, *The Idea of a Free Press: the Enlightenment and Its Unruly Legacy*, Northwestern University Press, 2006, ibid., p. 41.

17. ibid., p. 46.

18. Professor John Carey, *The Intellectuals and the Masses: Pride and Prejudice among the Literary Intelligentsia 1880–1939*, Faber and Faber, 1992, p. 7.

19. ibid., p. 15.

20. ibid., pp. 7, 15, 121.

21. See Mick Hume, *There is No Such Thing as a Free Press*, op. cit., p. 78.

22. Cited in BBC News online, 21 April 2005.

23. *Guardian*, 12 June 2007.

24. BBC News online, 14 July 2011.

25. *New Statesman*, 30 April 2012.

26. New Orleans *Times-Picayune*, 9 December 2014.

27. Cited in *New Republic*, 13 February 2015.

28. See Daniel J. Boorstin, *The Image: A Guide to Pseudo-events in America*, 1962 edition.

29. Tom Watson MP and Martin Hickman, *Dial M for Murdoch: News Corporation and the Corruption of Britain*, Allen Lane, 2012, pp. 317, xvii.

30. Douglass, 'A Plea for Free Speech in Boston', op. cit.

31. www.webarchive.nationalarchives.gov.uk/20140122145147/http://www.levesoninquiry.org.uk/evidence/?witness=professor-barones-oneill

32. Copeland, *The Idea of a Free Press*, op. cit., p. 99.

33. 'A Manifesto for Media Reform', Media Reform Coalition and the Campaign for Press and Broadcasting Freedom, 2015, www.mediareform.org.uk/get-involved/a-manifesto-for-media-reform

34. Tim Wu, 'The Right to Evade Regulation: How corporations hijacked the First Amendment', *New Republic*, 3 June 2013.

35. Cass R. Sunstein, *Democracy and the Problem of Free Speech*, Free Press, 1995; review by Daniel E. Troy, *Commentary Magazine*, 1 January 1995.

36. Orwell, 'The Freedom of the Press', 1945, cited in Appendix I to George Orwell, *Animal Farm*, Secker & Warburg, 1987, p. 100.

37. Karl Marx, 'On Freedom of the Press', *Rheinische Zeitung*, no. 135, 15 May 1842.

A short summation for the defence

1. The *Sun*, 27 March 2015; The Conversation, 27 March 2015, www.theconversation.com/germanwings-coverage-a-kick-in-the-teeth-for-people-who-suffer-from-mental-health-issues-39446

2. *New York Times*, 11 April 2015.

3. Rosa Luxemburg, *The Russian Revolution*, 1918.

4. http://www.imdb.com/title/tt0117318/quotes

5. *Whitney v. California*, 1927, www.law.cornell.edu/supremecourt/text/274/357